THE UNCENSORED TRUTH AND PRIVATE LIVES OF COUNT

NASHVILLE BABYLON

RANDALL RIESE

ANAYA PUBLISHERS LTD
London

First published in Great Britain in 1989
by Anaya Publishers Ltd, 49 Neal Street, London WC2H 9PJ

Originally published by Congdon & Weed Inc.
A subsidiary of Contemporary Books, Inc.
298 Fifth Avenue, New York, New York 10001
Distributed by Comtemporary Books, Inc.
180 North Michigan Avenue, Chicago, Illinois 60601

The author and original publisher apologize to those photographers and
photograph owners who, despite our efforts, have not been traced, and who
therefore are not credited in this book.

A CIP catalogue record for this book
is available from the British Library

ISBN 1–85470–010–3

Printed and bound in Great Britain by Redwood Burn Ltd.

CONTENTS

I'm not one of those hard-bellied rock 'n' roll singers with a bulging crotch and Vaseline smeared on my pectoral muscles.
—Chinga Chavin, a country music singer

ACKNOWLEDGMENTS

Many thanks to:
- Mark Goins—for his inestimable, unconditional friendship and support.
- Aaron Kass and Linda Laucella—for creating an environment of affinity and inspiration.
- Jack Artenstein and Nancy Crossman—for the opportunity.

I would also like to thank the following individuals and organizations, who have generously lent their contributions to this work: The Academy of Motion Picture Arts and Sciences in Los Angeles, Donna Adkins, Nancy Artenstein, Kent Arnwood, Gary Bryson, Charles Carr, Gilbert and Bernicia Carreira, Cinema Collectors, David Allan Coe, Columbia Records, the Country Music Foundation in Nashville, Ranney Draper, Frank Driggs, Lydia Encinas, Christopher Esposito, Cindy Ford, Fletcher Foster, Kinky Friedman, Kathy Gangwisch, Gilley's, the Grand Ole Opry, the Hendersonville Police Department, Troy Hess, Donald and Sydney Hitchens, Gerald Holly, Billie Jean Williams Horton, Angela Hynes, Thomas Jacobs, Kayla Landesman, Les Leverett, Laurie Lico, Robert and Joyce Luzader, Sheldon MacArthur, Jim Malouf, Joe Martinez, Julie McFadden, Erin Morris, *Music City News*, Alanna Nash, Nashville Area Chamber of Commerce, the *Nashville Banner*, the Nashville Metropolitan Police Department, Ellis Nassour, Q Pearce, Wendell Pitzer, Ronnie Pugh, RCA Records, Linda Reisman, Ginger Rodriguez, Ronna Rubin, Georgene Sainati, Paul Schrader, Chris Skinner, Bill Spencer, Jerry Strobel, *The Tennessean*, Betty Lou Travis, Dorothy Travis, the University of California at Los Angeles (Department of Special Collections, University Research Library), the University of Southern California (Special Collections of Doheny Library), Dale Vinicur, Julie Pheiffer Walski, Warner Brothers Records,

Glenda Washam, Mickey Welsh, Kathy Willhoite, Lise Wood, and others who wish to remain unnamed.

A personal expression of thanks to Neal Hitchens, my assistant on this work, which commemorates the tenth anniversary of our relationship. We've laughed together, dreamed together, grown up together, and retained the purity of our friendship amid the destructive forces that lurk in the crevices of the hand- and foot-printed forecourt of Mann's Chinese Theater, in that infamous Babylon out West known as Hollywood.

PREFACE

You know, I'm so damned unlucky, if I died and got reincarnated, I'd probably come back as myself.
—Freddy Fender

*N*ashville Babylon examines the pitfalls of the peculiar, indulgent, and torturous world of country music. It pays homage to those who have suffered and survived, and it pays posthumous tribute to those who have died too young, as well as to those who have died under sensational circumstances. It also casts a voyeuristic gaze upon the turbulent love affairs that have rocked the puritanical Opry and enthralled the legions of country music fans worldwide. Naturally, the focus is on the colorful individuals, bespangled, bewigged, and bewildered, whose talent and torment have made the music and the headlines . . . who have kept us all vicariously and unabashedly entertained.

The following pages have been written with a little humor, a little arsenic, and a lot of affection. I expect that some will be offended. I hope that more will be entertained.

PRELUDE

The first time I met Norma was in a coffee shop in Nashville. I was ordering a hamburger. She was my waitress. There was something about her eyes, the innate youthfulness despite the obvious age, the molasses over gravel-scratched voice, and the way she prefaced each sentence with "Listen, honey . . ." that piqued my interest.

Norma first went to Nashville in 1939. She was twenty-three. Motivated by the Grand Ole Opry radio broadcasts that she religiously listened to every Saturday night, Norma packed her cardboard bag and said goodbye to her friends, family, and home in Pike County, Kentucky, or some such place. She was going to be a star. After all, Norma reasoned, if Miss "I Wanna Be a Cowboy's Sweetheart" Patsy Montana could do it, so could she. Moreover, not only was she going to become a star, she was also going to become, with a little amorous persuasion, Mrs. Roy Acuff.

Naturally, there were a few obstacles. First, she hadn't yet obtained a divorce from her husband, Euple, who had deserted her several months before. Second, she was the mother of two young children and would have to work as a cocktail waitress to support them. Third, she had no formal musical training. And fourth, she didn't have the slightest notion of *how* to become a star, nor had she ever even met Roy Acuff. All Norma knew was that she had to be in *Nashville*.

The years went by, but for Norma nothing happened. She saw Hank Williams come and go in a great puff of chemical exhaust, and she saw Kitty Wells become a star by way of "It Wasn't God Who Made Honky Tonk Angels." Still undaunted, Norma continued to audition, make and remake the regular rounds, and pitch her songs to record executives, producers, established singers, aspiring singers, and any of her beer-swilling customers who would listen between bottles. She also divorced Euple and fell in and out of love with several men who happened to resemble Roy Acuff.

And then "it" happened. The success of Kitty Wells created a sudden market for "girl singers." Norma was signed and recorded by a record company. It was an independent company, but at that time independent labels had proven to be powerful launching pads for new artists. Norma plotted and fantasized and even bought the dress she would wear for her debut at the Grand Ole Opry. She was *finally* on her way, or so she thought. Before her record was released as a single, fate unleashed a swift blow to the heart as Norma's record company was forced into bankruptcy. Norma clutched at her insides, summoned her southern-bred fire, and circulated her disc to the other labels, which had, by then, filled their quota of girl singers. Besides, they intimated to her, "Wasn't she getting a little too old to be a 'girl singer'?"

Devastated and embittered, Norma retreated deep within, away from the world, and away from her dreams. The man she was married to at the time left her. Her children, then grown, moved away from home. Alone, Norma washed away her ambition and pledged allegiance to the bottle—whiskey, gin, whatever was available. Failed country music stars took what they could get. When she got fired from one cocktail waitress job for drinking more than she was selling, she simply got another one. And so she went on, for many years.

It wasn't until she approached fifty that Norma began to reconcile with her disillusionment. She met a man named Hiram, who was decidedly *not* a Roy Acuff look-alike, and she—albeit begrudgingly—fell in love. Hiram has since died from a heart attack, and their time together was brief, but he inspired Norma to adopt a new perspective and to make the most of the life that she had remaining. Thus, when her previously estranged grandchildren recently visited her in Nashville, Norma took them on a tour of the Country Music Hall of Fame, and she told them, with unforced pride, the story of how she too was *almost* a star, just like the coal miner's daughter from Kentucky.

Today, at age seventy-two, Norma no longer drinks, and she no longer works in a cocktail lounge. She works in a soda fountain/coffee shop in Nashville that caters to the music industry. Rarely a day goes by when she doesn't meet some star or another. One day, she even met her idol, Roy Acuff, and served him a blue plate special—on the house. On the last day that I was there, she was sufficiently aroused to sing along with the jukebox. As I got up to leave, Norma waved at me, and said with a smile of unconditional approval, "Listen honey . . . y'come back here, anytime!" And then, she went back to entertaining some of her other customers with the story of her days in the music business, of her sudden "discovery," and of the dress that she never got to wear on the Opry.

After all these years, Norma has finally attained her goal: to become the center of attention, and to be loved by everyone. So what if her stage *is* a coffee shop and not the Opry? After all, there are many Normas in Nashville, all seeking the same dream, many of whom have suffered—and will continue to suffer—far worse fates than Norma the waitress. But that won't stop the perpetual pilgrimage to Tennessee, nor will it stop those already there from striving to become the next Hank or Tammy or Dolly or Willie. After all, in Nashville, as in Hollywood, *everybody* wants to be a star.

To Norma . . . and life's other beautiful losers

Grand Ole Opry.

GRAND OLE ORGY: AN INTRODUCTION

It was November 1925, only a few weeks after [radio] station WSM was founded in Nashville, Tennessee, that a mountain fiddler came to town to see the sights. Uncle Jimmy Thompson had heard of radio, so he went to the station and asked to be shown around. The manager at the time, a former newspaperman named George Dewey Hay, was a mountain music enthusiast. He not only showed Uncle Jimmy around, but put him and his fiddle on the air for an hour. The next week the old fiddler was asked to bring other mountain talent with him. Uncle Jimmy has since died, but every Saturday night for seventeen years mountaineers and their wives and children have streamed down from the hills on foot, wagon, or jalopy to Nashville to listen to the folk-music festival which grew out of this broadcast.
—*Newsweek*, October 18, 1943

So began the birth of the white man's blues and the emergence of the locality that became, for better or worse, its home. Welcome to Nashville—"Music City, U.S.A.," as it has been termed over the years by the tourist and recording industries. Rhinestone City, the country music glitter mecca, where the men grow up to be cowboys who cheat on their wives and who flaunt their boots, belt buckles, and beer-laden bellies as symbols of their masculinity; where the ex-cons become idolized singing stars (the more time served, the better the publicity); where the women stand by their men and smile through their tears or, if liberated, sing protest songs like Loretta Lynn's "Don't Come Home a-Drinkin' with Lovin' on Your Mind"; and where many preach the gospel by day and play musical bedsheets by night. This is a city with its own players, its own stars, and its own code of ethics.

This is also a city with its own personal tragedies, heartaches, embarrassments, dishonor, and history.

Originally named "Nashborough" in 1780, after General Francis Nash of North Carolina, present-day Nashville is a city in adolescence with a severe identity crisis. For the past five decades or more, the public face of Nashville has been, much to the chagrin of its populace, the capital of country music. In 1943, then-Tennessee governor Prentice Cooper was invited to attend a party at country music's worship palace, the Grand Ole Opry, in honor of singing star Roy Acuff. Governor Cooper declined and delivered a pompous blow to the Opry and its music with his declaration that he would be no party to a "circus" and that Acuff was disgracing the state by establishing Tennessee as the hillbilly capital of America. Ironically, 1943 was the same year that the Opry began to be broadcast nationally for the first time, thus vastly enlarging its audience.

Today, despite the fact that country music annually draws some seven million visitors and inestimable revenue to Nashville, many residents remain contemptuous of the music and mockingly refer to the city itself as "Nash-Vegas," drawing unfavorable comparison to the painted desert out west known for its plastic glitz and decadence.

Instead, Nashville's intellectual elite would prefer to bill their city the "Athens of the South," or at least "The Next Boom Town of the South." For years, Nashville has been the small town with the big reputation. That is changing. It is rapidly on its way to becoming an industrial and financial metropolis. In 1980, Nissan built its first United States assembly plant just outside of Nashville. By 1987, Tennessee had attracted the business of forty-one Japanese companies, which accounted for approximately 10 percent of Japan's total investment in the United States. Moreover, many accurately and assertively point out that country music is surprisingly *not* Nashville's most profitable enterprise. That distinction belongs to publishing. Bible publishing, that is. With a Baptist publishing house so big it has its own ZIP code, Nashville is the Bible publishing center of the country.

The culturally refined Nashvillians would also have us discount such colorful old relics as the Ryman Auditorium and Tootsie's Orchid Lounge in favor of Nashville's prize replica of the Parthenon, located in Centennial Park, and Vanderbilt University—home of several Nobel Prize–winning dignitaries. What these same cultivated citizens will *not* promote, however, is that Nashville ranks near the top of the nation in quantity of marriages (with almost as many divorces), and near the bottom in

Nashville, 1950.

Nashville, 1980.

quality of education (only 56 percent of adults twenty-five years and over have graduated from high school). Nevertheless, as far as music is concerned, the *Wall Street Journal* aptly wrote in 1987, "Mention music and many Nashvillians will tell you about their new symphony orchestra [which went defunct in 1988], or about the time Fisk University's Jubilee Singers performed for Queen Elizabeth." Still, despite the efforts of many, for most Americans and foreigners, Nashville is, and probably always will be, synonymous with the Grand Ole Opry, southern accents and mountain yodels, fiddles and Dobros, singing cowboys and cowgirls, and other things that go twang in the night.

> [Country music is] a salve for the beleaguered housewife who grits her teeth as destiny dumps its slops on her head.
> —*Newsweek*, August 2, 1971

Granted, when it's bad, it's awful (as in Johnny Cash's "Flushed from the Bathroom of My Heart"), but country music *has* come a long way from the days when musicians used to insert rattlesnake tails into their fiddles for added vibrato; from the days when Vernon Dalhart's "The Prisoner's Song" cost seven cents to record and sold 2.5 million copies; from the days when publications like *Collier's* would prophesize, "The cult of the hillbillies may be a passing fancy" (1938); and from the days when the music itself was referred to, often condescendingly, as "hillbilly

music" or "honky tonk music" or even "country and western music."

Through its many incarnations—from hillbilly, to rockabilly, to the rigidly formulated "Nashville Sound," to the "Outlaw Movement," to the alluring "crossover" threat of pop, to the "Urban Cowboy" rage, to the current nostalgic trend back toward "traditionalism"—country music appears to have come full circle. Not only has it survived the advent of Elvis, Motown, and the Beatles, it has thrived across seemingly impenetrable regional, racial, cultural, and societal boundaries. Still, regardless of how popular, or poetic, or soulful, or sublime, the best of country music can be, it is, as evidenced by the following, unequivocally *not* for all tastes:

> To allow this invasion [a country music concert] is to invite the anti-American, anti-Christian, hippie subculture right into our homes. Drinking and drunkenness (already a terrible problem in our schools), illegal sale and use of marijuana and hard drugs, nudity and immorality, lawlessness and total disrespect for law officers, and anti-patriotism and *crude music that stirs up the viler impulses of the human psyche.*
> —James Darnell, Fundamentalist preacher, Citizens for Law, Order and Decency in opposition to Willie Nelson's fourth of July country music picnic, 1976

Nashville's dueling landmarks, The Ryman Auditorium (left) (former home of the "Grand Ole Opry") and the Parthenon.

On March 16, 1974, President Richard M. Nixon attended the opening of the new Opry and swapped yo-yo techniques with Roy Acuff. He also joined the cast in "Will the Circle Be Unbroken."

Today, while the music has metamorphosed into a legitimate art form, the *industry* has exploded in scope from backyard barn dances and local state fairs into a multimillion-dollar enterprise. Naturally, this has changed the *way* business in Nashville is conducted. Arguably, the Grand Ole Opry has always resembled a fascist regime of sorts—with careers made and broken by the whim of Opry powers—but there used to be a sense of community in country music found in no other entertainment milieu. Everybody knew everybody else. Today, that has been replaced by a steely smile and a sometimes slimy handshake, and it would be of no great social consequence if the members of Alabama didn't know or care to know the members of the Oak Ridge Boys. Business is conducted with the head, not the heart, and occasionally lurking behind the crevices of those good-ole-boy smiles are cons and cutthroats, who are sufficiently sophisticated to rival the sharpest sharks that Hollywood and New York have to offer.

As the industry expands and competition intensifies, the odds of attaining stardom on Music Row have worsened. In Nashville, as in Hollywood, nepotism and casting couch practices are evident—though dropping one's blue jeans or opening one's legs certainly do not guarantee an Opry booking. Contrary to popular belief among many pop/rock fans and other assorted nonbelievers of all musical persuasions, it takes more than gimmickry, sexual favors, and a ticket to Nashville to become a country music star. Even such divergent personalities as Burt Reynolds, Clint Eastwood, Lynda Carter, Barbi Benton, Twiggy, and Tiny Tim have attempted to sing country music—with less than successful results. Nevertheless, since that 1925 radio broadcast, aspiring singers and songwriters have flocked to Nashville armed with guitars under their arms and rhinestone stars in their eyes. When David Allan Coe arrived in Nashville he used to park his car—a hearse, no less—in front of the Grand Ole Opry's Ryman Auditorium every Saturday night just to attract attention. He succeeded. Wynette Pugh, before she became Tammy Wynette, employed a similar tactic: she belted out "Your Cheating Heart" while standing perched on a makeshift stage in the back of a flatbed truck, which was also parked in front of the Ryman. Then there was the Memphis truck driver who drove to Nashville for an appearance on the Opry show in 1954—and flopped. An Opry official suggested to him that he go back to driving a truck. His name, of course, was Elvis Presley. In those old days, the struggling many used to convene at bars like Tootsie's Orchid Lounge (which opened its doors next to the Ryman in 1960) in hopes of befriending an established star to pitch their songs to. Today, Tootsie herself is dead, and her lounge is no longer what it once was.

Stirring up "the viler impulses of the human psyche," at the Willie Nelson picnic.

Tammy Wynette, who, early in her career, told a reporter, "I love to do m'own cookin,' Southern soul food, black-eyed peas, grits, almond dumplings, chicken dumplings, fried okra, buttermilk pancakes, and my special, banana marshmallow pudding."

> I have plans to do volunteer work at the hospital for children. If I hadn't gone into singing, I think I would have gone into nursing because I always wanted to be a nurse.
> —Former Alabama beautician Tammy Wynette, in her best
>   Miss America contestant repartee

If attaining stardom in Nashville is difficult, *maintaining* stardom is equally—though less desperately—challenging. Country music stars are expected to uphold a certain, albeit unspecified, decorum. After all, country music fans may be the most loyal in the world, but rarely do they tolerate a *moral* violation (it's okay for a star to be a murderer, but not an atheist). Consequently, when it comes to a star's *image*, Nashville is extremely policelike and protectionist. It is no longer a close-knit society, but it certainly is a closemouthed one. This isn't to suggest that there isn't gossip in Nashville, because there is—in abundance. But the gossip is usually confined behind the closed doors of executives' boardrooms and the stars' bedrooms, where it is exchanged with breathless abandon.

> My mother's a little embarrassed to admit she likes to eat squirrel brains. But back home it's a real delicacy. You put the head in a pot of boiling water and then crack it open with a spoon.
> —Dwight Yoakam

Dwight Yoakam, the new, old hillbilly star. A controversy erupted over whether the holes in his tight jeans were natural wear and tear or strategic design.

And just what is the preferred country music image? Generally, the ideal country music star was born of poverty-stricken parents, was undereducated (if you were well-schooled like Minnie Pearl, Tex Ritter, or Bill Anderson, for example, it should be kept quiet), and hails from the backwoods, the mountains, the hollows, or the cotton fields. It is also an advantage if the star was particularly precocious (though this word should not be in his or her public vocabulary), such as Loretta Lynn, who was married at thirteen and mother of four at eighteen, or 1970s recording artist Freddie Hart, who had been a Marine at fourteen and a veterinary surgeon not long after that. Female stars have such names as "Rattlesnake Annie." Male stars call one another "Hoss." Female stars are vigorously hairsprayed and overcoiffed and are expected to keep their legs crossed until marriage (however, multiple marriages are looked upon favorably—they mean she's suffered), to require frequent hospitalization for "exhaustion," to be antiabortion, and not to publicly endorse the Equal Rights Amendment. Male stars are tough, leathery, and pink-skinned and are encouraged to be obsessed with railroads,

Even well-educated stars like Minnie Pearl forgo words like "hello," "charmed," and "pleased to make your acquaintance" in favor of . . . "HOWDY!"

When Tanya Tucker was fifteen, her thirty-year-old brother used to accompany her into public restrooms.

guns, prison, mistreated Indians, and pro baseball (Roy Acuff, Jim Reeves, and Charley Pride were all pro or semipro aspirants). Female stars are forgiven for not knowing how to dress properly. Male stars are forgiven for obesity, adultery, wife beating, and alcoholism. Stars of both sexes also are expected to espouse the virtues of Mom, the flag, and pecan pie; wear their battle scars in public (as long as it's good publicity); and always preface each award acceptance speech by thanking Him, the Man Upstairs, or some other such acceptable euphemism for God.

> What do you mean, "peasant music," you goddam son of a bitch?
> —Faron Young to Zsa Zsa Gabor

> You talk about country music in a bad way and that's like sayin' my momma is a whore!
> —Dolly Parton to biographer Alanna Nash

Male country stars tend to have an obsession with firearms: Marty Robbins, Glen Campbell, and Kris Kristoffersonn brandish guns for the movie camera.

11

Country music stars are also encouraged to defend their genre of music with adámantine verve, to protect the purity of country music, and to profess the evils of rival pop (music) whenever possible. An amusing and symbolic illustration of this occurred in 1975 when Charlie Rich drunkenly stumbled onto the stage at the annual Country Music Association's awards show. Rich managed to articulate the nominated names for the Entertainer of the Year award. However, when he saw the card with the name of the winner, John Denver, Rich took out his cigarette lighter and promptly set the offending card ablaze. For months afterward, Nashville simmered with scandal—not because of the public spectacle of the drunken star and the flammable name card, but rather because the Country Music Association had elected to bestow the most coveted award in country music to a *pop singer*! Further, the same awards organization had previously named an Australian, Olivia Newton-John, as the top female country singer of the year over country *queens* Loretta, Tammy, and Dolly! Disgruntled, to say the least, a band of fifty country music stars assembled in the living room of Mr. and Mrs. (Tammy Wynette) George Jones, and organized a union dubbed ACE, which was designed to free country music from the contamination of pop. Interestingly, and to the shame of some, the association disbanded after founding members like Barbara Mandrell and Dolly Parton strayed toward the far more lucrative field of pop. Nevertheless, *pop* remains a dirty word in Nashville, and country stars are discouraged from seeking "crossover" successes. As Waylon Jennings exalted in his often quoted and widely applauded remark, "I couldn't go pop with a mouthful of firecrackers!"

But it isn't the image, or the industry, or even the music that has propelled country music to its current level of popularity—it is the *stars*, based in Nashville and elsewhere, whose lives are often more lurid than the lyrics they record.

> When you're a country boy just a month from the plow, and suddenly you're a star with money in your pocket, cars, women, big cities, crowds, the change is just too fast. You're the same person inside, but you're a star outside, so you don't know how to act. You're embarrassed about the way you talk, the way you eat, the way you look. You can't take the strain without a crutch. For me it was booze—I've seen the bottom of a lot of bottles. I was a mess, a wreck for years.
> —country boy Carl Perkins

Charlie Rich, one of Nashville's premier talents, battled with the bottle behind closed doors.

Country music fans love to pluck their stars not from the heavens, but straight from the ranks of the impoverished—which, as should be expected, sometimes causes casualties. An unsuspecting waif who happens to sing can be uneducated, uncultured, and unworldly one day and expressed onto that lonely country road from rags to rhinestones to Nudie designed suits the next. Before they were catapulted to stardom, Jimmie Rodgers was a railroad brakeman, Roger Miller rode bulls, Merle Haggard was a dishwasher, Kris Kristofferson swept floors, Glen Campbell was a garbage truck driver, Johnny Cash sold appliances, and, up until March 1986, Randy Travis washed dishes at a Nashville restaurant. About a year later, Travis had a platinum album, and the entire country music kingdom was lodged firmly beneath his stage-tapping cowboy boot. Willie Nelson, born dirt poor and abandoned by his mother at age six months, picked cotton and sold Bibles door to door. In 1983 his assets were listed as a 122-acre spread near Denver, a 400-acre ranch in Utah, a 200-acre farm near Nashville, two houses in Hawaii, a 44-acre ranch in Austin, the 1,700-seat Austin Opry House, an 80-unit apartment complex, a motel, a recording studio, a 775-acre country club near Austin, and a $1.7 million, seven-passenger Lear jet! Another case in point, country music's Cinderella, Tammy Wynette, went from picking cotton as a child to working

13

Former door-to-door Bible salesman, Willie Nelson (pictured, here in *The Electric Horseman*), deliberating whether to vacation, via Learjet, at his home in Hawaii or his home in Aspen.

Kenny Rogers (at top) shrewdly swapped pop for country, which created somewhat of a problem. Explained Kenny, "I've got a custom-built Stutz, a Rolls, a Mercedes, a Ferrari, a Corvette, and a station wagon, but I've only got a three-car garage!"

Randy Travis went from washing dishes in a Nashville restaurant to having a platinum album—in a year's time.

as a beautician to owning an opulently appointed Nashville home that had fifteen bathrooms and seven telephone lines.

It is this kind of extravagant excess and often annihilating *success* that has provided the impetus for the eventual psychological and financial breakdown of many country music personalities. Vernon Dalhart (real name Marion Try Slaughter) and Kelly Harrell are just two examples of country music stars who simply were not equipped to handle their success. In the 1920s, Dalhart recorded 5,000 releases and amassed sales of 75 *million* records. Harrell was a country music pioneer who recorded many hits, including "Cuckoo," "A Pretty Bird," and "The Butcher Boy." However, by 1942, through a series of misfortunes, both had fallen from hillbilly grace. Dalhart was reduced to working as the night checkout clerk at a small hotel in Connecticut. Harrell became a laborer in a rural Virginia towel factory. Not long after their falls from star status, they were both dead—victims of heart failure and faded glory.

It is certainly not unusual for country music stars to die destitute and destroyed after succumbing to crime, drugs, alcohol, sex, or other assorted temptations. After all, in country music, there is never a shortage of demons.

15

"**Y**'all don't worry, 'cause it ain't gonna be all right nohow."
—Hank Williams

1
COLD, COLD HEART

As an entire nation drunkenly ushered out the debris of an old year and festively celebrated the emergence of a new one, the biggest star country music had ever produced was dead or dying on a lost highway going nowhere. It was December 31, 1952, and Hank Williams was in the back seat of his baby blue Cadillac, wrapped in black leather upholstery and cuddled up in his bed of morphine, chloral hydrate, and alcohol. He was on his way to a New Year's night performance in Canton, Ohio, only he didn't know it. Charles Carr, his young chauffeur/companion, *did* know it, but he had just devoured a T-bone steak, charged to Hank, and was quite content to digest his thoughts—and the steak—in silence. Miles passed, and hours later Carr pulled into a filling station outside of Oak Hill, West Virginia. Hank was still quiet. Too quiet even for Carr, who finally turned around to ponder his famous and pathetic employer. But it was too late. Hank's hands were stiff and his heart was cold, and the long night's journey to death was over, reportedly without incident. He was twenty-nine years old.

There had been others before him—Roy Acuff, Eddy Arnold, Ernest Tubb—but Hank Williams was country music's first sex symbol. He was a gaunt 6'2" tall, balding on top and not inordinately attractive, but that wailing moan of a voice of his had a way of crawling up a woman's skirt and caressing her in places that her daddy hadn't seen and her husband hadn't found. And, in performance, when he parted those long legs and buckled those knees—way before Elvis did a variation of the same—there was rarely a dry female crotch in the house. Years after Hank's death, country singer Bobby Bare explained the difference between country and rock by quipping, "In country music, we want wet eyes, not crotches." Suffice it to say, Hank Williams wanted—and got—both.

Hank Williams: Tall, dark, and strung.

Despite grandiose claims to the contrary by overeager publicists and less deserving title contenders, Hank Williams is and always will be The King of Country Music. Granted, Roy Acuff has endured for what seems like centuries and Willie Nelson has perhaps made more money, and George Jones may have the better voice. But make no mistake about it: over thirty-five years after his death, Hank is still the King.

Like Marilyn Monroe, his Hollywood counterpart, Hank died young and perhaps by his own hand, and is a bigger commodity in death than he ever was in life. Also like Monroe, he has been used in death to billboard an industry that despised him while he was alive. As Hank Williams Jr. would later remark with characteristic candor, "I got so fuckin' sick of hearin' people say, 'Oh, God, your poor ole daddy, he wasn't treated right. He was the King and we loved him.' Well, they *hated* daddy in Nashville." By

1952, prominent members of the country music industry openly disapproved of Hank's drinking and his tendency to miss performances. Further, they felt that his rather salacious image conflicted with the desired homogenized image of the industry. Thus, shortly before his death, officials of the Grand Ole Opry fired Hank—a devastating jolt not unlike Monroe's firing from Twentieth Century–Fox—inarguably accelerating his demise. Still, since his death, Nashville has romanticized the memory of Hank Williams with unabashed hypocrisy. Time and money, it seems, rescind all truth.

Nevertheless, it wasn't Nashville that lured Hank down that unmarked and dimly lit street of self-destruction. He had been hitchhiking up and down that backwoods country road since he was a boy. Born Hiram Williams in Mount Olive, Alabama, in 1923, Hank grew up poor, without a father, and under the auspices of a mother who wore an apron with strings made of steel. He wasn't well-educated. Comic books were his preferred lifetime reading material. He wasn't smart, but he had balls. He also had an obvious inclination toward music. At six, he joined the church choir. At fourteen, he formed his first band, the Drifting Cowboys. In between, he was tutored by a street Negro named Tee-Tot in a musical style that fused hillbilly and pop with the blues. He also started drinking beer. While other kids toyed with immortality, Hank flirted with death. By fifteen, he was an alcoholic.

He had obvious talent but not much drive. And talent without drive is like sex without a partner. Just another hand-job. Hank needed a vehicle and a *driver*. He found the latter at the unlikeliest of places, a traveling medicine show in a small town in Alabama. He was onstage. She was in the crowd. After reportedly living together for two years (at a time when such things were thought to be crimes against decency), Hank Williams and Audrey Mae Sheppard Guy were married in a gasoline station in Andalusia, Alabama. Little did they know that just eight years later, with road maps of torturous anguish behind him, Hank would make one final trip to another gas station in another city. The not-so-full-service wedding was conducted in December 1944 by the gas station owner who sidelined as a justice of the peace when business was slow.

The marriage quickly escalated from young love to volatile drama, but it nonetheless proved to be a judicious business partnership. Not only did Audrey inspire Hank to write some of his most wrenching lyrics, she also fueled his talent with un-bridled ambition. It was Audrey who coerced Hank into the office of Acuff-Rose in Nashville, which led to his first songwriting contract and launched his career. With Audrey's approval, Acuff-Rose became the catalyst in Hank's initial contract with Sterling Records, his subsequent graduation to MGM Records, his first hit record, "Lovesick Blues," and his performer's membership on the Louisiana Hayride, which was based in Shreveport. By then it was 1949, and Hank Williams was just one performance away from his vehicle to stardom.

Although it isn't the case today, invited membership on the Grand Ole Opry in Nashville used to be a commonly accepted prerequisite for country music stardom. First, of course, there had to be an *invitation* to audition. Hank's audition took place on the stage of the Grand Ole Opry before a paying audience. It was a Saturday night, June 11, 1949. Although many of the country fans who packed the pews at the old Ryman Auditorium had heard of Hank Williams, they didn't know *who* he was or what he looked like. As he took center stage, they couldn't have been very impressed. He was all bones and legs and hollowed eyes. But when he unleashed the opening tortured wail of "Lovesick Blues," Hank devastated the usually staid Opry faithful—who demanded, and got, *six* encores of the *same song*! His performance remains, to this day, the single greatest moment in the history of the Opry.

Although Audrey Williams was overwhelmingly successful with her primary goal of prodding her husband to stardom, she was virtually ineffectual in eclipsing his alcoholism. On the contrary, Hank swapped beer for whiskey and increased his daily toxic intake. It's not that he didn't wage a battle with the bottle, because he did. Many of them. But Hank was a spree drunk. He'd go for weeks without a lick and then, provoked by some unknown torment, descend back into that warm, liquid rush toward oblivion. Once, after a particularly abusive round of verbal sparring with Audrey, Hank got drunk, checked into a Nashville hotel, and fell asleep with a lit cigarette that set his bed and hotel room on fire. Hank survived the scare. After all, legends don't die in a sudden blaze of 100-proof glory. They live in it.

"Lovesick Blues" spent forty-two weeks on the charts. Many, many other hits followed, songs like "Long Gone Lonesome Blues" (1950), "Why Don't You Love Me" (1950), "Moaning the Blues" (1950), and "Cold, Cold Heart" (1951). In a startlingly short time, Hank Williams had become the biggest attraction in country music.

He also became its biggest embarrassment. As fame held out

its sweaty palm with leering anticipation, Hank's drinking intensified, and he began to miss performances with increased regularity. Worse, his performance on the dates that he did make began to suffer perceptibly. He started forgetting the lyrics to his songs. At one show in Canada, he fell off the stage in mid-performance. Then, in late fall of 1951, he reinjured his back and was introduced to pain medication. And Hank was in desperate pain. His marriage to Audrey was rapidly falling apart.

As Hank was catapulted to the foreground, Audrey Williams was consigned to the background. However, as anyone who knew Audrey would vouch, she was not the type to dwell passively in anyone's shadow. Thus, while Hank was on the perpetual road that country stardom entails—shooting up some hotel room television set with his everyday-use pistol or greasing his most prized gun with a groupie of the night—Audrey was wrapping herself in furs, jewels, and allegedly, the comforts of other men. (Reportedly, Hank wrote "Your Cheating Heart" in protest of Audrey's philandering.) Still, it wasn't just jealousy or infidelity that destroyed their marriage. The critical factor, Hank's drinking, had been there at the start. With stardom, he merely acquired other destructive devices, and Audrey simply grew too rich, too detached, and too tired to play nursemaid.

Hank Williams, a profile in self-destruction.

In January 1952, Audrey filed for a separation, which precipitated the beginning of the end for Hank Williams. As he slipped further into abysmal decline, Hank employed a self-professed Doctor of Science and Psychology and Alcoholic Therapist by the name of H. R. Toby Marshall. "Dr." Marshall's treatment, for which he was paid $300 a week, consisted of supplying Hank with regular doses of chloral hydrate, a powerful knockout drug, presumably to have been used in lieu of alcohol. It was later learned that unbeknownst to Hank, Marshall was actually not a doctor at all. He had purchased his medical certificate at a gas station for $35, and was an ex-con and paroled forger (who later had the audacity to present Hank's widow with a bill for $736.39 for services rendered). Meanwhile, Audrey's divorce was granted, and she was awarded the house, custody of Hank Jr., $1,000 a month, a Cadillac, and one-half of all of Hank's future record royalties.

The autumn of 1952 signaled the final, desolate fall of a troubled man, unable to find a livable place somewhere between stardom and mortality. The most devastating blow was delivered by the forum that had insured his stardom just *three* years before. On August 11, after continued drinking and more missed performances, Hank was fired from the Grand Old Opry. As Nashville shut its doors, and as he was almost literally run out of town, Hank packed his belongings into a borrowed Chrysler and headed back home to Steel Apron Strings, Alabama.

Hank lost Audrey and the Opry, but he still had his mother, the Louisiana Hayride (which was a second-rate Opry), and a nineteen-year-old girlfriend by the name of Billie Jean Jones Eshlimar, whom he had met a few weeks earlier backstage at the Opry. Perhaps he was motivated by love on the rebound, money, or the desire to make Audrey jealous. Or maybe he was simply grasping, desperately, at whatever sustenance he had remaining. Whatever the reason, in October 1952, Hank married Billie Jean not once, but *three* times—twice before a paying audience. The theatrical wedding took place at the Municipal Auditorium in New Orleans. The Nashville community, though invited, cocked its disapproving eyebrow and declined to attend. Patrons paid seventy-five cents and $1.50 a ticket. It sold out twice (a matinee and an evening "performance"), and reportedly netted $30,000.

By the end of 1952, Hank Williams was still at the top of the charts with "Jambalaya." Furthermore, he had returned to Nashville in September to record "Your Cheating Heart" and "Kaw-Liga." Both would become enormous hits. The industry may have turned its back on Hank, but the rest of the country had not.

Meanwhile, his marriage to Billie Jean got off to an inauspicious start and never seemed to recover. First of all, Hank was too drunk to attend his proposed honeymoon in Cuba. Second, and more critically, Billie Jean was not prepared to treat the severity of Hank's decay. Furthermore, Nashville aligned itself behind Audrey. But some believed that Hank planned a return to Nashville in February 1953. It was also believed (though many have disputed this—including Charles Carr, the last man who saw Hank alive) that he intended to leave Billie Jean, court Audrey, and win back a spot on the Opry.

But Hank Williams did not make it back to Nashville. He didn't even make it to Canton.

> Billie, I think I see God comin' down the road.
> —Hank Williams to his wife, December 30, 1952

He braced himself in the black-leathered back seat of his baby blue Cadillac, which had been purchased in cash by the American dream, and gripped a nearby bottle of beer for support on his final trip on the road that New Year's Eve. It was midmorning, and Hank's young driver, Charles Carr, drove out of Montgomery, and headed north toward Birmingham on Route 31. Their eventual destination was Canton, Ohio, where Hank was set to perform on New Year's night. The highway blurred as Hank dulled the vacuous journey with sleep, chloral hydrate capsules, and more beer.

Shortly after 7:00 P.M., Charles Carr checked into the Andrew Johnson Hotel in Knoxville, Tennessee. Carr instructed the bellman that he had a sick man in the Cadillac and would need assistance. Two black porters carried Hank up to his room. With Carr, they undressed the famous star and put him to bed. Carr then phoned room service to order two T-bone steaks and phone a local doctor, who arrived shortly thereafter, armed with a needle. His name was Doctor Cardwell and—presumably without knowledge of Hank's dangerous history of addiction, the chloral hydrate, or the beer—he allegedly gave Hank two shots of morphine. Sleep consumed time. Wasted hours passed until Charles Carr received a mysterious phone call. After receiving the call, Carr prepared to resume the road journey to Canton. The two porters returned at 10:30, messenger boys of some god or demon, and dressed and carried the still sleeping, ever-stiffening, star back down to the Cadillac. Carr checked out of the hotel shortly before 11:00. At 11:30, he was stopped and ticketed for reckless driving by Corporal Swann Kitts. Kitts observed the backseat passenger and remarked, "He looks like he might be dead." Carr told Kitts that his passenger was Hank Williams and that he was merely sleeping. Unimpressed, but with his curiosity *temporarily* pacified, Kitts escorted Carr before the county magistrate, where Carr was fined before being released.

Hours later, Charles Carr pulled into a gas station, *the* gas station in Oak Hill, West Virginia. It is not known whether or not he filled the tank of Hank's Cadillac in that particular gas station. What is known is that he rushed his cold corpse of a passenger to the Oak Hill Hospital. It was a futile act. You can't revive the dead. After all, this *was* the age before the birth of evangelical television.

For thirty years, it has been accepted that Hank Williams died on January 1, 1953, in the backseat of his Cadillac somewhere between Knoxville, Tennessee, and Oak Hill, West Virginia. However, that belief was challenged when the original, long-lost handwritten police report, filed by patrolman Swann Kitts finally surfaced, in the *Knoxville Journal* just a few years ago. The report read:

> *On Wednesday, Dec. 31, 1952, Hank Williams and his driver, Charles Carr, caught a plane out of Knoxville and left their car at the airport at 3:30 P.M. They returned to the [Knoxville] airport [reportedly due to bad weather] at 5:57 P.M.*
>
> *At 7:08 P.M. Carr checked in Williams and himself at the Andrew Johnson Hotel. Dan McCrary, assistant hotel manager for the night shift, said Carr seemed nervous. The hotel manager didn't see Williams as the porters helped him to his room. They carried him up.*
>
> *He spoke only a few words as he was so drunk that he was almost out. Carr ordered two steaks. Carr ate his, but Williams was out and couldn't eat.*
>
> *Dr. P. H. Cardwell arrived. He said Williams was very drunk and that he talked with him. He gave Williams two injections of morphine and B-12. He said he noticed Williams had some capsules, 3 or 4, but didn't know what they were or if Williams had taken any of them. Dr. Cardwell stayed only a short time and left.*
>
> *In about an hour and a half or two hours Carr talked*

with someone on the phone and said he and Williams had to leave for Canton, Ohio. Carr and the porters had to help him dress Williams.

He was lifeless as they put his clothes on him. The porters carried him out and put him on the back seat of the car. Williams never moved at all. He seemed to make a coughing like sound (only twice) as they carried him, but was lifeless and didn't move. Carr checked them out at 10:45 P.M., spending only 3 hours and 44 minutes at the hotel, after telling the manager that they planned to spend the night there.

Carr, driving Williams' car, was stopped near Blaine, Tenn. at about 11:45 P.M. by S. H. Kitts of the Tennessee Highway Patrol after Carr almost hit head-on with the patrol car.

Carr said he was driving Hank Williams. I noticed Williams and asked Carr if he could be dead, as he was pale and blue looking. But he said Williams had drank 6 bottles of beer and a doctor had given him two injections to help him sleep.

He asked me not to wake him up as he was very sick and looked that way. I had him (Carr) to stop at Rutledge. I wrote him a ticket (for reckless driving) at 12:30. He was tried before Justice of the Peace, O. H. Marshall, and was fined $25 and costs.

I talked with him about Williams' condition in the presence of Sheriff J. N. Antrican and Marshall. We thought he (Carr) was a little nervous over paying the fine and he asked us not to bother Williams.

Carr had a soldier with him at the time he was in Rutledge. He paid the fine, thanked us, and left at about 1 A.M.

After investigating this matter, I think that Williams was dead when he was dressed and carried out of the hotel. Since he was drunk and was given the injections and could have taken some capsules earlier, with all this he couldn't have lasted over an hour and a half or two hours.

A man drunk or doped will make some movement if you move them. A dead man will make a coughing sound if they are lifted around. Taking all this into consideration, he must have died in Knoxville at the hotel.

It is curious that very few have paid much attention to the implications of the Kitts report. If it is to be seriously considered, then two issues are blatantly apparent. First of all, according to Kitts, Hank Williams died in a Knoxville hotel room and not in the backseat of his Cadillac. Second, if Hank Williams died in Knoxville, it can easily be deduced that he died on the evening of December 31, 1952, and not on New Year's Day, 1953. In addition, the report provokes several disturbing questions: (1) *Who* telephoned Charles Carr at the Andrew Johnson Hotel? (2) If Hank was obviously drunk and drugged, *why* was he given, or allowed to be given, two shots of morphine? (3) If Hank Williams was dead at the hotel, *how* could *anyone* not have known it? (4) Was Dr. Marshall ever questioned by the police, and if not, *why not*? (5) *Why* was there no further investigation into the death of Hank Williams?

As for Charles Carr, he is now in his early fifties and categorically denies the thirty-five-year-old Kitts report. He also dismisses Kitts as an overzealous cop with a poor memory, who was eager to jump on the Hank Williams postdeath bandwagon. Carr's version of the events that transpired on that junction between 1952 and 1953 is far less colorful.

In December 1952, Charles Carr, age seventeen, was home in Montgomery on Christmas break from Auburn University, where he was a freshman. Carr had met Hank Williams through his father, and had worked for Hank on various odd jobs for which he was well paid. Thus, when Hank approached him about the Canton trip, Carr readily accepted. On December 31, Carr drove Hank to Knoxville, where they both boarded a plane to Canton. However, the plane was unable to land in Canton and was forced to return to Knoxville. Thus, with their plans thwarted, they checked into a Knoxville hotel, where they planned to spend the night. Doctor Cardwell arrived a short time later, but according to Carr, he administered vitamins to Hank, not morphine (Carr is quick to point out that Hank's autopsy report does not include mention of morphine). A few hours later, Carr received a phone call from a man he doesn't remember. He thinks it may have been the show manager in Canton, but this seems unlikely because whoever made the call was in a position to insist that Williams and Carr check out of the hotel and resume their journey, despite the lateness of the hour and the perilous condition of Hank's health. At any rate, they went on—according to Carr, with Hank still alive. When asked how he was sure, Carr answered that he had spoken to Hank in Bristol, though he didn't recall the conversation. Carr also had a vague recollection that

Hank Williams, Sr. 1953 Cadillac
Hank Williams, Jr. Museum

The car that Hank may or may not have died in.

they may or may not have stopped for a sandwich somewhere along the way. Then, outside of Oak Hill, West Virginia, Carr pulled into a gas station/discount store, where he noticed that the blanket that had been covering Hank had fallen off. He repositioned the blanket over Hank and realized that Hank seemed stiff. Alarmed, Carr requested the assistance of the gas station attendant, who remarked, "I think he's dead." Carr then drove to Oak Hill Hospital, where Hank was laid out on a steel table and pronounced dead.

With the two conflicting accounts, and without benefit of any kind of formal investigation, it still remains questionable *where* and *when* Hank Williams died. For years, the Nashville country music industry had even denied that Hank died of an overdose. Allegedly, Hank's mother, Lilly Stone, had seen to it that "heart

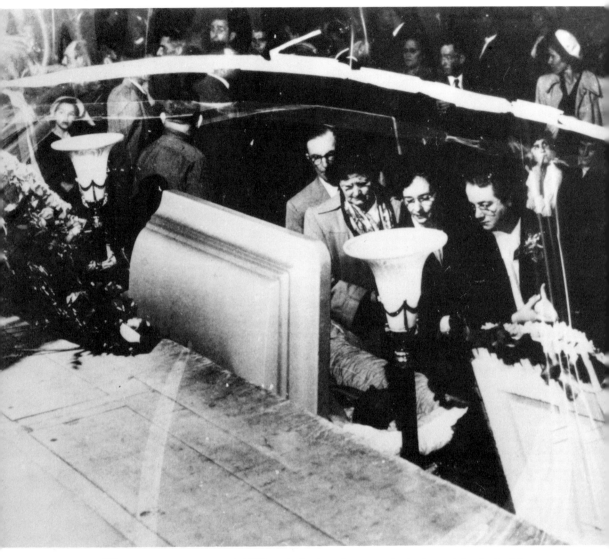

"Hey, Good Lookin' ": Hank Williams's final performance took place at the foot of the stage of Montgomery's Municipal Auditorium.

failure" was listed as the cause of death on his death certificate and that "morphine" was eradicated from his autopsy report. Nevertheless, ask almost anyone in Nashville today how Hank Williams died, and they'll tell you, with almost awed reverence, that he died from a combination of drugs, alcohol, heartbreak, and too much living. What they won't tell you is that he probably died choking on his own vomit.

Y'all don't worry, cause it ain't gonna be all right nohow.
—Hank Williams to his audience

The funeral in Montgomery was a country music carnival, complete with a roster of stars who sobbed; 20,000 mourners, some of whom fainted and 3,000 of whom stampeded the Municipal Auditorium to view the body in open casket; hysteria on the streets; *two* widows in black; and a marble replica of Hank's cowboy hat. Roy Acuff, who Hank had replaced as the nation's top country star, sang "I Saw the Light." Red Foley, who had introduced Hank at his first, momentous Opry performance, sang "Peace in the Valley." Ernest Tubb sang "Beyond the Sunset," and Little Jimmy Dickens wept the Mississippi. A two-ton truck was required to cart the floral tributes from Nashville alone, and the services were broadcast by two radio stations. It was a gaudy, maudlin display of sorrow—some of which was heartfelt and some which was not—and a DeMille-like spectacle that rivaled Hollywood's passing of Rudolph Valentino.

Perhaps no one is interested in investigating exactly what transpired that New Year's Eve because, as time has proven, Hank Williams is more valuable to the country music industry dead than alive. His legend almost singlehandedly expanded the boundaries of country music and has kept those Nashville cash registers happily ringing with resonance for four decades. Besides, *alive* he was a man with a drinking problem who was booted out of the city. *Dead*, he is the most revered star in country music history, and Nashville, like the former lover eager for reconciliation, has appreciatively lifted her gingham skirt and embraced him in warmth and glory.

2
THE WAR OF
THE WIDOWS

First, there was "The War of the Worlds." Then, there was The War of the Widows.

The battle began at the funeral. As the body of Hank Williams lay at the foot of the auditorium stage for public inspection, Audrey Sheppard Guy Williams and Billie Jean Jones Eshlimar Williams sat, side by side, in the front row of the auditorium, each vying for the title of Chief Mourner. Audrey seethed beneath her veil, amazed that this little, pubescent Billie Jean thing had the audacity to compete with *her*! Billie Jean mused over Audrey's painted-on eyebrows, and quietly resented that she had been banned from participating in the funeral arrangements. He was, after all, *her* husband. Billie Jean later commented, "I felt like any minute someone was going to say, 'Will the real Mrs. Hank Williams please stand up?'" Legend has it that, before the day was over, the two widows closely compared wedding rings in a fist-to-face fight. Regardless of the outcome of that particular encounter, the final blow was years away from being delivered.

The biggest mistake Audrey Williams ever made was divorcing Hank Williams. She had been with him for ten years. Billie Jean had been with him for two months. If Audrey could have held out just a little longer, Billie Jean *might* have been banished forever to obscurity.

One of the biggest mistakes Billie Jean Jones Eshlimar ever made was marrying Hank Williams—ten days before her first marriage ended in divorce. The error eventually served to increase Audrey's stock, and it tainted Billie Jean's credibility as the widow Williams.

As is the case in any war, sides must be chosen. Hank's mother, Lilly and his sister, Irene, pledged allegiance to Audrey. Audrey also had the admittedly biased, but nonetheless powerful, back-

30

Audrey Williams, her daughter by a previous marriage, and the two men that she groomed (some would say, browbeat) to stardom.

ing of three-year-old Hank Williams Jr., whom Audrey paraded about whenever she required additional leverage. Billie Jean had the current marriage certificate and the support of her own family.

Lilly, despite protest by Billie Jean, was named administratrix of the estate, which included only $13,000 in real and personal property. In a combined effort to eliminate her from the picture, Billie Jean was paid $30,000 to forfeit her interest in the estate. Two years later, Lilly died and Irene succeeded her as the administratrix, a post she held until 1969, when she was imprisoned for possession of illegal drugs.

With Billie Jean temporarily quieted by the $30,000, Audrey posed for the world as though she had never divorced Hank. She had a poem that she had written to him engraved in granite on his gravestone. She took out a large advertisement in the music trade publication *Billboard* announcing that, the law aside, *she* was the *real* Mrs. Hank Williams. For years after Hank's death, she kept the Cadillac that he may or may not have died in parked in her Nashville driveway. It became a regular stop on bus tours. And, on the first anniversary of Hank's death and on every anniversary thereafter, Audrey sent a dozen red roses to his grave with a card that read, "With Love, from Audrey and the children."

Shortly after her husband's death, Audrey took out this ad for herself in *Billboard* to spite Billie Jean.

Audrey's most flamboyant gesture, however, was a shameless, self-serving exercise in bad taste. Audrey had always wanted to be a singing star. With her ex-husband's death and his burgeoning posthumous popularity, she grasped what she thought was her shot at stardom. Unfortunately, she was not equipped with much of a voice. Nevertheless, gussied up in her finest cowgirl regalia, Audrey embarked on a tour, billing herself as "Mrs. Hank Williams" and singing the songs of the deceased. Not to be outdone, Billie Jean filed an injunction against Audrey to pro-

The woman who inspired the songs . . . and the pain.

hibit her from using the marquee name, "Mrs. Hank Williams."
Subsequently, Audrey was forced to bill herself, "Mrs. Audrey
Williams." In addition, Billie Jean went on a singing tour of her
own, also dressed in cowgirl attire, and billed, of course, as the
real "Mrs. Hank Williams."

The War of the Widows subsided a short time later when Billie
Jean stopped touring and married aspiring country singer
Johnny Horton in September 1953, only eight months after the
death of Hank Williams. Horton became Billie Jean's third
husband in less than a year. All of which undoubtedly pleased
Audrey, who formed an all-girl band, the Drifting Cowgirls
(Hank's nickname had been the Drifting Cowboy), and con-
tinued to tour with Hank's songs for over a decade.

Meanwhile, Johnny Horton became a major country music
star. In 1959, his "The Battle of New Orleans" was a smash hit. At
twenty-six, Billie Jean was finally on the threshold of claiming

A dying star and his blossoming bride, Billie Jean.

the glass slipper as country music's Cinderella bride. And then tragedy struck. Again. In November 1960, while en route to a performance in Texas, Johnny Horton was killed in a car crash.

While vicious speculation that she might be a black widow of some sort circulated through Nashville, Billie Jean mourned the only way she knew how: she went on tour. She also renewed animosities with Audrey by beginning a lengthy legal battle to win her share of the Hank Williams estate.

On October 25, 1968, in Atlanta, Georgia, Billie Jean Jones Eshlimar Williams Horton Berlin (she had married businessman Kent Berlin), filed a $1.1 million dollar lawsuit against MGM films for its movie version of Hank Williams's life, *Your Cheating Heart*. Audrey had served as the adviser on the film, and Hank Jr., then nineteen, had sung his father's songs on the soundtrack. Thus, it was rather predictable that the film depicted Audrey as Hank's one and only wife and widow. Audrey had always wanted to excise Billie Jean from Hank's life, and with Hollywood magic at her disposal, she was able to do precisely that. The only character in the film who even faintly resembled Billie Jean was seen briefly and portrayed as a hillbilly harlot. In her lawsuit, Billie Jean contended that MGM had deliberately misrepresented her marital status with Hank. By November 1969, Billie Jean's suit multiplied to $4.5 million. In 1972, the jury ruled in Billie Jean's favor but finding no deliberate malice on MGM's part, declined to award any damages. Further, the court ordered her

34

George Hamilton and Susan Oliver, Hollywood's Hank and Audrey.

Audrey giving Hollywood a little piece of Hank.

to pay all court costs. Billie Jean later appealed the decision, with the same result.

Billie Jean may have lost the battle but not the war. Although the jury failed to deliver the substantial financial compensation she requested, the judge did conclude that, despite the fact that her divorce hadn't been finalized at the time she married Hank in 1952, she was nevertheless his legal, common-law wife at the time of his death. Armed with this confirmation, Billie Jean filed another suit, this time in a Nashville court. Billie Jean's objective was to replace Audrey as the recipient of Hank's extremely lucrative copyright renewal royalties.

Battle-scarred but still in the ring, Audrey Williams did not age particularly well, a fact she lamely tried to hide under an assortment of blonde wigs. Furthermore, despite years of effort, she never attained her dream of singing stardom. Instead, she was forced to achieve success vicariously, first through Hank and later through her son, Hank Jr. However, by the early-to-mid-1970s, Hank Jr. grew increasingly determined to seek independence from Audrey and to have an identity separate from his dead father. Thus, Audrey had to console herself with the task of carrying the torch for Hank by herself.

Unlike her nemesis Billie Jean, Audrey never remarried. Nevertheless, she allegedly found frequent comfort with the young, aspiring male singers who camped out on her doorstep seeking her tutelage. After all, *she* had made Hank Williams a star—perhaps she could do the same for any one of them. But by the 1970s, Audrey had long since lost her touch and, some think, her sanity.

Certainly, she grew increasingly despondent. Shortly after the 1972 court ruling in which Billie Jean was legally named Hank's wife at the time of his death, Audrey was arrested in Florida on charges of drunk driving, resisting arrest, and destroying county property. In 1973, to commemorate the twentieth anniversary of his death, Audrey sent twenty *dozen* roses to his grave. She also campaigned for the city of Montgomery to erect an eighty-foot-high cowboy boot as a memorial to Hank. However, the structure would have cost a reported $750,000; thus the rather absurd proposal was shelved. Next, in 1974, Audrey announced plans to transform her Nashville home into a Hank Williams museum. However, Nashville zoning regulations prohibited converting a residential property into a commercial enterprise, so Audrey's plans were thwarted once again. Still obstinate, Audrey circumvented the city, to a degree, by hosting a "garage sale," to which she charged $2 admission, and selling Hank Williams momentoes.

In October 1975, twenty-three years after Hank had married another woman, Audrey Williams was finally stripped of her share of Hank's copyright renewal royalties. Nashville judge L. Clure Morton ruled that even though Billie Jean was married to Hank for only two months, she was still entitled to the widow's share of Hank's royalties. They were an exceptionally expensive two months for Audrey. With a stroke of a judge's gavel, Audrey lost her primary source of support, and Billie Jean became a very rich and happy woman. For Audrey, the defeat was crushing. Just a few months before, Hank Jr. had almost died in a devastating tumble off a Montana mountain. The Internal Revenue Service seized her home, and the rumor around Nashville was that Audrey became heavily dependent on sleeping pills. She stopped eating and her weight dropped to eighty-five pounds. According to one of her friends at the time, Audrey "was groggy, half-asleep and half-awake. She just got to where she wouldn't get out of bed." For Audrey, beaten and bitter, the court decision

Billie Jean, the southern beauty, with country music hubby number two, Johnny Horton.

had been the final agony. One month later, at the age of fifty-two, she was found dead in her bed, wearing only her bra and panties. Officially, she had suffered a convulsive seizure and died of "natural causes." Nevertheless, there are some who believe that Audrey simply lost the will to live and took one too many pills.

When she was last heard from, Billie Jean Williams Horton was in her mid-fifties, divorced, and living in Shreveport, Louisiana. She was still prom-queen pretty and had metamorphosed from the naive teenage ingenue who married Hank Williams before 28,000 paid spectators on a New Orleans stage into a shrewd businesswoman with more than a few battles, legal and otherwise, tucked under her cinch belt. She was—after years of playing musical courthouses—not terribly unlike her rival of nearly three decades, Audrey Williams. Only much happier. Billie Jean—who once became an ordained minister in the Pentecostal church—admitted that wasn't always the case. "At one point," she recalled to the *Nashville Banner*. "I considered suicide. But then I went to a revival meeting and not only found religion, but [I also] got rid of my chronic headaches."

Up until the time she died, Audrey Williams contended that she and Hank had planned to reconcile in Nashville after he got back from Canton. Thus, even though Billie Jean claimed Hank's royalties, and won The War of the Widows, it seems only appropriate that it is Audrey who won the right to be buried beside him in Oakwood Cemetery.

There was no widower at the Audrey Williams funeral. There was no crowd of 20,000 sobbing, fainting mourners. There was no truckload of floral arrangements and no radio broadcast. And there was no country star who made an appearance and sang his or her parting praises.

But there *was* a New Orleans preacher who sang "Hey, Good Lookin' " as her casket was lowered into the ground.

3

MAMAS, DON'T LET YOUR BABIES GROW UP TO BE COWBOYS

"Are You Sure Hank Done It This Way?"
—Waylon Jennings

Hank Williams was not the first or last country star to be ravaged by drugs and alcohol. But he was the one who romanticized the pathos of its devastation and lured a legion of awe-inspired desperados to scavenge for a place in his twisted shadow.

Hank Williams *Jr.* has spent more intimate time with Jim Beam than he ever did with Hank Williams Sr. Yet, there has probably never been a son who has tracked his father's deeply imbedded bootprints with more reckless voracity, with more instinct to self-destruct, than has Hank Jr.

It was a role he was born to play. While other infants rigorously sucked off their pacifiers, little "Bocephus" cradled a miniature guitar and posed, all gums and no teeth, for publicity pictures with his parents. By the time he was eleven, eight years after his father's premature exit, Hank Jr. made his debut on the Grand Ole Opry. With Audrey, the quintessential stage mother, critiquing his every move, Hank Jr. spent his childhood lip-synching to his father's records, mimicking his vocal inflection, memorizing his jokes, and impersonating his mannerisms and stage patter. From the start, Hank Jr's self-concept was based upon one overriding criterion: how well he could recreate the image of his father.

Perhaps, in retrospect, he was too adept at his job. For awhile, Nashville stood up and applauded, bemused by the little boy all dressed up in his dead father's voice. Hank Jr. toured with his mother's Caravan of Stars extravaganza, which featured his band, the Cheatin' Hearts. Exalted Audrey, "Everyone who knew and saw Hank Williams work on the stage can see an image in

Hank Williams Jr., all dressed up in his dead father's voice.

40

Hank Jr. as he sings, walks, and performs." By fourteen, he signed a reported $300,000 recording contract with MGM Records, and was being spoon-fed backstage groupies to accompany his cookies and milk. He didn't object. He recorded albums with titles like *Hank Williams Jr. Sings the Songs of Hank Williams* and *Songs My Father Left Me*. He also sang the soundtrack to the Hollywood film biography *Your Cheating Heart* and even went into the studio and recorded harmonies over his father's vocals. The latter provoked contemptuous commentary from factions of the music industry that Hank Jr., as Audrey's puppet, had been milking the corpse of Hank Sr. and was planning to take his father's coffin on tour. The novelty had worn off.

> I'd just put daddy's record on the jukebox and get a nice fifth of whiskey and a couple of downers and sit there and try to communicate with him.
> —Hank Williams Jr.

Hank Jr. spent the first half of his life working to impersonate his father. He has spent the second half trying to exorcise his father's ghost. As early as age sixteen, he publicly wrestled with the monster legacy that he had been bequeathed. He recorded his first self-penned hit, "Standing in the Shadows (of a Very Famous Man)." By 1970, he had grown increasingly despondent over dwelling in the padded cell of his father's fame. Instead of seeking therapy by writing autobiographical songs, he grasped the nearest escape valve.

Country music stars have always been inordinately subjected to the temptations of drugs and alcohol. By the nature of the business, many stars are required to spend up to three hundred days a year on the road, where life is a blur of highway dividing lines and revolving Holiday Inns, where performances are played out in a succession of indistinguishable one-night stands in Nowhere, U.S.A. It's an exhausting exercise in monotony. The mileage takes its toll, and for many additional fuel of some sort is required. In the backstage babylon of country music, drugs and alcohol are readily accessible. Generally, country music performers work in a honky tonk environment, where there is always a greasy agent, overzealous groupie, or supposed friend eager to produce a pill to gain some unspoken favor. For country music stardom has the power to instantly transform those who had nothing into those who have *everything*. While some stars manage to revel in their sudden riches with a level head, many find it difficult to adjust to the deluge of everything that "everything" comprises, and they seek solace in the bottom of a bottle.

Hank Jr. getting some fatherly advice from Ed Begley Sr. in *A Time to Sing*.

Hank Williams Jr. was twenty-one years old when he purchased his first-class ticket to oblivion. He started taking pills.
Anything and everything. With his foot firmly planted on the
accelerator, he speeded his young life away. After all, if he was
going to die, it wasn't going to be a passive death in the backseat
of some Cadillac convertible; it was going to be in a massive
explosion of high-octane wrath and fury that Nashville would
never forget. In 1973, at the age of twenty-three, Hank Jr. was
hospitalized in Nashville after a suicidal overdose of barbiturates. Close to death, a psychiatrist warned him, "You've been
taught, you know, live like, act like, be like, sing like your daddy.
Your lifestyle is exactly like his, and, you're going to be gone,
too." Another psychiatrist remarked, "He had fully taken over

the image of Hank Williams, the only difference being that Hank Jr. would probably die by the time he reached his twenty-sixth year." (Hank Sr. had died at twenty-nine.)

Hank Jr. survived the overdose, but his death wish, conscious or not, persisted. In August 1975, after recording his album *Hank Williams Jr. and Friends*, he went to Montana to rest and regroup. Prophetically, his album included a song that lamented about going to Montana to rest his soul. On August 8, accompanied by friends, Hank Jr. climbed atop Mount Ajax. The journey going up was infinitely more enjoyable than the journey going down. As Hank Jr. and friends crossed the 9,000-feet elevation mark, Hank slipped. He plummeted off the side of the mountain and smashed face first into a sharp boulder, crushing his flesh—right between the eyes. Said witness Dick Willy, "About the only thing he had left was the one eye. It literally tore his nose off, drove it up through his head, and blew a hole in his forehead which exposed the brain. And, as far as his lower part of his head, his jaws, teeth, gums, they were pretty much ruined." So, with one eye ripped out of its socket, all the bones in his face shattered, and his blood splattered like a memento all over the

Hank Jr. has loved some ladies and has loved Jim Beam.

mountain, Hank Jr., dead from the neck up, was carted off to a Montana hospital.

But he survived. Talk about tempting fate. Perhaps, Hank Jr. might have thought while mummified in bandages, there was nothing to this legacy thing, after all. At any rate, with major reconstructive surgery behind him, one thing was certain: he was still alive, but he was not quite ready to accept it.

> About 1978, I began to notice there was something wrong in the way some of the artists sounded in recording sessions. There was this nasal tone. It was like they were singing through their noses. I found out what the problem was—cocaine.
> —Rick Blackburn, CBS Records executive in Nashville to the *Tennessean*, September 8, 1984, about cocaine usage in the country music industry

> Sex feels good, Jim Beam tastes good, but cocaine will kill your ass.
> —Hank Williams Jr.

By 1979, Hank Jr.'s new nose developed a craving for cocaine. Said one former band member to *The Tennessean*, "After we'd do a show and go back to the hotel, he'd get so messed up drinking his Jim Beam and snorting his coke that he'd go berserk, breaking up furniture and kicking in the walls." One night, in a Florida hotel room, Hank Jr. took out one of his guns—as his father's ghost nodded in silent empathy—and blasted the room to shattered glass and wood. Like his father, Hank Jr. has an obsession with guns. But it wasn't *gun* powder that he had been cramming up his nose. By the end of 1979, Hank Jr. had been hospitalized three times for near fatal overdoses of cocaine.

Nashville aired out its mourning clothes in anticipation of his death. Elaborate memorial services were designed in the minds of some, while others, who knew his father, shook their heads and mumbled how Hank Jr. was still just like Hank Sr.

But Hank Jr. survived the overdoses, and he has claimed to have been off cocaine since late 1979. Still, Nashville waved its wary finger when he was sued for $1.2 million by a Sherman, Texas, nightclub owner who charged that Hank Jr. had been drunk during a 1981 performance. In court, a security guard testified that he had delivered a quart of whiskey to a stumbling, incoherent Hank Jr. shortly before show time. Hank Jr. lost the suit and was ordered to pay $160,000. In 1982, he was sued by

In the 1975 tragedy that almost killed him, one of Hank Jr.'s eyes was ripped out of its socket. Today, he still wears dark glasses—*wherever* he goes.

concert promoters who claimed that Hank Jr. had missed a performance in Orlando, Florida, because of drugs. He lost the suit and was ordered to pay $98,606.

Nevertheless, at nearly forty years old, Hank Williams Jr. has outmuscled his father's legacy with good ole boy rowdiness and a decidedly rocking beat. He has stepped out of the shadows and defined his own niche in country music. In 1986 and again in 1987, he was selected "Entertainer of the Year," the most coveted award in country music. On one of those occasions, Hank Jr. later remarked that he felt his father's presence accompany him to the winner's podium.

And why not?

Better there than to the grave.

Portrait of a dying man: Johnny Cash, circa 1960.

Most everybody had written me off. Oh yeah, they all acted like
they were proud of me when I straightened up. Some of them
are still mad about it though. I didn't go ahead and die so they'd
have a legend to sing about and put me in hillbilly heaven.
—Johnny Cash

Nearly all of Nashville knew that Johnny Cash was dying.
Hank Williams Jr. would go on to become the city's prodigal son
by carrying out the family tradition, but in the mid-1960s, it was
John R. Cash who was the primary heir apparent to the Williams ·
death sentence. Live fast, hard, and with a finger on the trigger at
all times.

Whispered gossip had it that it was Johnny Horton's tragic
death in November 1960 that precipitated Cash's drug abuse. The
two were extremely close. Others contend that Cash had discovered pills before Horton's death. At any rate, by the end of 1960,
Johnny Cash had been a star for several years, by way of "Folsom
Prison Blues," and "I Walk the Line." He was performing up to
300 dates a year, and his increasingly erratic behavior had the
public salivating.

By 1965, at age thirty-three, Cash was walking the precarious
line between breath and death, and putting on quite a spectacle
in the process. Although the music industry suppressed reports
of his addiction and upheld its placid visage, some stories managed to leak out. There were colorful accounts involving Cash of
public restroom toilets exploded by firecrackers; a reproduction
of the Mona Lisa, with a bowie knife flung in its face; hotel room
doors chopped down by an axe; a hotel floor flooded with a
firehose; and a hotel wall ripped to devastation by Cash's bare
hands. On the less amusing side, Cash, heavily doped, smashed
some footlights at the Grand Ole Opry, and was promptly informed that he would no longer be welcomed there. He was also
accused by the U.S. government of starting a brushfire near a
wildlife reserve near Ventura County, California. The fire required 450 men, eight aerial tankers, four helicopters, and two
days to contain. Cash was later court-ordered to reimburse the
government $82,000 in damages.

Then, hell-fire raged. On October 4, 1965, Cash was lassoed at
El Paso International Airport by federal narcotics agents. He was
charged with smuggling, concealing and facilitating the con-
cealment of 688 Dexadrine (pep pill) and 475 Equanil (tranquil-
izer) tablets, which he had obtained from nearby Ciudad Juarez,

Johnny Cash (pictured here in *Five Minutes to Live*): Living with a finger on the trigger.

Mexico. The pills had been stashed, half-heartedly, in his pockets and guitar. Cash pleaded guilty and was given a thirty-day suspended sentence and fined $1,000. He spent one day in jail.

However, if the wrist-slapping sentence was intended to encourage rehabilitation, it had the opposite result. Cash deteriorated with pathetic alacrity. He was doing about a hundred pills a day. In 1966, he was thrown in a Starkville, Mississippi, jail for public drunkenness after he was caught picking flowers and roaming the city streets at 2 A.M. Incensed at what he thought was an unjust arrest, Cash kicked in the walls of his cell and broke his left big toe. The following year, he was again arrested for public drunkenness, this time in Lafayette, Georgia, where he spent another night behind bars. Meanwhile, his long-term marriage was falling apart, and in mid-1966 his wife, Vivian, filed for divorce on grounds of extreme cruelty. His weight dropped to 140 pounds. His face, haunted and frightening, was all eyes and withdrawn flesh. His body was all bones, dressed, appropriately, in funereal black. He resembled, not surprisingly, Hank Williams before he took the cowboy's last ride.

Johnny (Blues Brother) Cash, lassoed in El Paso.

Early one morning in Toronto in 1967, Cash's longtime partner and friend, Marshall Grant, found Johnny unconscious on the floor of his tour bus, slumped over a pile of potato peelings. He was, by all appearances, dead. He wasn't. Not quite.

Shortly after the near fatal overdose and his brief stint in the Georgia prison, Cash abruptly switched gears and made an audacious jump off the speeding freight train destined for tragedy. Supported by his new wife-to-be, June Carter, Cash locked himself into a room and sweated out the nightmare of his addiction.

By September 1979, rumors widely circulated in Nashville that Cash was back on drugs and that his marriage to June was in trouble. He denied both. "As for narcotics, I swear I have never, repeat never, used heroin or sniffed cocaine. And, I am *not* on

The man in black (pictured here in *The Gunfight*): Back in the saddle again.

pills, nor have I been since I was cured years ago," he told the press.

A few years later, Johnny was attacked by an ostrich. It was sudden and it was lethal. The brawling bruiser of a bird slammed its feet into Johnny's chest, kicking and clawing and going for blood. Cash fought back. Perhaps he envisioned the following morning's headlines: JOHNNY CASH: MURDERED BY A KILLER OSTRICH! It wouldn't have been a pretty obituary. However, the bird's attack was warded off, somehow, by Cash's heavy metal belt buckle. With five broken ribs, he was rushed to the hospital, where he was given prescription drugs for pain.

> A man who is strong emotionally and physically, a lot is expected of him. And I felt at times there was too much expected of me. I guess I wanted a security blanket. I wanted to hide from that.
> —Johnny Cash to Barbara Walters

Within a few months of the bashing bird incident, Johnny Cash was rehooked on pills. Then, in November 1983, he was rushed to

Baptist Hospital in Nashville, reportedly for blood poisoning due to an insect bite. On November 22, he underwent surgery for treatment of a bleeding ulcer. Reportedly, Cash's treatment included ten days of morphine injections. From Baptist Hospital, he was flown to the Betty Ford Center in Rancho Mirage, California, for rehabilitation from his addiction to drugs. He was there forty-four days.

In May 1987, Cash collapsed onstage in Council Bluffs, Iowa. Press reports cited "exhaustion" and a failure to take his blood pressure medicine as the reasons for his breakdown.

Certainly, his career was in trouble. In 1986, after *twenty-eight years*, Columbia Records unceremoniously dropped Johnny Cash. With the label, Cash had sold millions of records, had a network television series, collected innumerable awards, and established himself as one of the biggest stars in the history of country music. But he hadn't had a Top 10 solo hit since "The Baron" in 1981. Besides, Columbia was more interested in investing in its new hotshots—like Ricky Van Shelton, the O'Kanes, and Johnny's daughter, Rosanne—than in reviving the sagging career of a country music patriarch. Though not intended to be, it was a backhanded slap to an extremely proud man. It was also, in a way, Nashville's revenge on Cash for not having died twenty years before as he was expected to. Columbia's Nashville honcho Rick Blackburn was repentant. "This is the hardest decision that I've ever had to make in my life . . ." Blackburn announced, rather lamely. And he got away with it. Country music personages kept their mouths shut and conducted business as usual.

It took relative newcomer Dwight Yoakam to shatter the dignified decorum and lambaste Blackburn: "What kind of decency is

Johnny Cash.

that? The man's been there thirty fuckin' years makin' them money. He paid for the son of a bitch's office that the prick sits in and lets him leave the label. He built the building, man."

For a while, Johnny Cash, *the* Johnny Cash—who, like Hank Williams before him, had greatly expanded the periphery of country music—was a man without a label for the first time in thirty years. He resurfaced in May 1987 on Polygram Records. However, the first album, *Johnny Cash Is Coming to Town*, was released to less than enthusiastic response. It peaked in only its tenth week on the *Billboard* charts at number thirty-six. The first single didn't do much better, and peaked at number forty-three. It was a duet with Waylon Jennings, his old roommate, and was titled, appropriately, "The Night Hank Williams Came to Town."

> I crave amphetamines. Today, I'm not taking them, and I don't intend to take them tomorrow. But, it's something that I can't help; it's my chemical make-up. The least little mood-altering thing that I might take, my system cries, "Drugs, drugs, drugs . . . more, more, more." It's like one's too many and a thousand is not enough.
> —Johnny Cash, *Music City News*, 1987

Today, the man with the lived-in face is still wearing black (does anyone really care *why* anymore?), is still married to June Carter, and, is still standing on the mountain tops, making the sound of his music, and slaying those pesty dragons.

> You can't take a poor fellow, take him out of a pair of overalls and dress him in a three-piece sharkskin suit, set him in a Fleetwood Cadillac with a gold record fixin' to come and a royalty check that's bigger than what the bank has in that little town he was raised in, and expect that dude to stay like he was. Somewhere or another, it pushes something away.
> —Carl Perkins, *Rolling Stone*

> His mother was the only thing he ever loved. He never really progressed beyond that. One time I was sittin' across a table from him, and his wife came up from behind him to hug him, and he knocked her away with his elbow, and then gave me this crooked grin like he'd done something great.
> —Waylon Jennings, *Penthouse*

Before he was "the Pelvis," he was "the Hillbilly Cat."

The last time I saw Elvis was at the Hilton in Las Vegas. He sent
his security guards down to the lobby to get me, because he'd
invited me up to a party and I hadn't gone. So me and Jessi
went up there. Sonny West was waving a gun around and
pointed it at Jessi. I told him to stop it, and he did it again. I said,
"Hoss, you better grease up that gun, because I'm fixin' to stick
it up your ass." And Elvis laughed at that. He really liked that.
—Waylon Jennings, *Penthouse*

Elvis Presley went to the bathroom at about 9:00 A.M. on
August 16, 1977. A short time later, he was found dead, sprawled
out on the bathroom tile, 226 blubbering pounds of wasted
brilliance. A book, *The Scientific Search for the Face of Jesus,* lay
beside him. The subsequent coroner's report claimed death due
to "cardiac arrhythmia." But nearly everyone outside the clutching gates of Graceland thought otherwise. After all, at the time of
his death, there were reportedly fourteen different drugs in Elvis'
body: including codeine, three sedatives, five varieties of
downers, two antidepressants, and a decongestant.

Elvis was never a cowboy, but he certainly *did* get his start in
country music. When he recorded "That's All Right Mama," at
Sun Records in July, 1954, he also recorded Bill Monroe's "Blue
Moon of Kentucky." In 1955, he cracked the country charts with
"Baby, Let's Play House," and later hit number one with "Mystery
Train" and "I Forgot to Remember to Forget." Keep in mind that
Elvis did not register on the national *pop* charts until he recorded
"Heartbreak Hotel" (written by Nashville's Max Axton) in Nash-
ville in *1956.* Shortly after he was rejected by the Grand Ole
Opry, Elvis became a big hit on The Louisiana Hayride, based in
Shreveport, where he was billed as the "Hillbilly Cat." It was with
this moniker that he went on the road and toured with the
Singing Ranger, Hank Snow.

After "Heartbreak Hotel" and the rock and roll steamroller
that ensued, many thought that Elvis Presley had, with a swing
of his hips, single-handedly killed country music. In retrospect, it
is rather obvious that he didn't. He just killed himself, one way or
another.

It was August 22, 1977, just one week after Elvis Presley's death.
The world was still in mourning and perhaps wondering who the
next show business victim would be. According to newspaper
accounts, the manager of a New York courier service pondered a

package that he had just received. It was a large manila envelope, addressed to Waylon Jennings in Nashville, which read in big, bold, black letters, CONFIDENTIAL: DO NOT OPEN. His curiosity aroused, the courier opened the package and was not particularly surprised when three little plastic packets tumbled out onto his desk. He knew immediately what he had uncovered—pure cocaine.

Waylon Jennings was recording at American Sound Studios in Nashville, producing an album, *The New South*, for Hank Williams Jr. Together, they were in the process of recording "Storms Never Last," a song written by Waylon's wife, Jessi Colter.

The courier informed his boss of his discovery, who notified the Drug Enforcement Agency. The following day, federal agent Bill Rosenberger inspected the envelope and confirmed the findings. According to some sources, as much as twenty-seven grams of cocaine were found. For some curious reason, Rosenberger retained twenty-five grams of the coke, and sent only the remaining two grams on their intended route. He also alerted the narcotics agents in Nashville.

Later that afternoon, Waylon's secretary, Lorri Evans, was sent to the Nashville Metro Airport to retrieve the package. She then drove back to American Sound Studios, where the recording session was still in process. Shortly after Lorri's return, there was a knock at the door. A Jennings associate later recalled, "Somebody flushed the coke down the toilet when the drug agents knocked on the door. When the agents came in, they found the little plastic bags lying on the bathroom floor." The wet plastic bags tested positively for cocaine. Jennings and Evans were arrested, fingerprinted, and photographed. The sender of the package, Mark Rothbaum, an aide to Neil Reshen, Waylon's manager at the time, was also arrested. Waylon was charged with conspiracy to possess and distribute twenty-seven grams of cocaine. Each charge carried a maximum penalty of fifteen years' imprisonment and a $25,000 fine. Nashville rocked. It was the first time that cocaine had been directly and publicly linked to a country music star.

But then, Waylon Jennings had always romanced rebellion. After all, he was the *country singer* who once performed on the same bill with the Grateful Dead (which led some wags to inanely pronounce that he had gone "acid rock"); who, along with a few others, popularized the hybrid between country and rock; who, along with musical compadres Tompall and Willie, tackled Nashville's corporate hierarchy—and won; and who treasonously hired a *New York* manager (worse, a New York

Country boy in a black leather wristband.

Jewish manager), instead of the standard good ole boy Nashville manager.

He was dangerous in a hot, whiskey-breath kind of way. He strutted and postured, all wrapped up in black leather and with a cigarette hanging menacingly out the side of his mouth. Men locked their doors, women went weak, and the Nashville hotline scorched with stories that Waylon's guitar wasn't the only instrument that he performed with nightly.

Strikingly handsome when he was younger—before he grew bearded and blowzy—Waylon was known in some circles as the cowboy Warren Beatty. Former professional groupie Pamela Des Barres, was even inspired by Waylon's instrumental prowess to "cross over" from the preferred rock, roll, and raunch of Jim Morrison, Mick Jagger, and others to the more basic pleasures of country. In her autobiography, subtitled *Confessions of a Groupie*, Des Barres wrote of Waylon: "We were honestly crude and crudely honest . . . such a huge hunk of a man."

Waylon further rattled the puritanical Opry when he publicly acknowledged that his sexual appetite was racially integrated. Said Waylon, "I've been with some pretty foxy little black chicks, and the devil had nothing to do with the first time, and the second time, the third time, the fourth time, it was all mine." A daring statement, considering that the country music constituency still resides primarily within the confines of the Bible Belt, where interracial harmonizing is discouraged and where interracial sex, or even a *song* about interracial sex, is strictly taboo.

> In some ways, Hank Williams unfortunately did a great injustice. A lot of little boys were out there watching him when he was on top, and they've tried to grow up [and be] just like him.
> —Jessi Colter to the *Tennessean*, 1984

Then, of course, there were the drugs.

In 1965, Waylon moved from Phoenix to Nashville and shared a $150-a-month apartment with Music City's resident bad boy at the time, Johnny Cash. The two became renegade horses trapped in the same corral. They popped pills with a vengeance, and dwelled in degradation. As Waylon later reflected, "Neither one of us could handle it and the other one knew it. It got to the point where it nearly killed both of us. I weighed 135 pounds soaking wet."

For Waylon, like Hank before him, major stardom accelerated the tunnel vision ride toward self-destruction. By way of the counterculture, immensely lucrative "Outlaw Movement" of the mid-1970s, Waylon Jennings became one of the biggest stars in

Former roommates, former pillmates.

country music. He also became addicted to cocaine. Nashville awaited his seemingly imminent demise. In his battle to reach the top, Waylon had left many ego-wounded adversaries eager for his fall.

Then came the Bust of the Little Plastic Bags and Nashville nearly wet its designer dungarees in anticipation. The day after the 1977 arrest, Waylon reportedly left the Forest Hills home that he shared with Jessi and checked into a Nashville hotel. At the arraignment, his drummer, Richie Albright, attacked an overly ambitious television cameraman and was subsequently charged with criminal assault and battery. In court, charges against Lorri Evans were dismissed, but Waylon and Mark Rothbaum were ordered to appear before a grand jury. A three-ring circus would have been more descriptively accurate. In court proceedings it was learned that an audiotape had been made at American Sound Studios on the night of the drug raid. U.S. District Court Judge L. Clure Morton ordered Waylon's attorney, Dale Quillen, to turn over the tape to the grand jury. However, Waylon's attorney protested that the tape would have been "very detrimental to Mr. Jennings." Anticipation was further raised when acquaintances of Waylon's pleaded the Fifth Amendment after being questioned about reputed "coke parties" in the country music industry.

But charges against Waylon were dropped on October 4, 1977. Some speculated that it was another case of the rich being able to purchase their way out of possible purgatory. To others, however, the results seemed to be a matter of a boggled investigation and insufficient evidence. After all, didn't the federal agents stop to think that Waylon and gang might have been alerted when *the* package arrived with only two grams, instead of the expected twenty-seven? Further, if Bill Rosenberger had airmailed the entire package of twenty-seven grams, instead of the paltry two grams, perhaps there would have been more actual physical evidence to confiscate. At any rate, the bottom line was that Waylon was not found with the cocaine in his actual possession, and the case was dismissed.

But the chemical abuse continued. After a performance at the Northern Arizona University Dome in 1978, Waylon and band terrorized the Little America Motel in Flagstaff, Arizona. They tore up four rooms, shredded a banquet room, heaved sand into the air conditioners, emptied the ice machines onto the floor, and ripped down the curtains and light fixtures. Ironically, Waylon's single at the time was "Don't You Think This Outlaw Bit's Done Got Out of Hand?"

Cocaine was depleting Waylon of other resources as well. His addiction, at its dizzying apex, was costing him a reported $1,500 a day. As he later recalled, "When it was time to eat, I would go take a snort of cocaine before I sat down at the table." In 1980, he went broke. In October, he was sued for $750,000 by Alan Cartee, owner of American Sound Studios, the same studio where he had been arrested just a few years before. Cartee contended that not only did Waylon fail to keep up his rental payments of $16,641 a month, he also, abetted by Richie Albright, had stolen $40,000 worth of recording equipment and abandoned the studio in a state of disarray. Waylon, by then swathed in legal and financial turmoil, said, "I think my own mother might sue me next."

Meanwhile, Nashville industry insiders were growing increasingly nervous. In 1981, eight people involved in a local drug ring were arrested. Allegedly, the ring had supplied drugs to figures prominent in the country music publicity profile. And word spread that some stars had even hired staff drug-runners to keep them supplied.

Still, Waylon continued to be his own worst enemy. In 1981 he told an interviewer, "An artist of any kind becomes dependent on drugs if he does them very much. When they start ruling you, you're not in control of your life, no matter what you do. When you're not in control of your life, it's going to ruin you. Several of *us* got into it too heavy. I think it's pretty well leveled out now. I don't know of anybody who is really into it now. They got busted a lot. I just stopped. Everybody was amazed." Two years later, he was asked by another reporter what caused him to stop drugs. Waylon joked, "They quit making any good ones." Then, more seriously, he said, "I just got sick and worn out. I had to stop, literally, and go in the hospital."

However, contrary to what he told the press, Waylon's cocaine abuse continued. By the spring of 1984, his health had deteriorated appallingly. He wouldn't eat. Jessi was reduced to force-feeding her husband with a variety of home-concocted protein shakes. As Waylon later realized, "Jessi went through hell. She was watching me die."

In March 1984, Waylon and family moved to Phoenix. He would later explain, "I finally ran up against the wall. I was drawing up into a shell, ruining my health and not liking anything, anybody or anything I did. I can look back now and tell what a wreck I was. Then, I couldn't tell. I was really, really sick. A lot of folks tried to tell me that for a long, long time, but I wouldn't listen." In Phoenix, after twenty-one years of life on drugs, Waylon quit. Perhaps he was inspired by his friend and ex-

Waylon Jennings: Dangerous in a hot, whiskey-breath kind of way.

Waylon, who narrated television's "Dukes of Hazzard," here with Tom Wopat: Unlikely heroes.

roommate, Johnny Cash, who underwent treatment at the Betty Ford Center. Perhaps he was inspired by the piercing innocence and questioning eyes of his young son, Shooter. Or perhaps he simply confronted himself in front of the mirror and saw death reflected back. And so he quit. And he did it by himself. He didn't consult a psychiatrist. He didn't check into a hospital. He just moved out of Nashville.

Kris Kristofferson arrived in Nashville in 1965. An army captain at the time, he seemed to step gallantly out of the pages of an F. Scott Fitzgerald novel. He was beautiful and brilliant and bound for glory. But he was also a displaced identity, a clashing dichotomy of contradictions, a poet trapped in the body of a jock, a rabble-rousing good ole boy, with the tortured soul of an artist. Within that context, then, it seems somehow appropriate that, at the age of twenty-nine, he discarded his military brass and previously earned accolades (including a Rhodes Scholarship to Oxford University) in favor of a bottle of tequila, a pair of faded

Musical compadres Kris and Willie, buzzing through life.

blue jeans, a janitorial job at Columbia Records in Nashville, and aspirations of songwriting stardom.

Within a few years, as the rest of the country muscled its way through cultural revolution, Nashville embraced a renaissance of renegade songwriters, led by Kristofferson. With "Me and Bobby McGee," "Sunday Morning Coming Down," and "Help Me Make It Through the Night" in his denim back pocket, he was inundated with saccharine laudations.

He nearly suffocated in the praise. He shifted uncomfortably in his new constraining suit of fame. For, despite his previous successes, he had always felt out of place, always the outsider, always the lurking sense within of underlying *separateness.* It was there in Brownsville, Texas, where he was born. It was there at Oxford, England. It was there in the army in Germany. And it was there amid the pomp and circumstance of stardom in Nashville.

With his newfound celebrity and come-hither blue-eyed looks that one arduous female fan described by saying, "He could be standing in a pail of garbage and he'd still be beautiful," it only seemed a natural progression for Kris Kristofferson to become a movie star.

The Big One, of course, was *A Star Is Born.* Kristofferson was to be the film's designated slab of beef, portraying an over-the-hill, alcoholic rock musician who is fatally overshadowed by the Barbra Streisand character's emerging star. It seemed an appropriate role. During the shooting of the film, Kristofferson's personal boozing intensified dramatically. According to an *Esquire* article, Kris started drinking each day at dawn, but was nonetheless one of those fortunate unfortunates who could drink and still function.

While Kristofferson sought solace in the bottom of a bottle of tequila or Jack Daniels or Tia Maria, turmoil raged on the set. In addition to being the film's star, Streisand was the producer and, reportedly, the substitute director. Her boyfriend at the time, former hairdresser Jon Peters, was credited as coproducer. To compound the tension on the set, Streisand had, in years previous, dated Kristofferson. One particularly delectable verbal barrage took place, fortuitously, in front of reporters and went like this, according to *Esquire*:

STREISAND TO KRISTOFFERSON:	Shut-up goddamn it, and listen to me!
KRISTOFFERSON TO STREISAND:	I'll be goddamned if I listen to anything more from you!
PETERS TO KRISTOFFERSON:	You owe my old lady an apology!
KRISTOFFERSON TO PETERS:	If I need any shit from you, I'll squeeze your head!

As the story goes, Peters then offered to fight Kristofferson on the final day of shooting. However, perhaps in view of Kristofferson's background as a Golden Gloves boxer, the proposed boxing-for-Barbra's-honor fight never took place. Nevertheless, Kris-

Kristofferson, the poet/artist as a slab of beef in *A Star Is Born*.

Kris and Rita in *Pat Garrett and Billy the Kid*: No simulation necessary.

The Sailor Who Fell from Grace with the Sea, the movie that launched a thousand creams.

tofferson is said to have hurled the ultimate insult at his costar and the costar's boyfriend with, "I ain't trusting my career to the judgment of a Vegas singer and a hairdresser!" However, Kristofferson's next major media decision was not so wise.

It was shortly after the shooting of *A Star Is Born*. Sarah Miles, Kristofferson's costar in another completed film, *The Sailor Who Fell from Grace with the Sea*, suggested that they reunite to pose for promotional pictures to appear in *Playboy*. The angle was that they would simulate the film's erotic love scene for the still camera. Kristofferson, resplendent in his alcoholic haze, consented. The resultant shoot was like a dream—a wet dream for the many readers of *Playboy* who snatched the issue off the shelves when it was published a few months later. Whether by spontaneity or by design, the publicity shoot, presumably to the delight of the *Playboy* photo crew, became far more sexually graphic than the actual film. One photo featured Kristofferson's naked, well-muscled back and butt as he thrust himself into his understandably agreeable costar. Another one showed him with his face buried in her bosom. Other shots captured the couple in various states of lust and agony and exploration. But the photo that caused the biggest sensation was shocking, even by *Playboy* standards. It illustrated Miss Miles, standing on a bed, back arched toward the ceiling, hands pressed against the wall, head thrown back in ecstasy, as Kristofferson unmistakably buried his face between her thighs and ate lunch on her freshly mowed front lawn.

While women all over America envied Sarah Miles, Kristofferson's wife, singer Rita Coolidge, was none too pleased. After all, extramarital affairs were one thing, but having them flaunted in your face from the pages of a magazine was another matter entirely. Kristofferson later explained publicly, "That was just about the worst thing I ever have done. My face where it was for ten million people. We were acting our roles in the movie, and I just, uh, got into it, y'know?"

On September 20, 1976, in an effort to salvage his faltering marriage, Kris Kristofferson stopped drinking. The catalyst had been seeing an initial screening of *A Star Is Born*. He later said, "When I watched the movie for the first time, I saw the character I was playing, a boozy rock star, lying there drunk, and I felt I was seeing myself through Rita's eyes for the first time."

However, by 1981, with the eventual dissolution of his marriage to Rita and the dismal catastrophe of *Heaven's Gate* close behind him, Kristofferson turned increasingly to drugs, particularly marijuana, which he referred to in interviews as "laughing tobacco." It was also at about this time that Kris was sued for

"Jesus, fuck! This is it, you know. This one's just about done me in, this fucking one. This fucking thing is . . . crazy. I'm just a basket case!"
—Kristofferson on the shooting of the film *Convoy*

paternity. A woman named Peggy Hanson contended that Kris had fathered her son in 1969, when Kris was still a struggling Nashville songwriter. The suit sought past child support payments of $250,000. Kristofferson acknowledged that he knew Hanson, but he denied paternity (he was not vindicated in court until 1987).

For Kristofferson, the early 1980s were a tumultuous exertion in love and pain and the whole damn thing. He later reflected, "Life was hard. It was hard enough to take care of the twenty or so employees I've got and to try to keep supporting my families and ex-wives and raise a little girl [daughter, Casey] at the same time." He also admitted, "I was pretty heavily into chemicals around that period and the farther I get away from it I can see there was also a lot of misdirected rage."

At one particularly significant interview for *Esquire*, he greeted the writer, Laura Cunningham, with "Let's have some dope." The interview and subsequent cover story came back to haunt him. Wrote Cunningham, "I remain high just by breathing Kris's exhaust." The article reportedly infuriated Kristofferson, who nevertheless acknowledged, "I had already quit drinking years before that article. But I was just loading up [on pot] instead. The article kind of pointed that out to me. I was real embarrassed that it was in public."

> I could end up a drunk tomorrow, but I doubt it. I think I have all the chemistry to be a full-fledged alcoholic or drug addict, because I welcome oblivion like an old friend sometimes.
> —Kris Kristofferson, 1985

Kristofferson on fame: "It's like being in a public shithouse, and everybody's writing on the wall."

Today, at fifty-two, Kris Kristofferson seems somehow too grounded to be perpetually high or in hiding. With a third wife and three more children in three years, he appears to have found his space on earth. He is still strikingly handsome, still a mass of contradictions, and still searching for a poetic vision of the world. While Nashville has essentially dismissed him as a former great gone Hollywood, he seems less concerned with commercialism and more concerned with personal conviction. In 1987, he postponed a promotional tour of his album *Repossessed* to attend peace talks in Russia; he has visited Central America; he has openly and harshly criticized Ronald Reagan and the United States involvement in Nicaragua; he makes "small" movies that don't compromise his soul; and he sings songs about Martin Luther King Jr. and other passions that arouse his pen. In the late 1960s and early 1970s, Kris Kristofferson was the voice of his generation. Today, he is more the conscience of his generation. Unfortunately, nobody pays much attention to his conscience anymore.

Larry Gatlin's *talent* is undeniable. But, for a long time, a lot of people in Nashville did not like Larry Gatlin. Some still don't. In Gatlin's own self-appraisal, he was "a selfish, self-centered, egotistical, cocky little runt."

One incident in particular seemed to stir sentiment against him. It was a musical festival of some sort that took place in 1978. Now, as everyone in the industry knows, unlike other entertainment genres, country music stars are expected to treat country music *fans* with almost as much reverence as they receive themselves. For years, megastars like Loretta Lynn have routinely spent hours after a show signing autographs and chatting with the faithful. After all, country music personalities are supposed to be down-to-earth, and if they're not, they're encouraged to fake it. The collective consensus in the industry has always been that the fans want songs and stars that they can relate to. But Larry Gatlin was not one for such humbling protocol. After the 1978 music festival, he was heavily attacked by the press and public for his allegedly abrasive treatment of his fans. Gatlin retaliated in the *Nashville Banner*:

> *I think it's unfair to step off a stage after I've been singing my butt off and be met with 200 people sticking pencils in my face. The fans don't belong backstage or anywhere around the stage. Their place is out front. I don't care if they come to see me from Mars. Coming from Mars and paying $10 does not give them a piece of my life. The fans don't understand. You're not supposed to criticize people until you've walked in their shoes and since they obviously will never walk in mine, they should keep their big mouths shut. [After a performance] the last thing I want to do is sit there and hear from some little ole lady from Indianapolis that Leroy didn't send the alimony check.*

Larry Gatlin: Just Say No?

Nashville was scandalized, and for a while there seemed to be a "get-Gatlin" attitude in the industry. Thus, some were secretly delighted in December 1984, when it was learned that Larry Gatlin was hospitalized for cocaine addiction. Eyebrows were raised in June of that year when the Gatlins were forced to cancel an appearance at the White House after Larry was rushed to a Nashville hospital for what was publicly described as "a viral infection." It wasn't cocaine that put Gatlin in the hospital. It was hepatitis. It was, reportedly, the first time in the twenty-nine-year history of the Gatlins that they had missed a date. Larry was quoted at the time as saying, "I've been sick before, but never this sick. It would have to be something important for us to cancel a performance for the president of the United States."

> I've watched them ol' boys take that stuff. Cocaine costs $2,000 an ounce, you just stuff it up your nose, and it's gone. There's a lot of the entertainers who take it. Some of the biggest ones take it.
> —Faron Young to Dolly Carlisle, *Hustler*

Then, on December 7, 1984, the Gatlins performed at Billy Bob's, the famed, now defunct, country nightclub in Fort Worth. From there, Larry flew to California to tape a special series of shows for "Family Feud." On December 10, after finding himself crawling around the floor of his hotel room, gathering up pieces of lint to smoke in a pipe because the lint resembled coke, he decided to seek help. He checked into the CareUnit rehabilitation center in Orange, California. He was joined by his brother Rudy shortly thereafter.

During the five-year period from 1979 to 1984, Larry Gatlin had spent approximately $500,000 on cocaine, sometimes, as much as $10,000 in a single day. As he later reflected, "I have an addictive personality. I wanted the fastest car. I wanted the prettiest girl, so I married her. I wanted to beat you a hundred to nothing in every ball game. I wanted the best of everything. The very best." And, "I had emotional problems. I didn't really know how to love anybody, least of all myself."

Following treatment, Larry Gatlin exalted, "I feel almost virginal!" His first performance, appropriately, was at Ronald Reagan's second presidential inaugural gala on January 19, 1985. He has since joined First Lady Nancy's "Just Say No" antidrug campaign.

Ernest Tubb, the beloved Texas Troubadour.

Unlike Larry Gatlin, not all country music cowboys, genuine, imagined, and otherwise, have cleaned up their noses, conquered their addictions, and been invited to dinner at the White House. Some have simply swallowed and snorted away their careers. Others are still trying to crawl out of the bottle and back up the charts. And there are others who never lived to see the Tequila sunrise.

Their names read like a *Who's Who* of country music.

The Delmore Brothers, Alton and Rabon, were Opry favorites from 1932 to 1938. But after the death of his daughter, Alton began drinking heavily. Rabon became seriously ill and died of cancer in 1952. Alton moved to Huntsville, Alabama, where he was reduced to becoming a door-to-door salesman. He died in 1964 of a liver disorder.

In 1957, Ernest Tubb, assuredly one of the most beloved performers in country music history, brandished a .357 Magnum pistol and shot up the lobby of the National Life Building in Nashville, which housed the Opry's radio station, WSM. Tubb, victorious over the phantom villain, was arrested and carted off to jail, where he served three hours for public drunkenness.

Rod Brasfield, diminutive Opry comic and sometime partner of Minnie Pearl, drank himself to death at the age of forty-eight.

Rex Griffin, who unsuccessfully recorded "Lovesick Blues" a decade before Hank Williams shot to stardom with it, had a lifelong drinking problem and died in 1959 at the age of forty-seven.

Red Foley, once the number one star in country music, was once rushed to a hospital and saved from death due to an overdose of sedatives. A fan of Foley's was not so lucky. Legend has it that a Los Angeles woman tried to drive her husband crazy by repeatedly playing Foley's record, "Old Kentucky Fox Chase," on the phonograph. The enraged husband picked up a frying pan and bludgeoned his wife to death, presumably to the beat of the music. Foley had wife problems of his own. His first wife, Pauline Cox, died giving birth to their daughter, Betty. His second marriage, to Eva Overstake, was reportedly stormy and ended with her unexpected, peculiar death. Foley himself continued working one-night stands late in his life because, despite his former hillbilly glory, he was broke. In 1968, he was found dead in an Indiana motel room, due to what was termed acute pulmonary edema.

Lefty Frizzell, traditionalist honky tonk singer and musical forefather to Randy Travis, Merle Haggard, Willie Nelson, and others, had a serious drinking problem throughout his career.

Multifaceted country music star Merle Travis was heavily addicted to barbiturates. In fact, while enroute to some tour

An addiction to pills put the talented Merle Travis into a California mental institution.

The former "King of the Road," Roger Miller, scored a major success in the 1980s with his Tony-winning Broadway musical *Big River*.

dates, he and Johnny Cash used to pop pills in the backseat of his car. Like so many others, Travis's addiction threatened his career. According to his third wife, Betty Lou Travis, who occasionally sang onstage with Merle, he was once committed to Camarillo State Mental Hospital in California (it was either there or jail), where he was incarcerated for three months. A while after his release, however, he reverted back to pills and ended up spending time in various California hospitals. It was Merle's addiction to pills that eventually brought on the dissolution of his marriage to Betty Lou in 1977. Merle remarried in 1980 and, according to his fourth wife, Dorothy, he finally gave up pills several years before his death in 1983.

After the fatal 1956 car crash that killed his brother and crippled his career, country boy Carl Perkins drank himself to near oblivion. When he joined "The Johnny Cash Show" in 1966, he and Cash used to camp out in the back of the tour bus, Carl with his bottle and Cash with his pills.

Roger Miller, the wit of Nashville, was another fanatical pill popper. His ascent to stardom was fast and furious, but unfortunately his decline was equally rapid. At one point, the former king of the road was eating ninety pills a day.

After Charlie Rich's drunken fire-act at the 1975 Country Music Awards (which was later explained to the press as the side effects of a poisonous insect bite!), his career collapsed and the less talented but nonetheless sober Kenny Rogers inherited Charlie's "countrypolitan" throne and became, arguably, the richest country music star in the industry's history.

Johnny Rodriguez exploded onto the country music scene in 1972 at age twenty-one. It was a lethally sudden success for a Tex-Mex poor boy. As he later recounted with graphic description, "I pigged out on cocaine and I paid. Cocaine was everywhere. I mean, everywhere. Fans had it. My friends had it. Everybody was doing it—like beer back in Texas." Reportedly, once Rodriguez sidled up next to Waylon Jennings and the two of them proceeded to snort coke—while being interviewed. He later explained, "All of a sudden, I had all these people depending on me for a living. And if you are any kind of person, you fill that responsibility. I tried to, but it was hard." In 1981, with his marriage and career destroyed, Rodriguez entered a drug rehabilitation center. Within a year afterward, he was back on coke. In the spring of 1984, he entered another treatment center, this one outside of San Antonio. He left after only four days. However, he returned to the same center in August of that year and reportedly has been straight ever since. Today, he is trying to resurrect his career, which once held such promise.

"Hell, I ain't got any problems. I'm just Johnny, J.R., having fun."
—Johnny Rodriguez

"I'm not in bad shape for a tequila-drinking doper."
—Willie Nelson (pictured here in *Honeysuckle Rose*)

Y'all hear about ol' Willie Nelson passing out onstage in Dallas the other night? Somebody said Willie got his pillboxes mixed up and took downers when he meant to take uppers. Well, hell, I been to the drugstore a time or two myself.
—David Allan Coe, *Esquire*, July, 1976

"Hee Haw" star Lulu Roman is one of the few country music women to go public about a drug problem. Said Lulu, "I was so involved in the drug scene that I'd eat handfuls of the garbage." She was "saved" when she turned to God. In 1987, the 300-pound Lulu announced that she would be going out on tour with Jim and Tammy Faye Bakker.

Junior Samples, another 300-pound "Hee Haw" star, died of a heart attack in 1983. His biggest hit was titled "The World's Biggest Whopper."

Nearly forty years after the death of Hank Williams, the men of country music are still fulfilling his sad and foreboding prophecy. Although they don't necessarily condone their idol's lifestyle of drinking, drugging, and eventual self-destruction, they do *empathize* with it. So many have been down that lost highway themselves. It is something inbred, something that, as men, they can share in the name of brotherhood. There *have* been some Nashville women who have suffered the ravages of drug and alcohol addiction, but the Hank Williams legacy is a decidedly masculine thing. Like growing up wanting to be a cowboy. Like longing with melancholy at the sound of a lonesome whistle from a passing freight train. Like drinking beer straight from the bottle. Like pissing in the wind.

4

QUEENS IN A QUANDARY

Roba Stanley was the first country music woman recording soloist. Pasty Montana was the first to have a million-selling single. Molly O'Day was on her way to becoming the top female singer in the land when, in 1952, she contracted tuberculosis and gave up her career to become a minister in the Church of God. A few years later, Kitty Wells went on to become crowned the "Queen of Country Music." Her successor, Patsy Cline was the very first female star to become a country music legend and remains the most gifted vocalist in the history of the music.

But today Kitty Wells, no disrespect intended, is more the Dowager Empress than the Queen. And Patsy Cline died too soon, leaving far too little musical vinyl behind.

So make no mistake about it. Today there are only *three* women who deserve to hold court in the royal circle as the true "Queens of Country Music." They are the same three who have admirably worn the crown at various times over the past three decades. Many others, younger and prettier, all aflutter in false eyelashes, pouffed bouffants, and sashaying gingham, have come and gone, and still only Loretta, Tammy, and Dolly remain at the top.

There is a touching, frail beauty about Loretta Lynn that's like a thin cotton summer dress on a brutally windy day. You just want to wrap her up in a warm winter jacket and take care of her. Everybody loves Loretta Lynn. Still, there are those in Nashville who are convinced that ole Loretta has gone off her Butcher Hollow rocker.

LORETTA

Loretta Lynn:
A thin cotton summer dress on a brutally windy day.

Okay, okay. So, she is always a-passing out on stage. And she does seem to have frequent skids of depression. And she does tend to ramble when she talks, going off and out into unexplored galaxies. And she has sometimes forgotten the lyrics to her own songs while onstage. And she is awfully *honest*, too honest for the comfort of some. And she did once denounce her early Christian teachings in favor of palm reading. But, is all this really sufficient evidence to brand her a country music mental suspect?

Where does it end? When am I going to slow down?
—Loretta Lynn

Loretta Lynn has always gone too fast. She was married at thirteen, a mother of four at eighteen, a grandmother at twenty-nine. At twenty-five, she was a star. And she has gone fast and faster ever since. Too fast to take a breath and look over her pretty shoulder and see the expansive distance that she had placed between herself and real life.

Her health was the first thing to go. Over the years, Loretta has had breast surgery and been stricken by and cursed with ear infections, blood poisoning, bleeding ulcers, migraine headaches, and her infamous spells of blackouts and "exhaustion." It is the latter, of course, which has provoked the most concern and commentary.

Not a year goes by, it seems, when Loretta isn't hospitalized for exhaustion. In 1972, she was hospitalized nine times. Sometimes she passes out on stage. Most times, though, it's backstage or at an airport or hotel. As Loretta's former manager David Skepner once stated, "She does what she has to do and collapses later." Loretta explained, "I just pass out. Go into a sort of coma, when I don't even know it's comin' on."

When she isn't in a state of collapse, Loretta seems to be threatened by some other physical calamity. In 1986, while en route from Nashville to Memphis, she and her husband, Mooney, were involved in a car accident. Their Mercedes was demolished. Mooney escaped unscathed, but Loretta was hospitalized with a concussion and an injured right arm and leg. The following year, while doing a USO tour of military bases in Korea and the South Pacific, Loretta took a nasty spill, was treated for injuries, and had to recuperate in Hawaii. Still, it is her *mental* health that is in question, and that seems to be most in peril.

I just get all torn up by harsh words and violence. Like one time Doo [her name for Mooney] got mad at a dog that was barking too much. So, right in front of me, he just hit it once with a club and killed it. I just went to bed and stared at the ceiling for twenty-four hours.
—Loretta Lynn

In 1977, Loretta told a writer for *Esquire* that she once almost committed suicide. Explained Loretta, "These migraines—if you was to cut your arm off it wouldn't be no worse. My husband gave me a little pearl-handle gun for Valentine's Day. Well, a while back the migraine was starting to get so bad I was about to vomit and I reached into my pocketbook and there wasn't no Darvon, wasn't no Demerol, I came to that little pearl-handle gun. It's a good gun; it's hard to pull the trigger. If you don't want to die, you won't do it by accident. But I had the gun to my head. The doctor asked me the next day, 'Why would you want to kill yourself?' I said, 'I didn't want to kill myself. I just wanted to kill the pain.' " To a *Rolling Stone* reporter, Loretta likened herself to Marilyn Monroe: "I was just about that depressed, you know. The way I got to thinkin' was that I was being used on every—every time I moved. My family used me, my kids, my husband, everybody. I was just like a piece of machinery. I'd come in, I was treated like a stranger. I'd come in home and I was just like somebody visitin' the house. So, I could have endin' up like Marilyn because I did try it. I was scared."

> I think I'm one of the unhappiest people in the world. Never
> hardly a night goes by on the road when I'm in the back of the
> bus, that I don't cry. 'Bout half the time I cry myself to sleep.
> —Loretta Lynn, *Esquire*, 1977

In 1978, Loretta publicly confessed that she was seeing a psychiatrist and that she had been addicted to "nerve pills." Said Loretta, "Every time I felt nervous, I took a pill. And, at bedtime I had me still other pills to get to sleep." She was nervous a lot. In fact, sometimes she got so nervous in her own house that she had to check into a Nashville hotel. Said Loretta, "[I had] too many responsibilities, too many conflicts, too many guilts." However, Skepner, Loretta's manager at the time, seemed to shrug off her depression. "About three years ago [1975] Loretta had a thing where everyone said to her, 'try this' or 'try that' for her nerves and headaches. If you know Loretta, she's the kind of person who will figure that if a doctor says to take one of something, two will be even better. It's a very common addiction. Loretta's addiction continued and she began taking daily doses of an antidepressant. The worst part, she admitted sadly, was that "I'm not allowed to drive a car because I might pass out. That makes me mad because I wrote some of my best songs while drivin' along." Loretta's drug dependency grew severe enough for her to check into a rehabilitation program at Nashville's Parkview Hospital. Explained Loretta, "[With drugs] I was trying to heal my mind, you see. It got where if I started crying I'd take one [Librium]. Later, it got to where I'd take two and still be shaking. Finally, it got to where things were so bad I'd just get up and do my show and say, 'Hey! I don't wanna think about nothing!' And I'd just take some Librium and go to sleep."

When her depressed state of mind wasn't getting her in trouble, her *mouth* was. Certainly, she is the most honest and straightforward of the country queens. She also seems to be completely free of any form of prejudice. Nevertheless, she was once sued for $2 million dollars by a black man who contended that she had humiliated him in front of 10,000 people. It happened at a 1982 performance in Richmond, Virginia. Loretta was in the middle of singing her trademark song, "Coal Miner's Daughter," when she stopped abruptly and turned to Caesar Gaiters Jr., a black security guard who stood near to the stage. Loretta then turned to face her audience again and said, without guile, "If you people don't know what coal looks like, here is somebody who knows what coal is all about." The spotlight then shone momentarily on Gaiters. Loretta turned her back to him and said, "Black is beautiful, ain't it brother?" She then resumed her song, and that, of course, should have been the end of it. It wasn't. Gaiters filed suit, claiming that Loretta's onstage repartee had provoked him to drink and led to impotence. Four *years* later, the case was dropped. But not before many had given Loretta a—uh—black mark for indiscretion.

Loretta, Dinah, and Crystal, taking home the gold.

But then this is the same woman who once fell asleep on the talk shown panel when feminist Betty Friedan was being interviewed. And who wrote and recorded a song called "The Pill" and quipped, "You know, I had four children by the time I was eighteen. And if they had had pills back when I had my first boy, why, I'd have eaten 'em like popcorn." And "Actually, I recorded it for poor little Tanya Tucker. There she is, just sixteen years old and singing, 'Would you lie with me in a field of stone.' She needs to know about the pill!" And who barked at singer Johnny Rodriguez, after Rodriguez had been out late one night, drinking with Mooney, "You shut up! I don't want to hear anything you have to say. This isn't any of your business. You do whatever you want to with your life, but stay out of mine!" And who advised a reporter backstage at the Opry after she had returned home from a European tour, "Put in your article about how bad the toilet paper is over there. I wish you could see it, hun, you wouldn't believe it!"

As early as 1977, *Rolling Stone* reported Loretta's public claim that she was psychic. "I look at someone's eyes, and I know what has really passed and I know what's comin'. I was about nineteen years old when I started feelin' this power comin' over me and I wondered what it was. People would say I was crazy if they knew the things that I do, but it's not crazy." Then she dropped the bomb. The front page of the *Nashville Banner* screamed, "Country music superstar Loretta Lynn says she can no longer accept some of her early Christian teachings and is now convinced she is the product of reincarnation." There are, of course, many highly intelligent and lucid individuals who adamantly believe in metaphysics; however, as previously mentioned, country music fans are traditionally rigid in their religious devotion, and country music stars are expected to be the same. The church is sacred and not to be questioned. Nevertheless, Loretta brazenly acknowledged that her beliefs did not reflect those of her church, the Church of Christ. Said she, "My church hasn't answered a lot of questions that I've asked. But what's happened to me now, does. I know people are going to say I'm going to hell and the preachers will tell me the same thing." Loretta also told of séances held at her house. "The scariest experience of all took place the night we made contact with a spirit who told us that he was a man named Anderson. We tried to ask him questions, but Mr. Anderson would have none of it. He got so all-fired angry that the table began shaking like you wouldn't believe! That was my most frightening moment, sitting there in the room and watching that table as it rocked from side to side and jumped up

Conway and Loretta, the most successful duet team in country music history.

and down. Finally, it jumped up and came down on the floor with so much force."

She also delved into her past-life incarnations, which she learned about while under hypnosis. "In one past life, I was a servant, bringing out platters of food to a bunch of men. And when the hypnotist asked me who my master was, I said, 'He's the king.' He asked me my master's name, and I said that it was King George and that I was his girlfriend on the side—the queen didn't know about it. I told the hypnotist I lived near a village called Claridge and that I was very unhappy, because the king was going to be killed. Meanwhile, the king's best friend was grabbin' me and making love to me behind the king's back, and I was afraid to tell the king about it because they were such buddies. Anyway, the king died before I did, and then his best friend choked me to death." Loretta also told of another lifetime, in which she had been married to an Indian chief. Said she, "I was an Indian princess once. My name was 'Little Flower.'"

Loretta also professed a talent for palm reading and claimed to have predicted the tragic death for "Big Joe," a bassist for Conway Twitty, Loretta's duet partner. "I told him to be careful of an accident or something else that was going to happen to him." Two nights later, according to Loretta, Big Joe was killed in a car crash.

Perhaps it is because of her psychic awareness that Loretta Lynn never learned how to swim and has always been afraid of the water. But even she was not able to forecast the tragedy of July 1984. She had been en route to Nashville from a concert in Kansas City when she collapsed at a truck stop and was rushed by ambulance to Good Samaritan Hospital in Mount Vernon, Illinois. While she was there recovering from another bout of "exhaustion," a rescue worker's boat propeller churned up the body of Jack Benny Lynn, thirty-four, Loretta's firstborn son, out of the Duck River, located near Loretta's Tennessee dude ranch. Said Assistant District Attorney Dan Cook, "It looks as if he tried to ride his horse across the river, the water washed him off, and he drowned." He had been wearing blue jeans, a T-shirt, and cowboy boots with spurs.

At first, Loretta was not notified of her son's death. And when she was told, the entire country music industry seemed to hold its breath in fear that Loretta would fall finally and irrevocably apart.

She hasn't. She still wears those wigs (overzealous fans had habitually butchered her natural hair) and those out-of-style ball gowns and looks as though she stepped out of a dream from somewhere back in time. For, despite the fact that Loretta Lynn became famous singing the songs of the soil and remains essentially what is termed "down to earth," there is something ethereal and visionary about her, some otherworldly strength and beauty. Just ask Daman Reynolds, whose pick-up truck crashed into Loretta's tour bus on a Texas highway in June 1986. Loretta, awakened by the crash, hurried outside and nursed the injured college student in her arms until paramedics arrived on the scene. Or ask the audience at the San Antonio Livestock Show. In the middle of her performance, the stage and house lights mysteriously blacked out. Undaunted, Loretta continued to sing on a stage lit only by the headlights of a police car.

> What is love? You know what love is? When you hold your little baby in your arms for the first time. That's it. That is love. After that, forget it, friends.
> —Loretta Lynn

"I don't know if I'd go into show business again. It's an unnatural life. And it's cut-throat. People are always doin' and a-sayin' ugly things."
—Loretta Lynn

Loretta has since "slowed down." Perhaps, she isn't crazy at all. Perhaps, she has just been in too many towns and seen too many highways from the back of a tour bus. Perhaps, after all these years, and like the fictional Dorothy, she just wanted to go home.

If Loretta Lynn is country music's Dorothy lost in the land of Oz, then Tammy Wynette is certainly its Cinderella. But where does the fairy tale end and real life begin? *Is* she the quintessential victim, the lovable but pathetic "Heroine of Heartbreak" as she has been proclaimed, or is she simply a star with a flair for the dramatic?

Her publicity biography reads, "She cooked in an open fire-place, carried her water from a spring down the hill and *boiled diapers in an iron pot over a backyard fire."* She grew up, cursed with the name Virginia Wynette Pugh, on a farm near Tupelo, Mississippi. Naturally, she picked cotton. Her father, blind and dying, sat at the piano and placed her fingers on the keys of the piano and told his wife, "If she has any talent at all, please see to it that she has lessons, music lessons. I would love for her to sing."

While still a teenager, Wynette married her first husband, Euple Byrd (which made her Wynette Pugh Byrd), to get away from her mother. They lived in what has been described as a log cabin shack, which Wynette insulated with cardboard boxes that she had ripped apart and nailed to the walls. When Wynette shared her dream of singing stardom with Euple, he reportedly snickered, "Dream on, baby, dream on." (Naturally, "Tammy" later gave Euple an autograph that read "Dream on, baby, dream on.")

In an effort to get away from Euple, Wynette, by then the mother of two young girls and with another one on the way, packed up and moved to Birmingham, Alabama, where she became a beautician at the Midfield Beauty Salon. It was 1965, and Wynette soon grew weary of life with her hands in someone else's dandruff. She continued at the salon to support her daughters, but she also began taking brief sojourns off to Nashville to make the proverbial rounds, meeting with record company executives, producers, and established stars. And then she got a break. Porter Wagoner, a big star of the era, was post–Norma Jean and pre–Dolly Parton, and he needed a girl singer. Wynette Pugh fit the bill and was hired for a one-week tour. According to excerpts from Porter's unpublished autobiography written with Ellis Nassour (author of the well-researched *Patsy Cline*), Tammy and Porter had a brief, loveless affair headquartered at the Anchor Inn in Nashville. However, to this day, Tammy bristles at the allegations of horizontal humping with Porter. Said she, "Let's put it this way: if Porter was Adam and I was Eve, there would have been no Cain and Abel."

But it was producer Billy Sherrill, not Porter Wagoner, and not Don Chapel, Wynette's second husband, who was cast as Wynette's Prince Charming.

> If we were recordin' tonight and I said, "Your next record is 'Three Blind Mice,' " she'd say just three words: "What key, Billy?"
> —Billy Sherrill

It was Billy Sherrill who transformed Wynette Pugh into Tammy Wynette. With Sherrill's tutelage, Tammy quickly became a star, singing songs like "Apartment #9," "Your Good Girl's Gonna Go Bad," "I Don't Wanna Play House," "D-I-V-O-R-C-E," "Stand by Your Man," and "Don't Liberate Me, Love Me." "Stand by Your Man" became the biggest selling single recorded by a female country singer. Tammy was also named the Country Music Association's "Female Vocalist of the Year" in 1968, 1969, and 1970, eclipsing even Loretta Lynn for a spell.

Billy Sherrill may have been Tammy Wynette's Prince Charm-

(Tammy Wynette and George Jones:) The Sonny and Cher of Country Music.

Georgia Department of Human Resources

VITAL RECORDS UNIT

STATE FILE NO. _____

COUNTY NO. 9 498 _____

CERTIFIED COPY

Marriage License

To any Judge, Justice of the Peace, Minister of the Gospel, or any other person authorized to solemnize: You are hereby authorized and permitted to join in the Holy State of Matrimony

GEORGE G. JONES _____ *and* _____ VIRGINIA W. BYRD

according to The Constitution and Laws of this State, and for doing so this shall be your sufficient license.

Given Under My Hand and Seal, this 25th *day of* FEBRUARY , 19 69 .

BOB ROLLINS Ordinary

Ordinary
Probate Judge

I Hereby Certify, That

GEORGE G. JONES _____ *and* _____ VIRGINIA W. BYRD

were joined together in the Holy State of Matrimony on this 25th *day of* FEBRUARY , 19 69 , *by me in the City of*
RINGGOLD , *County of* CATOOSA , *Georgia.*

Recorded MARCH 3 , 19 69. *Signature of Officiant* BOB ROLLINS

Book No. 25 *Page* 195 *Title* ORDINARY

BOB ROLLINS, ORDINARY *Address* RINGGOLD, GEORGIA
Judge of the Probate Court

I hereby certify that the above is a true and correct copy of Marriage Record as it appears in my office.

Witness my hand and seal this 12th *day of* APRIL , 19 88 .

Lois T. Queen

LOIS T. QUEEN, CLERK

ing, but country music superstar George Jones was her shining, though not entirely sober, knight on the charging white horse. One night in 1968, Tammy and hubby Chapel were in the midst of a heated domestic argument when Jones dropped by the house to visit Tammy. He ended up in confrontation with Chapel. When Chapel reportedly cursed at Tammy, Jones retaliated by blurting out, "You don't talk to her like that!" Chapel responded, "Why? She's *my* wife." To which Jones gallantly countered, "Because I love her." Tammy's hit single at the time was "D-I-V-O-R-C-E."

So Tammy and George scooped up her three daughters and fled, never to return to the scene of the fair maiden's rescue. Chapel filed a $100,000 alienation of affection suit against Jones that was subsequently settled out of court. Meanwhile Tammy moved in with Jones, and the collective sentiment in Nashville seemed to be that ambitious Tammy had dumped her loving husband for a more famous bedfellow.

Their eventual marriage fulfilled the Cinderella theme quite nicely. As Tammy herself exulted often enough, "Very few people get to marry their idol. I did." As for George, he released a single called "I'll Share My World with You." Despite having told the press that they had married in August 1968 (they were, after all, *living together*), the actual wedding did not take place until February 16, 1969, in Ringgold, Georgia. They began recording together in 1971. Many hits, duet and solo, followed. They had sell-out crowds everywhere they went. They had residences in Tennessee and Florida, a houseboat, a nightclub, a country music theme park, a large collection of antique cars, and eventually a daughter named Tamala Georgette. They were, much to the delight of their fans, the Liz and Dick of country music.

They ended it as the Sonny and Cher of country music. Tammy initially filed for a divorce in August 1973. However, the couple reconciled a month later and released a new single to commemorate their renewed togetherness. It was called "We're Gonna Hold On." In an interview that appeared in October 1974, Tammy cooed demurely, "I wouldn't live without him. I know that. I just couldn't." Two months later, the couple separated again, and in early January 1975, Tammy filed for divorce, contending cruel and inhuman treatment. The couple's single at the time was "We Loved It Away."

Tammy was through standing by her man. George later filed a countersuit, charging that Tammy, in conjunction with his agent Shorty Lavender, had conspired to damage his career. Tammy responded with a charitable public statement: "George is sick and badly needs help. Many of my friends in the music business have tried to help him over the last several weeks. It is painful for me to endure this, but my real concern is that George get some help to protect him against his own worst enemy—himself." As for her love for George, Tammy said, "There's no love in the world that can't be killed if you beat it to death long enough." Tammy was awarded the house, $1,000 a month; child support for Georgette; George's band, the Jones Boys, which Tammy renamed the Country Gentlemen; and the couple's twelve-bunk touring bus with its logo "Mr. and Mrs. Country Music."

Still, George continued to carry the torch. On November 8, 1976, he attempted a reconciliation by flying from Nashville to London to be at Tammy's hospital bedside. She was reportedly suffering, from acute bronchitis. Nashville newspaper photographers shot Jones boarding the plane to be at Tammy's side. He told reporters, "There will never be anyone else for either of us." The public, awash as usual in sentimentality, ate it up. Tammy and George's hit single at the time (they had continued to record together) was entitled "Near You."

But for Tammy, George's knight-on-white-horse act had lost its veneer. As for George, he didn't seem to recover from losing his Cinderella bride, and he went into personal and professional decline that lasted several years. He grieved to reporters, "Let's say I was happiest when I lived with Tammy." Tammy's career also waned. She lost tour bookings. Promoters and fans, it seemed, wanted them both or not at all. As late as June 1977, George was still proclaiming his love for Tammy. Said he, "I think we still love each other. I know I love her." He even started a rumor that they were about to remarry. Said George, "Maybe Tammy'll hear it and come on home."

Tammy's career recovered somewhat, due to her renewed and highly publicized love life. There was Tom Neville, tackle for the New England Patriots, and there was Rudy Gatlin, Larry's brother and Tammy's back-up singer, who was ten years her junior.

But it was Burt Reynolds who was Tammy's most impressive escort. At the time, Reynolds was the biggest box-office attraction in the world, the King of Hollywood, and Tammy was still battling with Loretta for the title of Queen of Nashville. It was, in the eyes of some, the ultimate crossover. At first, Tammy was coy and secretive to the press about their relationship, which of course only intensified public interest. Said she, "It's not an ordinary relationship. And other than that, if things worked out, yes, I would [marry]. I mean, if we can. Well, I don't know how to put this. I'll just have to give it time and see. I'm afraid to try again with somebody in the business, which, well, I'll just have to put it, the guy I'm talkin' about is in the entertainment business."

The guy she was talkin' about *was* the entertainment business. Tammy's fans, of course, were enthralled by her potential replacement for George Jones. But the match made in press agents' heaven was not to be, and some wags have since speculated that perhaps Tammy had exaggerated the extent of her friendship with Reynolds. Certainly she acquired a lot of publicity at a time when her career was in a lull. Further, since her initial attempt at discretion, she has openly discussed their relationship. She even publicly described an incident in which Reynolds lost consciousness in the bathtub of her home. Tammy, understandably in a panic, yanked the famous movie star out by his head, and hauled him off to the hospital.

But it wasn't Burt Reynolds who Tammy Wynette married on July 18, 1976. It was a realtor named J. Michael Tomlin. Tomlin was quoted at the time as saying, "I never had any idea about marrying anybody. A lot of my friends can't believe I am getting married at all, but I am ready to settle down and Tammy is a lady I can settle down with. It all seemed very quick to a lot of people who didn't know the situation, but for the first time I'm really in love and this is what I want to do." Tammy just gushed, "I've never been so nervous. My name will be Tammy Tomlin."

Not for long. The honeymoon was over almost before the ceremony. The couple lived together for three weeks. Officially, the marriage lasted two months. Tammy later insinuated that Tomlin was a hustler who had married her for her money. Shortly after their marriage, Tammy had to be hospitalized for gallbladder surgery. While she was in the hospital, according to Tammy, Tomlin went to the bank and told the bank manager that he needed $8,000 to pay off her hospital bill. The bank manager gave Tomlin the money and also alerted Tammy's attorney, John Lentz, because, as Tammy contended, "There was actually no balance due on my hospital bill." Tammy filed for an annulment, and Tomlin countercharged that she had damaged his reputation and threatened to sue her for $300,000. For Tammy, it was an expensive wedding. As she later bemoaned, "The flowers alone cost me $7,200."

George and Sheila Richey were Tammy's best friends during this period. Richey, a songwriter and record producer, had played the organ at Tammy's wedding to Tomlin. Sheila, Tammy's girlfriend, confidante, and former secretary, had been her matron of honor. In June 1975, the Richeys were having marital difficulties of their own and Sheila filed for divorce, claiming cruel and inhuman treatment. In her legal complaint, Sheila contended that on June 2, the night of their first wedding anniversary, she and Richey had gone out to celebrate at a Nashville restaurant. Upon returning home, Sheila claimed, Richey physically beat her; took her pocketbook, her clothes, and her keys to the home; and bodily threw her out of the house, partially nude. She was subsequently forced to walk, half-naked, to the home of a friend. Sheila also contended that she was "dreadfully afraid" of Richey and sought a restraining order to prevent him from approaching her. Nevertheless, by December 1975, the couple reconciled and the suit for divorce was dismissed.

However, in October 1977, the case was refiled, with one intriguing, additional element: Sheila Richey charged her husband with adultery. Sheila contended that she had been receiving phone calls from friends who told her that he had been seen in the company of "another woman" and that he had made a public announcement that he intended to marry this other woman. Sheila was, accordingly to her court papers, "greatly humiliated and hurt emotionally" by her husband's conduct.

Less than a year later, on July 6, 1978, George Richey became Tammy Wynette's fifth husband. Reportedly, they had lived together for several months prior to their marriage. In January 1981, Tammy was quoted in the *Star* as acknowledging that she and Richey had fallen in love *while* he had still been married to Sheila. The interview, which Tammy has since confirmed, read, "Our first night together was when he was still married. I had to do an overdubbing session in Nashville and while I was working Richey came by the studio. He had been drinking heavily, which is very unlike him. When I finished dubbing, I walked over and sat on his lap to listen to the playback and he said, 'You know, I've been in love with you for over two years.' From that night we were never separated. We slipped out of town and hid out for a few months. It was all so romantic."

But there were to be no storybook endings for Sheila Richey. On October 15, 1981, Sheila was found dead in her Nashville home. She was thirty-seven. Her pet poodle, Elsie, which had been a gift from Richey, was found dead beside her. There was no investigation, and the death was termed "accidental." Nevertheless, there was a plethora of speculation in Nashville that Sheila Richey, in a state of extreme depression, took an overdose of drugs and killed herself, and her dog as well.

Tammy had been having horrific problems of her own. They began shortly after her divorce from George Jones and before her marriages to Tomlin and Richey. For several years, there was terror at the mansion on the hill. During one particularly tumultuous period, there were seventeen break-ins in nine months at the Franklin Road home that Tammy had shared with Jones. They began when unknown vandals entered the home and, using

Tammy's lipstick, smeared words such as "Slut," "Pig," and "Bitch," across Tammy's expensive mirrors, television screens, bed sheets, and walls. They also blackened her back door with eight "X" marks. And that was only a scurrilous promise of what was to come.

On the evening of May 28, 1976, Tammy went to bed with an upset stomach. Unable to sleep, she got out of bed and went to the kitchen for a bottle of Pepto-Bismol. Thank God for small stomachaches. For while she was up, Tammy heard the sound of footsteps running in the rain outside of her home. She telephone Rudy Gatlin, her boyfriend at the time. Gatlin arrived armed with a gun but was unable to track the intruding footsteps. The scare was not yet behind them though. At about 12:30 A.M., the first two of three separate fires scorched through Cinderella's palace. The fire department arrived and left and, shortly before 3:00 A.M., was resummoned to battle yet another blaze. The final fire swept through Tammy's trophy room, turning her treasured accolades to ash.

The damages were estimated at $150,000, and the fire department assertively claimed, "It's definitely arson!" Mike Shumate, of the Brentwood, Tennessee, Fire Department, told reporters, "It looks like the three fires were set by one of the nine persons staying at the house at the time. I say that because it's highly improbable that someone could have gone inside the house and set it on fire with nine people in it." Subsequently everyone in the house at the time of the fires, including Tammy, Gatlin, Tammy's mother, her aunt, her four daughters, and one of their friends, was subjected to voice polygraph and stress evaluation tests. However, nothing was concluded from the tests, and the case was never solved. The fire department remains to this day in a state of bewilderment over the Wynette fires.

And then it was the police department's turn.

It was shortly after 7:00 P.M. on October 4, 1978. Nashville-area television stations broke into their regular programming with the following announcement, "[We] have learned that a woman tentatively identified by reliable sources as country music star Tammy Wynette has been found badly beaten and wandering along a country road in Giles County off I-65 South tonight. . . ."

Tammy had been at the Green Hills Shopping Center, shopping for a birthday present for daughter Georgette. She had $40 cash and *thirty* credit cards in her pocketbook. Absentmindedly, she left the keys to her canary-yellow Cadillac Eldorado in the car's ignition. At about 5:30, she returned to the car, which was parked in the mall's lot. She opened the door and was confronted by a stocking-masked gunman in the backseat. The gunman poked his gun in Tammy's side and ordered, "Drive!" Following her abductor's orders, Tammy drove to Franklin, Tennessee. She was then forced out of the driver's seat and told to lie on the floorboard of the car. Terrified, she scanned the gunman's face and figure searching for some identifying mark. But all she could see, as she would later recall, was "a brown glove, a lot of hair on his arm, and two inches of gun barrel." The abductor drove approximately eighty miles south on Interstate 65 to Pulaski, Tennessee. He then stopped the car. He got out, walked over to the passenger side, and opened the door with his right hand. In his left hand he held his gun. He dragged Tammy out of the car. As she later described, "I got out and he hit me upside the head with his fist" and, "I thought, Oh, God, I'm gonna die." The sadistic masked gunman then walked over to another car, a dark blue station wagon, and drove off in a cloud of exhaust and mystery.

For a while, Tammy hid in the bushes. Then, when she was relatively certain that her captor would not return, she staggered out onto the road. A pair of pantyhose dangled from her neck. Apparently her captor had contemplated choking her to death but opted against it.

Bobby Young, twenty-one, had pulled out of his mother's driveway to go to a gas station when he saw a woman, hysterical and stumbling, along the road. Bobby pulled up beside her. Just then Tammy fell to the ground and uttered, "I'm Tammy Wynette. I need help." Bobby led Tammy into his mother's farmhouse as Tammy repeated, over and over, "He tried to kill me, he tried to kill me, he tried to kill me. . . ."

> I think we found her just in time. She was choking, gasping for breath and I don't think she could have lasted much longer. I gave her a cold, wet rag. Her cheek was skinned. It looked like the kind of scrape you get when you fall on concrete. Her neck wasn't cut but was swelled and red from the pantyhose or whatever that had been tied around her neck. She couldn't breathe. It was real tight, in fact I had to cut it off. I hollered to one of the kids for a knife, then she gave my son the number to call her husband.
>
> After I looked at her, I knew right away it was Tammy. I'm a big fan of hers, she's my favorite singer. I couldn't believe it was the real Tammy Wynette! I wanted to say how I just loved her and George Jones together, but it wasn't the time or place to talk about her ex-husband.
>
> —Junette Young

The following morning, an article appeared in the *Nashville Banner* written by Tammy describing her ordeal. The headlines blared Tammy's vow, I'LL NEVER GO OUT ALONE AGAIN.

The Nashville police were clearly befuddled. After all, there had been no apparent motive, no demand for ransom, and Tammy had not been sexually assaulted. Two days after the abduction, the police centered their search on a gas station attendant who worked near Tammy's mansion. However, that angle was later dropped. Three weeks later, a mysterious handwritten note on a yellow legal pad was found attached to Tammy's front door. It read, "We missed you the first time. We'll get you the next time." The police were further confused. Whoever had delivered the note went undetected, despite a fortresslike security force stationed at Tammy's house. Said Lieutenant Sherman Nickens, who headed the investigation, "We just don't have a motive. If they wanted to kill her, they could have already done that, and they didn't ask for any money when they kidnapped her. We don't have any prime suspects, either. We have no motive, no nothing."

The press was equally confused and increasingly wary. The sentiment seemed to change from "Tammy Was Kidnapped!" to "Tammy *said* she was kidnapped." The case was further complicated when, a few weeks after the abduction, Tammy's husband, George Richey, told a reporter, "I think I know who is responsible for all this, and we're going to put an end to it." The October 15, 1978, Chicago *Sun-Times* announced, "Tammy Wynette declares that she and her 5th husband, George Richey, 'know who is responsible.' " But, did they really *know*? If so, why did she tell *Penthouse* in 1980, "In my mind, I feel I know who was responsible, but I'd prefer to let it be, if it will. They were people who had approached me about doing some things career-wise, very legitimate things in the business, and I'd said no." And then why did she tell another publication in 1984 that she had received a letter ("It made my blood run cold") in 1979 from a prisoner whose cellmate had acknowledged being her kidnapper? Claimed Tammy, "He [the letter writer] knew inside information that we had never made public. He knew things like what I was wearing."

For several months, years even, Nashville was fixed with fascination on the sordid possibilities. One popular theory was that Tammy had concocted the entire episode. After all, it was argued, her career was in decline, she had a new album to promote, and the alleged abduction took place just two weeks before the nationally televised Country Music Awards, and Tammy had been mercilessly snubbed in the nominations. The

Tammy: "He tried to kill me! He tried to kill me! He tried to kill me!"

speculation ranged from the inquisitive to the snide. One country music executive was quoted as having joked, "I think I'll go down Broadway and see if I can't stand around and watch Tammy Wynette being raped." Others conjured visions of a kinky bedroom game gone astray, in which the abduction was merely a cover-up of an illicit affair of some kind. There were many other theories, of course, but the most popular ones seemed to involve George Jones in one way or another. After all, it was reasoned, he *was* still in love with Tammy, and George Richey, whom Tammy had married only a few months before, had been one of Jones's best friends. In addition, at the time of the abduction, Tammy had just completed writing her autobiography, which was not particularly kind to any of her ex-husbands, Jones included. Further, just two weeks before the abduction, Tammy had won a court case against Jones, in which he was ordered to pay her $36,000 in back child support.

Nevertheless, despite the lengthy police investigation, the seemingly endless public speculation, and Tammy's own assertion that she knew who the culprits were, the case, like the arson case before it, has never been solved.

Tammy herself somewhat dispelled the notion that George Jones had had anything to do with her abduction when she announced their professional reconciliation in early 1980. Jones had sworn off drugs and alcohol, and Tammy, for one, was convinced: "I know him pretty good, and I think he means it this time. I've never seen him with such enthusiasm." George Richey agreed, enthusiastically claiming "Tammy and I could never have given up on George. We've both always believed in him. He's the absolute greatest country singer that ever drew breath on this earth and we both knew that one day he'd get his life together again. George looks great and he's singing great. We're all totally and terribly excited about this."

Their first duet single, "Two Story House," was a big hit. They then embarked on a joint tour. All went well until Jones, "The Possum," characteristically failed to show up for a performance. The missed date was in Ottawa, Canada. When he didn't show up in Cincinnati either, Richey stepped up on the stage and announced to the audience who had paid to see the George and Tammy reunion, "George Jones is drunk and won't be here tonight. Would you believe me if I said he was crippled and couldn't be here? I'm serious, folks. George Jones is not here tonight. He didn't show up in Toronto or Ottawa either, and we don't know where he is. We hope you will stay, but for anyone who wants a refund, the ticket window will be open for the next ten minutes."

Victimized again. But that, of course, had always been a major part of Tammy Wynette's appeal. She had always been the betrayed but valiant trooper; the protective mother, fighting to keep and provide for her children; the long-suffering wife, trying to rehabilitate and hold on to her wayward husband. She has been divorced four times (actually, one marriage was annulled), but the failed marriages have never been *her* fault.

In her autobiography, she claims that one husband tried to have her institutionalized, one husband swapped nude photos of her through a porno ring, one husband married her for money, and another husband drank. Almost everyone, it seems, had betrayed Tammy at one time or another—even her mother, her children's Vietnamese nanny, and her daughter Tina, who once ran away from home and filed papers calling herself a "neglected child."

And, physically, Tammy has made even Loretta Lynn resemble the perfect portrait of health. Tammy has checked into hospitals like other people checked into hotels. She has been through an appendectomy, a hysterectomy, a gallbladder operation, numerous operations for abdominal adhesions, a drug overdose, and electroshock therapy. In 1977, following a performance in Corpus Christi, Texas, she fainted in the arms of George Richey, who then stepped on her finger and nearly broke it! She had to have two operations just to straighten the finger out. In 1978, a dramatic military airlift transported her from a Seguin, Texas, concert and delivered her to a San Antonio hospital. Two hours later, after the doctors reportedly refused to administer the medication she requested, she walked out of the hospital. In 1986, Tammy entered the Betty Ford Center to treat her addiction to Demerol. In February 1987, she was rushed via helicopter and plane to the Mayo Clinic in Rochester, Minnesota, where she underwent major stomach surgery. According to Tammy, "They did a complete revision of my stomach and removed 25 percent of it." Other sources identified the problem as a "bowel obstruction."

> Tammy knows just which strings to pluck, and she plays them
> with the skill of an expert. [She creates a] pathetic appeal.
> —Neil Daniel, professor, Texas Christian University,
>   Fort Worth

No other star in any milieu, with the possible exception of Marilyn Monroe, has been more adept at transforming personal adversity into positive publicity than Tammy Wynette.

Directly due to her 1978 kidnapping, Tammy Wynette received

In the 1980s, Tammy's career floundered (she hasn't had a number one in over ten years). One music critic said her stage performance "fell flatter than a bad face lift."

more worldwide publicity than she has ever had in her entire illustrious career. And that, of course, is due to Tammy herself. The day after the abduction was her daughter Georgette's birthday. Tammy announced to the press that the party would "go on as scheduled." Then, just two days after the abduction, Tammy went back on the road. She traveled via Lear jet to Columbia, South Carolina, where she bravely performed onstage with heavy layers of makeup barely covering her bruises as photographers eagerly snapped away. To her audience that night Tammy confided, "*He* could possibly be here, I just don't know. I know he's still out there, somewhere, and I'm a little bit nervous going on stage. Not just here, but anywhere." And, to a reporter: "Since it happened, I find myself looking at people and looking at cars and thinking, you know, 'Is that the one?' " And, to another reporter: "At times like this, I have to say, I wish I weren't famous." And, defiantly, to yet another reporter: "I'm going to the pistol range next week and learn how to really shoot a pistol. Because I don't intend for this to go on forever." What newspaper, magazine, wire service, or country music fan, for that matter, could resist such dramatics?

Today, her career is no longer what it once was, but Tammy has managed to remain at the top thanks to her hits from the late

1960s and her past soap-operatic travails. But, several years ago, not one to rest prettily on her throne, Tammy began a daring image transformation. She clipped off her cascading ringlets, shed the accompanying southern doll persona, and strived for a more contemporary look and sound. Although it has yet to pay off in a big way, she is still equipped with that voice, and she has shown some signs of renewed vigor, particularly on the Jamie O'Hara song "Talking to Myself Again."

One other thing. Tammy Wynette seems to be happy. Perhaps the Heroine of Heartbreak has finally found in George Richey a man worthy of standing by. She hasn't been in the news like she once was, but as Tammy herself once acknowledged, "The sad part about happy endings is [that] there's nothing to write about."

NO DUMB BLONDE

The image of country music women is that of the bimbo in the sequined leather pants and mile-high hair. There's Dolly Parton, who wears so much makeup that you could carve your initials in her face and not draw blood.
—M. Howard Gelfand, *Minneapolis Tribune*, March 24, 1975

Sorry, Mr. Gelfand, but to equate Dolly Parton with a bimbo is to miss the point entirely. She might be invariably costumed as part prostitute, part cartoon character, and part K Mart fashion statement, *but* there has never been a more *brilliant* package squeezed between an out-of-control bouffant and a pair of cheap evening pumps.

Dolly Parton has, perhaps more than anyone, defied the stereotype of the dumb blonde and forced society to look beyond the makeup and the mammary glands, no matter how ample either might be.

But, alas, it has not been easy. Particularly not in Nashville, where "girl singers" have always been relegated to the secondary ranks of the strictly decorative variety. That is, of course, not only the fault of the men. Opry star Jean Shepard was once quoted as saying, "I can't stand for a woman to come up and say, 'I can do anything a man can do.' Maybe mentally she can, but I think it's still kind of a man's world and, to be frank, I kind of like it that way. I'd never like to see a woman president, for instance. A woman's too high-strung for that kind of job." Connie Smith, another Opry star, concurred, "I'd a lot rather have somebody brag on my supper than my new record." Granted, with the

"Lots of women buy just as many wigs and makeup things as I do . . . they just don't wear them all at the same time."
—Dolly Parton

liberation of the rest of the country, Nashville has evolved somewhat, but it predominantly remains good ole boy territory, and a decidedly sexist attitude still prevails. As Reba McEntire recently and succinctly stated, "If a woman wants to be her own producer, she's a bitch. For a man to do that, he's a strong person."

When Dolly Parton arrived in Nashville at the age of eighteen in 1964, she *knew* she was going to be a star. She had known it while growing up on a farm in Sevier County, Tennessee. She was talented, ambitious, and beautiful, and she was willing to play the "girl singer" game. Once in Nashville, she batted her eyelashes and dressed demurely in high-necked gingham. She sang pretty, she spoke softly, and she sat under her big blonde wigs awaiting the turn that she knew would come.

In 1967, she hit with "Dumb Blonde." The song was mildly political, but Nashville was too mesmerized by Dolly's appearance to listen to her lyrics. That same year she became Porter Wagoner's girl singer and joined his television and road show. Many hits, duet and solo, followed, all produced under Wagoner's totalitarian rule.

Dolly Parton was a star. But while others were content with a piece of the proverbial rock, Dolly dreamed with passion of the mountains, the hillsides, and the virtually infinite landscape. In 1974, after seven successful years, Dolly dissolved her partnership with Porter Wagoner. She had, after all, served her appren-

Dolly Parton and Porter Wagoner: The girl singer and the star.

Dolly upstaging Porter.

ticeship and paid her dues, and like the butterfly out of its cocoon, she was ready to spread her wings and chart her own course.

There are many in Nashville, including Porter Wagoner of course, who seem to have never forgiven her. At the time he partnered with Parton, the pompadoured and Nudie-clad Wagoner had been one of the biggest stars in country music for several years. Yet because it was he who got her her first recording contract and groomed her to stardom, he is, and probably always will be, remembered as the man who "discovered" Dolly Parton. Further, his association with Dolly, though extremely successful, precipitated the decline of his own individual stardom. Because, by the end of their pairing, it was blatantly apparent that Dolly had overshadowed him and become the bigger star.

Unfortunately for them both, the productivity of their partnership has been severely eclipsed by the feud that followed their

"I did nothing but great things for that lady."
—Porter Wagoner

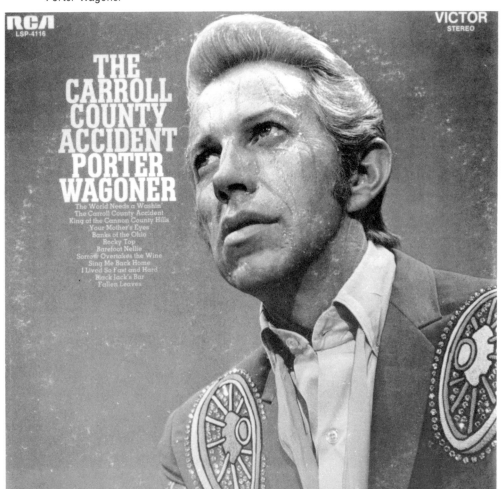

separation. Initially, Porter put on a gallant "let-me-step-aside-and-open-the door" public visage. At their joint press conference in February 1974, Porter acknowledged, "Dolly is now a super-star in every way. She's well prepared to go on her own. I am very happy that I have helped Dolly in preparing for this day." As for Dolly, she continued for a short while longer to play the modest, subservient "girl singer," announcing, "He [Porter] felt I was ready to go out on my own, which was a very unselfish decision on his part."

Later the fighting began. At first, they couldn't even decide who left whom. Dolly told an interviewer, "I haven't seen Porter since I left him. But I've been busy. I don't think he's over being mad at me. Me and Porter just couldn't talk there at the last, so we couldn't really work anything out. But I have tried." Porter retaliated, "No, no, no, she couldn't stay. *I let her go.* Dolly didn't quit me. I gave her notice in Tulsa, Oklahoma, that she needed to get her own band together because I wasn't going to travel and have a girl that I had to fight with on the road with us. I'm not bitter because Dolly left my show in any sense. I was just disappointed to find out she's not made of what I thought she was."

Over the years, the volleys continued, back and forth, in the Nashville newspapers and in publications like *Playboy* and *Rolling Stone.* For example:

DOLLY: We just got to where we argued and quarreled about personal things. We didn't get along very well. I'm sure he is bitter at this particular point. He is so strong-headed and bullheaded, he won't accept things sometimes the way they are. I won't either, sometimes.

PORTER: Dolly was not what I would call a great melody writer, and I would create some extra little tune or some rhythm pattern that would add a lot to her songs.

DOLLY: Porter was my first big break and I would be a fool not to be thankful and grateful. I was with him for seven years, went on his TV shows, went on the road with him, and we did the duets. They were seven of the best years and seven of the worst years of my life. I mean, we didn't get along that well. We disagreed because we were both stubborn and set in our ways, both extremely creative. I felt I knew what was best for me, and he felt he knew what was best for me, so we didn't totally agree.

PORTER: I don't believe a country girl singer would do things in the manner she's done them. Like the *Playboy* [cover] thing. Do you think Kitty Wells would do that? Dolly wants to do everything possible for her[self]. She's living in a fairyland. She wants to be in movies, she wants to be a playgirl, she wants to be the greatest songwriter, she wants to be the greatest singer, the greatest soul singer. She wants to be everything. That's fine, there's nothing wrong with that. But there's a way of doing things. Dolly's the kind of person that if you and I were sitting here with her and Johnny Carson and Huel Howser were sitting over there and they've got a bigger station, she'll go over there. She would do it if it were her mother and her sister sitting here.

DOLLY: Me and Porter, we just kind of said things, hurt each other's feelings and, you know, trampled around on territory that was real sensitive. I felt black and blue.

PORTER: [After Dolly won the Country Music Association's Entertainer of the Year Award in 1978] To me, Dolly Parton is the kind of person I would never trust with anything of mine. Regardless of what it was or who it was—I mean her family, her own blood—she would turn her back on [them] to help herself.

DOLLY: He owns half of my publishing company that I gave him for Christmas one year. At the time he was working hard on my career. I was writing the songs and he was helping me put them together and it was only right. He still works down there, runs the publishing company, but I own controlling stock. He still makes a percentage of my record royalties for another period of time through a contract he negotiated for me in the past. I could have stopped a lot of that stuff if I had wanted to, but you never hear that side. You only hear what a bitter, vicious person somebody is.

PORTER: I don't care about seeing her. I did nothing but great things for that lady.

DOLLY: Porter was upset at me pretty bad, and from things I read, is still pretty bitter at me, but I certainly had my reasons and he certainly knows what they were. I don't care what he says. He knows why I left.

PORTER: I don't want to be known as the person who discovered Dolly Parton. I've done many more important things in my career than just discover Dolly Parton.

As Dolly and Porter publicly laundered their consciences and sharpened their nails, Nashville took up sides. The Dolly camp contended, simply, that it was time for Dolly to move on. The

Porter faction argued that Dolly had gotten too big for her britches. Rumors filtered out of both battle zones. There was speculation that Porter had been notified of the split not by Dolly but by RCA officials. Another story, reported in Alanna Nash's biography *Dolly*, alleged that when he did learn of the impending separation, Porter threatened to kill or in some way harm Dolly.

In 1979 Porter Wagoner filed a breach of contract lawsuit against Dolly. He wanted what he claimed was his share of Dolly's earnings from 1974 to 1979, which were enormous. Reportedly, while with Porter, Dolly had earned $300 a night; by 1978 her fee was $30,000 a night. In his lawsuit, Porter asked for $3 million—$2 million from Dolly's net income, and $1 million for producer's royalties. Dolly retaliated that Porter had "intimidated" her into signing the 1970 contract that gave him a percentage of her income.

In November 1979, much to the dismay of the Nashville gossips, who were by then salivating with titillation, Dolly and Porter met and agreed to settle their dispute out of court. It had been their first face-to-face meeting in over two years. Nashville papers reported the obituary. "Attorneys for Porter Wagoner and Dolly Parton announced today that their clients have agreed to dismiss the current lawsuit filed by Wagoner and to equitably divide the assets of the businesses jointly operated by the parties for the last twelve years." At a further attempt at some semblance of reconciliation, Dolly, then the movie star, invited Porter to the Nashville premiere of *9 to 5*. He declined.

But he did have the last word. In his unpublished autobiography, *Hey, Porter!*, an excerpt of which was published in one of the tabloids, Porter seemed to confirm what many others had suspected (after all, in their years together, Porter *had* given Dolly fame, five rings, two Cadillacs, and two necklaces—everything *but* a wedding ring) all along; that he and Dolly had been lovers. The autobiography was never published because, according to its coauthor, Ellis Nassour, Porter decided it was "too hot." Nevertheless, according to the excerpt, the couple's first sexual encounter took place shortly after their professional union, at the Magnolia Motel in Hammond, Louisiana. The motel owner's widow has subsequently confirmed that Porter and Dolly used to frequent the place—albeit in separate rooms. The intense love affair that allegedly ensued ("I was in love with Dolly as much as she was in love with me") is, according to the excerpt, what fueled their eventual separation. Dolly responded to the allegations in her typically bemused and noncommittal fashion, "Some people will believe anything they read. Other people will just believe I have bad taste."

Sex is an overwhelming emotion. Natural as breathing. I will
say that if I feel the need to express any emotion, I'm gonna do
it . . . not to where I'm gonna get myself in a spot or do damage
to myself or to other people. I'm discreet, and I'm respectful. But
I really like it [sex], and I'm not ashamed to say it.
—Dolly Parton

Dolly Parton has always been something of a sexual suspect. Her
ideas about sex have always been so, well, *grown-up*. First, of
course, there is her longtime marriage to Carl Dean, whom she
met at a laundromat when she first moved to Nashville and
whom she calls "Daddy." Much ado has been made, over the
years, over Dolly's allegedly open marriage. But is it really an
open marriage? Certainly Dolly herself has stopped just short of
acknowledging that it is. To *Playboy* she teased: "I always loved
sex. I'm very aggressive. I don't mind bein' the [sexual] aggressor
if it comes to somethin' I need or want." And, "Nothin' better than
sex when you think you have to sneak it." And, "If I wanted to do

Proof for the stubborn disbelievers.

Georgia Department of Human Resources

VITAL RECORDS UNIT

STATE FILE NO._____

COUNTY NO. 6   1292

CERTIFIED COPY

𝕸arriage 𝕷icense

To any Judge, Justice of the Peace, Minister of the Gospel, or any other person authorized to solemnize: You are hereby authorized and permitted
to join in the Holy State of Matrimony
CARL I. DEAN   23   and   DOLLY R. PARTON   20
according to The Constitution and Laws of this State, and for doing so this shall be your sufficient license.
Given Under My Hand and Seal, this 30 day of MAY , 19 66

BOB ROLLINS, ORDINARY   Ordinary Probate Judge

I Hereby Certify, That

CARL I. DEAN   and   DOLLY R. PARTON

were joined together in the Holy State of Matrimony on this 30 day of May , 19 66, by me in the City of
RINGGOLD , County of CATOOSA , Georgia.

Recorded JUNE 6 , 19 66.   Signature of Officiant L. DON DUVALL
Book No. 20 Page 22   Title ORDAINED MINISTER
BOB ROLLINS, ORDINARY   Address RINGGOLD, GEORGIA
Judge of the Probate Court

I hereby certify that the above is a true and correct copy of Marriage Record as it appears in my
office.

Witness my hand and seal this 18th day of MARCH , 19 88

Lois T. Queen
LOIS T. QUEEN, CLERK

it [have an extramarital affair], I would; if I should do it, it would affect nobody but me and the person involved." And, to the *Los Angeles Times*: "I won't say I've never lusted after another man, 'cause I have. I'm human." And, to *Redbook*: "I could care less what Carl does, as long as he don't love somebody more than me. I think I would be hurt if he fell in love with somebody else, but I like the fact that he's got his friends. He takes his girlfriends to dinner and to lunch. Now, whether he goes to bed with them or not, I don't care, as long as it don't hurt me. He don't have to come telling me, but if he wanted to, that's fine. Same with me."

Because Carl Dean has rarely been seen with Dolly, there are those who believe that their marriage is merely a figment of Dolly's imagination invented for the sake of appearances. Very few people even know what he looks like, and many are convinced that he would be quite handsome—if he weren't so invisible. In all probability, though, he is just an extremely private individual with a life apart from his famous wife's public glitz.

Due mainly to the mystery surrounding her marriage there has been a ridiculous amount of speculative energy spent on Dolly's love life. Surely no other country music star has been placed under a pair of binoculars so often or with such scrutiny. For years there have even been rumors that Dolly's lifelong relationship with Judy Ogle extended beyond the realm of "best friends." After all, at one time Judy lived with Dolly and Carl, and it was Judy who accompanied Dolly on the road while Carl stayed at home. There was additional speculation about Dolly's closeness to her musical director, Gregg Perry. Perry was removed from his position in 1982 for undisclosed reasons.

Merle Haggard wrote in his autobiography, "I didn't just fall in love with the image of Dolly Parton. Hell, I fell in love with that exceptional human being who lives underneath all that bunch of fluffy hair, fluttery eyelashes and super boobs," and, "I was fool enough to believe that she loved me back." Dolly and Merle had spent a lot of time together when they were booked on several joint tours in the 1970s, when Merle was still married to his second wife, Bonnie Owens. In his autobiography, Merle implied that his love for Dolly precipitated the end of his marriage.

More eyebrows, fluttering and otherwise, were raised in 1982, when the usually stalwart Dolly, as she herself has acknowledged, was driven to the brink of suicide by a broken romance. As Dolly later related, "[I] was betrayed by someone close to me. . . . I won't say exactly who it was, except to say that it was an affair of the heart that left me shattered. Before I knew it, me, Dolly, the person who had always been strong—lost control. So I got sick—real sick." Dolly further said, "I had to make some decisions that I needed to make for years, but I kept holding on because I loved these people so much, *a* person in particular, but we were just destroying each other emotionally because we loved each other so much." When asked if it was someone she had been working with, Dolly termed the shattered romance "a personal business affair."

> I don't kiss nobody's butt.
> —Dolly Parton

Nashville, of course, was appalled. It might be okay for a male star to indulge in an extramarital affair or two, but for a female star to publicly *suggest* that she had done the same was unheard of. But then, after the Porter Wagoner debacle, Nashville—which had only a short time before lauded her as the last great purveyor of true country music—had begun to turn its back on Dolly. Those leading the movement against her proclaimed that Dolly thought she was too good for country music and country people. They cited the fact that, following her split from Porter, she had hired and fired her Travelin' Family Band, which included her own sisters and brothers; that she had rejected her old friends; that she had fired her Nashville management firm in favor of a high-powered Los Angeles company; that she had canceled country tour dates because of alleged vocal problems; and, worst of all, that she had compromised her country music in an attempt to broaden her commercial appeal. One Nashville music critic lambasted, "Dolly's sound has gone slicker 'n a greased pig!"

"It's a good thing that I was born a woman, or I'd have been a drag queen."
—Dolly Parton

Dolly as Doralee in *9 to 5*: Calling Hollywood.

More than anything, Nashville lamented, *their* Dolly had changed. The old Dolly wore only high-necked garments and told reporters things like, "I have really tried to not promote nothing but my talent." The new Dolly posed with a scantily clad Arnold Schwarzenegger for *Rolling Stone* (a *rock* publication!); posed for the cover of *Playboy*; posed for a poster in a haystack, bulging out of a Daisy Mae–like outfit; and flashed her breasts to friends at a stop sign in Beverly Hills ("I just pulled up my shirt and I flashed them with one of them"). Most shocking of all, she courted writers for mainstream publications and told them things like "I don't think I ever had a cherry. If I did, it got shoved so far back I was usin' it for a taillight!" Nashville shook its head and waited for Dolly to fall flat on her pretty face.

But Nashville forgot that Dolly Parton was impressively equipped with two attributes that would've made such a fall unlikely: brains and ambition. Not to mention talent, a powerful positive-thinking belief system, and an effective sense of self-deprecating humor ("I look like the girl next door . . . if you happen to live next door to an amusement park"). She has gone on to become arguably the biggest star ever produced out of Nashville. And one of the richest. Even for a box-office bomb like *Rhinestone*, Dolly was paid a reported $4 million. And for her less than successful ABC television variety series—it was canceled after the 1987–88 season—she grossed $44 million dollars over a two-year period.

"I guess it's like my daddy said. You shouldn't try to put fifty pounds of mud in a five-pound sack."
—Dolly Parton, after her bodacious bosom burst out of its bodice at a CMA Awards Show

There are many in Nashville who still condemn Dolly for having changed, but in actuality she hasn't changed that much at all. She is just more vocal about what she was really feeling all along. What she *has* done is to force change in the industry and in the way in which women are perceived in country music. Today female singers are no longer referred to condescendingly as "girl singers." A lot of that is due to Dolly Parton. She has given women in country music legitimacy and paved the way for those who will follow her. More than anything, though, she is the supremely gifted songwriter of art works like "Coat of Many Colors" and the possessor of that unmistakable voice—a tiny sliver of frill one second, a desperate full-throttle quaver the next. Loretta Lynn's voice may echo the mountains. But, at its best, Dolly Parton's voice recalls the heavens.

Other women, of course, have strived toward the country queendom, but none as yet have come close to dethroning Loretta, Tammy, or Dolly. If one of the three had to be chosen as the sole Queen of Country Music, it would probably have to be Loretta, for she has remained closest to the music, the culture, and the people. Tammy, for a while anyway, seemed a little too impressed by her mansion with the fifteen bathrooms and the other riches of royalty, and Dolly, though essentially still a country artist, is probably off charming some other orbit somewhere else in the universe.

Still, all three women deserve the crown, and one can't help but wonder, to employ the title of a George Jones hit, "Who's Gonna Fill Their [Ankle-Strapped] Shoes?"

For several years, Barbara Mandrell appeared to be the lady-in-waiting. In fact, the Statler Brothers once gave her the consolation title "Queenie" because she was not quite deserving of the top honor. In all likelihood, she never will be. Despite having been country when it wasn't cool, Mandrell has far too much Las Vegas élan and not enough pathos for the job. The latter applies to Tanya Tucker as well; despite being one of the best singers in the business, she is too brassy and provocative. A country music queen can be strong and outspoken, but she does not pose for album covers in skintight spandex. Emmylou Harris, though certainly beloved, is by choice too private an individual to enter the royal realm. Rosanne Cash has a shot at the top, though older country music fans might find her attitude too progressive. K. T. Oslin is an extremely gifted songwriter and a distinctive stylist,

Talented Rosanne Cash studied drama at the Lee Strasberg Theatre Institute and started her country music career with purple hair. Like her father, she underwent a drug withdrawal program. She had been addicted to cocaine.

Along with Wynonna Judd, k. d. lang may be the most gifted female vocalist in country music since Patsy Cline. However, time will tell if the ultraconservative country music establishment will accept her decidedly androgynous image.

"I have crawled over broken glass to get here. I'm divorced and I've been to the circus and seen the clowns. This ain't my first rodeo."
—Naomi Judd, the former nurse who went to the top of the charts with her daughter, Wynonna

Gifted singer/songwriter K. T. Oslin has defied Nashville's inherently sexist stance by taking women's songs out of the kitchen and into the eighties.

In April 1987, Reba McEntire, the hottest female solo act in country music, told an interviewer, "I'm very, very happy in my marriage. A funeral is cheaper than a divorce." Three months later, she filed for a divorce from her husband of eleven years.

but her openly feminist stance will undoubtedly offend many. k. d. lang is the most stunning explosion of talent to emerge from Nashville in decades, but her decidedly androgynous look might be too off-putting to too many. Next to k. d. lang, Wynonna Judd probably has the best female voice since Patsy Cline, but she has yet to project an image of any kind. Still, she is only in her early twenties and is definitely worth watching, particularly if and when she decides to go solo. Her mother and musical partner, Naomi, is hands down the most beautiful woman at the forefront of the business. But beauty alone does not make a queen.

At this point, the one with the strongest potential claim to the throne is Oklahoman Reba McEntire. She has most of the tangible qualifications. She is exceptionally talented, has won a string of consecutive Female Vocalist of the Year honors from the Country Music Association, and has the perception to select songs that communicate directly to a female audience. She was also given the endorsement of Loretta Lynn, who put her on an Oklahoma stage when Reba was fifteen and wearing pigtails. What McEntire has been lacking, though, (which isn't to say that she won't attain it) and what Loretta, Tammy, and Dolly all possess under their crowns, wigs, makeup, and ball gowns, is that innate light of radiance and recognition that distinguishes the routine from the regal.

5
THE FOOT-STOMPING KING OF WESTERN SWING

Daddy stomped on her stomach. He sat me down and said,
"You're going to watch me kill her."

That was the testimony of fourteen-year-old Melody Cooley who was forced to watch her father, country and western star Spade Cooley, the King of Western Swing, stomp her mother, Ella Mae Cooley, to death in the scandal that Nashville would like to forget. It was April 3, 1961. It had been a turbulent afternoon at Rosamund, the Cooley ranch in Willow Springs, which is located outside of Bakersfield, California. Country music band leader Spade Cooley and his wife, former "girl singer" Ella Mae Cooley, had been fighting all afternoon. After having suffered years of abuse, physical and otherwise, she finally told her husband that she wanted a divorce. However, he was not ready to let her go and accused her of sleeping around with some of his business associates. She denied it.

Melody Cooley arrived at the ranch at about 6:20 P.M., that evening. She had been staying at a friend's house when, at 5:30, she received a phone call from her mother, asking her to return to the ranch. As she entered her home, Melody saw Spade on the telephone. He was wearing a pair of tan corduroy pants. They were splattered with blood. Noticing his daughter, Spade hung up the phone, grabbed her arm, and led her into the den and its adjacent bathroom. The shower water was running. Spade opened the shower door and told Ella Mae that Melody had returned home. He ordered Ella Mae out of the shower. She was lying on the shower floor. The bathroom walls and tiles were splattered with blood. When Ella Mae did not exit the shower as instructed, Spade grabbed her by the hair and dragged her onto the den floor. She was naked. Then, in front of his daughter, he

Ella Mae and Spade Cooley: "Until death do us part."

Ella Mae joined Spade's band, fresh off the farm in the 1940s.

lifted his wife's head and crushed it onto the floor. He then ordered her to get up off the floor. When she did not comply, he turned to Melody and ordered her to witness her mother's execution. And so she watched. She watched as Spade kicked and stomped Ella Mae. And she watched in horror as he seared his wife's breasts with a burning cigarette. Then, brandishing a gun, he turned to Melody and threatened, "I'll give you three minutes to get your mother off the floor and into bed." And that's when Melody ran screaming from the house.

Donnell Clyde Cooley was born in Grand, Oklahoma, in 1910. A classically trained cellist and violinist, Spade (named for his proficiency at cards) arrived in Los Angeles in 1934 with a violin under his arm and six cents in his pocket. That's when he met Roy Rogers, who was then in the process of being transformed into a cowboy movie star by Republic Studios. Because of their physical resemblance, Rogers hired Spade as his stand-in. They became friends.

By 1942, Spade was leading his own successful band. He became a radio performer in the early 1940s and was booked at the Venice Pier Ballroom for seventy-four straight weeks, attracting 8,000 people every week. In 1946, Spade had his biggest hit with the song that became his theme, "Shame on You." By then, he was performing in the biggest dance hall on the West Coast, the Santa Monica Ballroom. Then, in 1948, he landed his own television show, "The Hoffman Hayride," in which he was introduced as "your fiddlin' friend and mine—Spade Cooley!" Every Saturday night, the program attracted 75 percent of the television viewers in Los Angeles. The King of Western Swing, as he was then proclaimed, had it all: wealth, fame, the house with a swimming pool, a fifty-six-foot yacht, and a personal wardrobe that included one hundred hand-tailored suits and thirty-six pairs of cowboy boots.

But by the mid-1950s evolving tastes in country music left yodeling cowboys out in the tumbleweed. Spade's career declined, and he had the first in a series of heart attacks. When his television show was canceled, he went into semiretirement and became a real estate developer.

> The large living room faces a green lawn in which is centered a kidney-shaped pool. A beautiful stone fireplace fills one wall with an inviting hearth which extends the entire width of the adjoining wall. On the opposite wall a maple spinet stands below a watercolor painted by Anita Lewis Cooley, mother of Spade Cooley's manager and close friend, Lee Cooley [not a relative]. The picture is a bouquet of California wildflowers for which Anita Cooley is widely known. It is in this atmosphere the Cooley family centers its desert living. Spade, when he is not out on a bulldozer helping to hasten the realization of his dream "to bring entertainment here" [he was building an entertainment complex], is on the phone, buying cattle for his ranch.

That is how Catherine Winston, a reporter for the local paper, the *Antelope Valley Press*, found the Spade Cooley household in November 1960. That day the Cooley family posed for numerous photographs and appeared to be the perfect portrait of domestic bliss. Spade, who told the visiting reporter, "I'd rather be a farmer than anything in the world," posed, smiling, with Ella Mae and their children, Donnell Jr., twelve, Melody, fourteen, and John, twenty-eight. Less than five months later, the familial façade would be shattered and drenched in blood.

Actually, there had been turmoil at the Cooley ranch for many years. Spade reportedly kept Ella Mae prisoner in her own home. She was not allowed her own friends or interests outside of the house. And, although he had been having an affair with the female violinist in his band, he was insanely jealous of his wife and even kept track of her telephone calls.

Spade Cooley and his
boys, posed behind
closed bars in
Everybody's Dancin'.

Fiddling around.

In the 1950s, Spade
released an album called
the *Sagebrush Stomp* and
a single called "You
Clobbered Me."

Roy Rogers:
The other man?

Three weeks before the murder, Ella Mae was hospitalized, probably by her own request. It was her only chance to get away from her husband. While in the hospital, she secretly plotted to leave him. And Spade did not like it when women tried to leave him. When Mary Virginia Jackson, a former singer with his band, told him that she was quitting, Spade tried to throw her off the Santa Monica pier.

After she returned to the ranch, Ella Mae virtually stopped eating. For several weeks she ate very little. But she did grow her fingernails. As she confided to a neighbor, she was afraid for her life, and she wanted her fingernails long so that she could at least scratch Spade when he attacked her.

On April 3, 1961, Ella Mae did not wake up until 3 P.M. When she did get up, she made the biggest mistake of her life. She told Spade that she was going to leave him. Spade later testified that their fight started when Ella Mae "confessed" that she had been having a three-way affair with two of his business associates whom he thought were homosexual ("They brought some boys up to my ranch that were completely on the limp wrist side"). That afternoon, she also confessed, according to Spade, to having an affair "with my best friend, my ex–best friend, Roy Rogers. He came to my home on Saturdays while I was at rehearsal." She also confessed, again according to Spade, to wanting to leave him so that she could join a sex cult of some kind.

The ranch house was quiet for over an hour after Melody had fled in horror. At 8 P.M., Barbara Bennett, a woman identified as Spade's business manager, arrived at the house. She met with

Spade for about an hour. Then, at about 9 P.M. Spade asked her to go into the bedroom to check on Ella Mae. Understandably alarmed at the battered flesh she found sprawled out on the couple's bed, Bennett suggested to Spade that they call an ambulance. He refused, but agreed to call a family friend who was a nurse, Dorothy Davis. When Davis arrived at 11 P.M., nearly five hours after the slaying, she insisted on calling an ambulance. The ambulance attendants later recalled that Spade kept saying repeatedly to the bloody corpse that was his wife, "I love you, please don't be dead."

Ella Mae Cooley was dead on arrival at Tehachapi Valley Hospital at 12:20 A.M. It was obvious that she had been viciously beaten. Ten minutes after she was pronounced dead, the coroner's office was called. Meanwhile Spade sat in the hospital waiting room. He told investigating police that Ella Mae had jumped from a moving automobile a few days earlier ("I grabbed her hair, and pulled some of her hair out when she jumped") and that she had slipped in the shower that night. The policemen nodded and noted that Spade's hands were swollen and bruised.

In court, Spade was in a daze. At one point, he didn't even recognize his eldest son, John. The prosecution termed Ella Mae's death a "torture murder" and pushed for first-degree conviction.

copy QA
6/6/61 steele

KERN COUNTY SHERIFF'S OFFICE
OFFENSE REPORT

Case No. __RO - 2392__   Date: __4-4-61__

Offense: __PC 187__   Investigator: __H. E. Cooper__

Name of Injured Party __Ella May Cooley__

Res. Address __Cooley Ranch, North of Willow Springs__

Phone __Blackstone__

Where Committed __Willow Springs in Kern County Cooley Ranch House located North__

Reported by __Tehachapi Hospital__

Address __Tehachapi, California__

Time Reported __Approx. 12:45 AM, 4-4-61__

Reported to __Desk Sgt.__

Investigating Officer __H. E. Cooper & Leo Blair__

Date Committed __4-3-61__
Time Committed __Bet. 6:00 PM and 8:00 PM__

Persons Arrested __DONNELL CLYDE COOLEY alias SPADE COOLEY__

By __Fote/Blair/Cooper__   Date __4-4-61__

Person Attacked __WFA, Housewife__

Property Attacked __Ranch house living area__

How Attacked __Beaten__

Means of Attack __Hands, physical force and other objects__

Object of Attack __Personal Motive__

Trademark __Suspect apparently beats victim to death.__

Vehicle Used __None__

Suspect _____

Hair Color _____   Eye Color _____

Height _____ Weight _____ Age _____

Nationality _____ Build _____

Occupation _____ Marks _____

Suspect _____

Hair Color _____   Eye Color _____

Height _____ Weight _____ Age _____

Nationality _____ Build _____

Occupation _____ Marks _____

Description of Property and Details of Investigation   Value of Property _____

At approximately 12:45AM, 4-4-61, I received a telephone call at my residence stating that the had been a victim of a beating brought into the Tehachapi Emergency Hospital and that upon the arrival of that victim, the victim had been pronounced dead.

At approximately 1:15 AM, 4-4-61, Chief Fote of the Criminal Divison of Kern County Sheriff's Office, picked me up at my home and we proceeded to the Tehachapi Hospital.

On arrival at the Tehachapi Hospital we were contacted by Sgt. Shuell of the Mojave Sub-station who had just been talking to SPADE COOLEY. This conversation wa s taking place in the waiting room of the Tehachapi Hospital. At that time Chief Fote and myself contacted SPADE COOLEY and he stated that he would gladly give us a statement of what happened at his Ranch house earlier on the evening hours of 4-3-61 and up until the time we talked to him in Tehachapi.

Along with Chief Fote and Sgt. Shuell and Coroner Stan Newman, SPADE COOLEY was taken into a Doctor's office at the Tehachapi Hospital where he was briefly interrogated on the surrounding circumstances of the injuries sustained by his wife. After talking to SPADE COOLEY for approx mately 20 to 25 minutes in the Doctor's Office, Mr. Cooley stated that he would free and volun tarily on his part proceed with Sgt. Shuell and myself to the Sub-station in Mojave where ther

(Do not write below this line)

(Cont'd

This offense is declared: CLEARED _____ By Arrest _____ By Recovery _____

INACTIVE _____ UNFOUNDED _____

Date: _____   By: _____

_____ Chief, Criminal Divisi

OFFICE OF THE CORONER

COUNTY OF KERN, CALIFORNIA

CORONER'S REPORT

RO 2392

#793   AGE ___37 years___

NAME OF DECEASED: ELLA MAY COOLEY

RESIDENCE: Cooley Ranch, Willow Springs, California

PLACE OF DEATH: DOA Tehachapi Hospital

DATE AND TIME OF DEATH: April 4, 1961 - DOA 12:20 A.M.

PLACE OR INJURED: The Cooley Ranch, Willow Springs, Calif.

DATE AND TIME OX INJURED: April 4, 1961 - About 6:15 P.M.

DATE OF CALL: April 4, 1961 - 12:30 A.M.

TIME CALL MADE: April 4, 1961 - 12:30 A.M.

TIME CALL COMPLETED: April 4, 1961 - 2 P.M.

INFORMANT: Dr. Vincent Troy of the Tehachapi Hospital

CALL RECEIVED BY: R. P. Gervais

BODY SENT TO: Turner Funeral Home

PROPERTY TAKEN BY: None taken.

REMARKS: Received a telephone call from Dr. Vincent Troy, of the Tehachapi Hospital reporting the death of this victim being DOA at the Tehachapi Hospital. Dr. Troy stated there were marks on the victim's body that he felt should be investigated by our office.

Accompanied by Coroner Stanley A. Newman, proceeded immediately to the Tehachapi Hospital. Upon our arrival observed the victim to be that of a Caucasion female of the apparent stated age of 37 years, Height; 5'4"; Weight; 110 pounds; Eyes; Brown; Hair; Red.

There were numerous marks of external violence noted on the body consisting of bruises over the entire body, indicating the victim had been beaten severely.

The victim was identified by her husband Donnell C. Spade Cooley. Upon arriving at the Tehachapi Hospital observed Donnell Cooley, husband of victim, to be seated in the waiting room of the hospital. After observing the victim's body, Mr. Cooley was questioned, he stated his wife had jumped from a moving automobile a couple days prior to this and had fallen in the shower on this particular evening, which caused the injuries.

Further questioning revealed the victim did admit slapping his wife two or three times while at their ranch in Willow Springs. Mr. Cooley was taken to the Mojave Substation where further questioning took place.

Daughter of Mr. and Mrs. Cooley was contacted at Mrs. W. P. McWhorter's residence at 301 Camden Street, in Rosamond. Daughter's name is Melody Cooley, 14 years old. Her address is also the Cooley

(continued on page 2)

Melody Cooley leaving her mother's funeral.

Spade admitted that he had fought with Ella Mae on the day of her death, because, as he testified, "Rockets ran through my brain when Ella Mae told me of her desire to join a free love cult." And so he hit her. With his fist. His next recollection was of Ella Mae taking the cigarette out of his hand, pulling open her blouse, and burning herself with it, while moaning, "I'm not worth it, Spade. I'm not worth it." Spade did admit, "I must have hurt her terrible. I must have hit her. She was half on the floor, half on the bed. I remember she was conscious. I felt horrible. I was ashamed of her. I was ashamed of myself, ashamed of being alive." Spade then told of how he "helped" Ella Mae to the shower. "She went into the shower alone. I didn't push or shove her. The next thing that happened, I'll remember as long as I live. There was a terrible thud . . . the glass [of the shower door] breaking." Spade then testified that he retrieved his wife's body from the bathroom floor and, "I rubbed her wrists, breathed in her mouth, put cold towels on her head—and, I prayed." When asked why he didn't immediately call a doctor, Spade replied that he didn't know. When asked about his daughter Melody's testimony, Spade called her a liar. He claimed that Melody had been upset with him because he had forbidden her to date men in their twenties.

The coroner's office classified Ella Mae Cooley as a 110-pound,

Spade in court: "Shame on You."

Melody exits the courtroom accompanied by her sister-in-law, Dorothy Cooley.

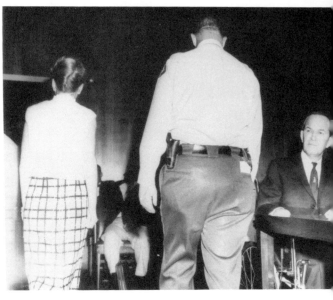

Spade watches as his daughter leaves the witness stand.

5'4", brown-eyed redhead. She was thirty-seven years old. The cause of her death was cited as "multiple injuries," including a ruptured aorta and lacerations on the inside of her vagina and anus.

During the trial, Spade collapsed twice and suffered one heart attack. Nevertheless, in August 1961, after what had been the longest trial in Kern County history, the jury reached a verdict of homicide at the hands of Donnell Clyde Cooley. Actually, it was at the hands *and* feet of Donnell Clyde Cooley. Spade was convicted of murder in the first degree and was sentenced to life in jail at Vacaville Prison. Asked what he thought of the verdict when leaving the courtroom, he replied, "Not much."

Eight years later, on November 23, 1969, Spade was granted a seventy-two-hour furlough to perform at a policeman's benefit at the Oakland Coliseum. He performed three numbers, including "San Antonio Rose," which he dedicated to country music legend Bob Wills. The audience of 2,800 gave him a standing ovation. He thanked them and expressed that it was great "to be free for a while." Three hours earlier, a television news team had asked him how he felt about his upcoming performance. Spade had explained that he was a heart patient and that he wasn't always well enough to perform. But he had a feeling that it would go well because, he had drawled, it was for a good cause. Prophesized Spade: "I think it's gonna work out for me. I have the feeling that today is the first day of the rest of my life."

After receiving his standing ovation, Spade Cooley retired to the wings and fell dead, the victim of an impeccably timed heart attack.

6
LOVE, MARRIAGE,
AND D-I-V-O-R-C-E

I n 1937, Nashville's Eunice Winstead married Charlie Johns. The marriage didn't create much excitement, despite the fact that Johns was twenty-two and Eunice was only nine and in the third grade. Eunice's dowry consisted of a large doll, which her husband had presented to her the Christmas before. Naturally, their first child, a girl, married by the time she was fourteen.

In 1977, Tennessee Reverend Claudius Vermilye was convicted on twelve counts of having "unnatural sex relations" with young boys ages eleven to twenty at his home for delinquent youths. He was also charged with taking nude pornographic photos of the boys, including nude photos of his own son. When asked in court "What kind of love did you have in that house?" Vermilye answered, "Christian love."

On January 21, 1978, twenty-year old Nashville plumber Danny Bass gave the term "Mama's boy" new meaning. He married his mother—without knowing it. Six years later, after discovering the news of his disturbing predicament, Bass informed the authorities and turned in his mother/wife. Mary Ann Garton Bass, then forty-three, pleaded innocent to charges of criminal incest and contended that her son/husband was merely seeking revenge because in 1961 she had put him up for adoption.

In 1984, few eyebrows were raised when Nashville resident Hal Warden married an older woman, Wendy Chappell. Warden was thirteen, Chappell fifteen. Later that year they had a daughter, Heather Nicole. When asked if he wasn't too young to become a father, Hal replied that he was but that he had been too embarrassed to ask his parents to purchase condoms for him. In 1985, the young couple divorced. A bitter $30,000 child custody battle ensued. In August of that year, a month before his divorce from

Wendy was final, Hal began dating thirteen-year old Catherine Trent. They married the following year.

Las Vegas may have more marriages and divorces, but in the name of Love and Litany, anything and everything happens in Nashville—and usually ends up on vinyl. Just ask Tammy Wynette and George Jones, who have nine marriages and seven divorces between them, most of which have been shamelessly paraded in the upper echelons of the *Billboard* country charts.

BAND MEMBER #1: Hey, remember that redhead we double-teamed in Seattle last month?
BAND MEMBER #2: You sure she was a redhead?
BAND MEMBER #1: She was the last time I looked close.
BAND MEMBER #2: That was Spokane, asshole!

There is no question that Nashville has its own peculiar perspective on love. For some star performers, love is romance on the road, watching some blonde in some audience in some city suck on her cigarette and roll her tongue around the rim of her beer bottle. Just as other forms of music do, country has its share of groupies—those glorious Glorias who are compelled, for reasons of their own, to travel from town to town with open minds, open legs, and a portable overnight toothbrush kit. For many years, the perennial favorite country music groupie was "Hurricane Shirley," who serviced all the major acts who toured on the West Coast, offering sexual solace not only to the performers but also to road managers, equipment men, and tour bus drivers. Other favorites were the "Black Rider," a groupie with a self-explanatory name, and the "Chicken Ladies," a cluster of female fans who followed their favorite stars on the road with batches of breasts and thighs of the poultry variety.

But regardless of color, skill, and anatomical dimensions, a groupie, for the most part, is a groupie. As songwriter John Hartford once surmised, "they're the same as other groupies insofar as they all want to ball you." And, as Willie Nelson acknowledged, "You could say that they're what keeps a lot of us on the road so many years."

Not only is love in Nashville not conventional, it is not entirely heterosexual. In fact, there are several well-known male country stars (who shall go unnamed) who have an underground reputation for their preference for muscles and meat over mascara and mammary glands. One star in particular, known for his voracious sexual appetite, is said to have a particular penchant for black men equipped with stereotypically large Texas Longhorns.

Nevertheless, the country music industry refuses to even acknowledge the presence of gays, preferring to discount homosexuality as some sort of West Coast affliction. As Faron Young, a devout heterosexual, once exclaimed to writer Dolly Carlisle, "I've seen some of those guys in Hollywood, those movie stars, turn queer because they've done had all the women they want."

Not many "traditional" marriages survive the eccentricities, the separations, and the inevitable infidelities of the irreconcilably different world of country music. Between Ferlin Husky, Jerry Lee Lewis, Tammy Wynette, Lee Greenwood, George Jones, Waylon Jennings, and Glen Campbell alone, there have been *thirty-three* pledges of "till death do us part." Even vanilla-veined Kenny Rogers has been married four times.

He tells me that he loves me and always wants to be with me one day, and then he disappears and files petitions for divorce the next day.
—Jana Jae Owens

In August 1977, Jana Jae Owens, thirty-three, filed a motion in Superior Court asking that her estranged husband, Buck Owens, forty-seven and twice divorced, be forced to undergo psychiatric evaluation. Said Jana, "[Buck is] mentally ill and was at the time we were married."

Just a year before, Buck had publicly admitted he had mental problems, provoked by the death of his extremely close friend Don Rich, thirty-two, who had bled to death when his motorcycle crashed at top speed into a highway divider near Morro Bay, California. Lamented Buck, "In the summer of 1974, I lost my best friend, my son, my brother, my music arranger, and my chief everything. His name was Don Rich and things really haven't been the same since. We were together nearly fifteen years. I was mentally depressed." Just weeks before his death, Rich said of Buck, "He couldn't drive me off with a pole." Reconciled to the loss, Buck mourned, "I just figured that whenever my mind ran across Don, I would just think of his smile."

Alvis Owens Jr. was born in Sherman, Texas, in 1929. In 1950, he moved to Bakersfield, California, where he pioneered the West Coast country music movement. From 1963 to 1969, Buck had twenty-one singles, all of which went to the number one position on the country charts. In 1965, he took out a full-page ad in the industry trade papers pledging that he "would not sing any song

Bucking tradition, Buck Owens (pictured with Roy Clark) advertised for a mail-order bride.

"[Buck is] mentally ill and was at the time we were married."
—Jana Jae, fiddler extraordinaire

that wasn't a country song." Nevertheless, a few years later he had major hits with "Johnny B. Goode" and "Bridge Over Troubled Water." In 1969, Buck was signed by CBS-TV to cohost a summer replacement show called "Hee Haw." It became the most successful country music show in television history.

In 1974, Buck went on "The Tonight Show" and announced that he was looking for a new mate. Subsequently, he was bombarded with 20,000 written proposals of marriage. It was at about that time that he met Jana Jae Grief and hired her as the fiddle player in his band. He fired and rehired her three times during her tenure with him, and courted her all the while.

On May 2, 1977, Jana Jae married Buck in Las Vegas after he reportedly made promises regarding her contract with his show. Following their wedding, Jana Jae and her two young children from a previous marriage moved in with Buck at his Bakersfield estate. Two days later, Buck disappeared. The next day, it was announced on his personally owned radio station that his marriage, albeit brief, was over. Jana Jae was served with annulment papers, reportedly on grounds that she was insane.

And then, just as quickly, he changed his mind.

> I love that pretty fiddle player and I won't stop until I get her back. I want her back but I can't get her on the phone. The whole annulment thing was all my fault. I'm just a poor country boy from Texas and I hadn't been married in a long time. I just got cold feet. Gee whiz, I thought here I play golf and tennis every day and I might have to give all that up. I'm used to going my own way. Then I thought that for the first time in my life, I am really in love. I spent two years talking her into marrying me and now I did this.
> —Buck Owens to reporters

Buck began sending truckloads of roses to Jana Jae—every day. More ostentatiously, and much to Jana Jae's chagrin, he began taking out ads in the Los Angeles area newspapers that proclaimed in bold black and white and for all the world to read: JANA JAE OWENS, I APOLOGIZE FOR BEING SUCH A FOOL. I LOVE YOU! BUCK. And JANA JAE OWENS, I NEED YOU, MATT AND KATHY! BUCK. Matt and Kathy are her children.

Jana Jae was not moved. Through her attorney, Marvin Mitchelson, she got a restraining order preventing the publication of further ads. She also filed a petition for divorce. Said Jana Jae at the time, "He's a chess master with people. He doesn't love me, he just wants to control me." And "He's using me and . . . there are other girls in his life."

Still, Buck persevered, telling reporters, "I love her and want her back. If I thought it would help, I'd find a World War II tank and drive it up in her front yard, waving a white flag."

Defeated or convinced, or a combination of the two, on July 21, 1977, Jana Jae returned to the Buck Owens ranch in Bakersfield. Reportedly, at Buck's request, she brought her children and her piano back with her. However, within twenty-four hours of her return, Buck disappeared without explanation. He returned home on July 30 and again begged the forgiveness of his befuddled bride. And then, four days later, he disappeared again.

In August, Buck filed his own petition for divorce. He offered Jana Jae no spousal support, no attorneys' fees, and no property settlement. Jana Jae, who reported that she had married Buck

Perhaps in an effort to reclaim Jana Jae, Buck posed buck naked for *Playgirl* photographers. They shot him cavorting on his horse, shooting pool, and romping in an alfalfa field. For whatever reason, the photos were never published.

only "at his insistence," changed the grounds of *her* petition from fraud to mental incompetence.

As best as can be ascertained from the series of legal filings and cross-filings, the couple did eventually receive their divorce. Jana Jae, after her circus sideshow of a marriage, has understandably avoided the extracurricular limelight. As for Buck, he never did undergo that mental examination. And to public knowledge, he has not remarried. At least not yet.

Willie Nelson has had a few stormy marriages of his own (granted, the Buck and Jana Jae Owens was more of a stormy *non*marriage)—but at least Willie's lasted for a respectable amount of time. Willie was sixteen at the time of his first marriage. Her name was Martha Matthews, she was a full-blooded Cherokee, and, as Willie later mused, "Every night we restaged

Custer's last stand." Three incidents in particular have attained near-legendary status in Nashville folklore. During one of their battles, Martha, armed with a knife, chased a naked Willie through a graveyard. During another fight, reportedly at the breakfast table, Martha flung her fork at Willie, and it stuck in his chest, and for a minute, quivered back and forth until Willie yanked it out. The most infamous account of their union, though, was the time that Willie came home drunk, stripped himself naked, and fell into bed. While he was sleeping, Martha either tied or sewed the four corners of the bedsheets and proceed to pummel her quickly sobering husband with the household broom. She left him there, a captive hostage squirming like a sackful of animate potatoes.

Another amusing scenario was related by Susie Nelson, Willie's daughter, in her biography of her father, *Heart Worn Memories*. While still married to Martha, Willie was in a Nashville hotel room tuning his instrument on a woman he had met while on tour in California. Unbeknownst to him, his wife was in the hotel room next door with a blackjack dealer from Las Vegas. The woman with Willie, Shirley Coolie, went on to become his second wife.

> This third marriage is the charm.
> —Willie Nelson

Willie met his third wife, Connie Koepke, while performing at a Texas honky tonk called the Cut 'n Shoot. They were married in

Real saints don't get divorced
. . or do they?

1971. It was Connie who saw Willie through the emergence of his stardom as the most distinctive vocalist of his generation and the advent of his image of part swami and part shitkicker with its accompanying trademark of beard, braids, and bandanna. In 1983, Connie was quoted as remarking, "I doubt that Willie's gotten any wiser about marriage—he just finally found somebody who could cope with him." Willie concurred: "It's not easy being married to a man like me. It's asking a lot to let your husband run around the world, flirting with pretty girls who flirt back." In 1987, after more than fifteen years of marriage, Connie filed for a divorce.

There is nothing novel about wife-swapping in Nashville. Once, while onstage at a Nashville awards show, singer Hank Cochran was reportedly decked by a Willie Nelson band member. Cochran, who had written several songs for Willie, had allegedly "stolen" the vindictive band member's wife.

Merle Haggard did not actually steal Bonnie Owens from Buck Owens—after all, Bonnie and Buck had gotten divorced twelve years before she married Merle in 1965. Merle and Bonnie

Merle Haggard has been living with women—off and on—ever since he shacked up with a waitress who worked in a waffle shop when he was sixteen. Recently, he cited his twelve-year-old chihuahua, Tuffy, as "the only consistent female in my life."

dueted successfully together in 1966 and remained married for the next ten years. The secret of their marital success was that they had an "open" marriage. Merle was once quoted as saying, "Bonnie always told me, 'I don't care what you do as long as you don't flaunt it in my face.' She realized that I was young and had a lot of things offered to me that I was not strong enough to refuse." It was during his marriage to Bonnie that Merle allegedly had an affair with Dolly Parton.

In 1976, Merle mysteriously disappeared for several weeks. According to his manager and Bonnie's ex-boyfriend, Fuzzy Owen, he had gone out "to buy a fiddle" and hadn't returned. For the first time in his career, Merle missed scheduled performances. A short time later, after his return, Bonnie filed for divorce.

On October 7, 1978, Merle married singer Leona Williams. His ex-wife Bonnie served as Leona's bridesmaid and remained a singer in his show. Leona had been a member of Loretta Lynn's backup group and had a hit of her own in 1971 with "Country Girl with Hot Pants On." In January 1979, just a few months after their marriage, an item appeared in the music trades that Merle and Leona were headed for the divorce court. However, it was not until 1984 that they were officially divorced.

The most notorious case of wife-swapping in country music has to be the titillating triangle of Mac, Sarah, and Glen.

Mac Davis was born in Lubbock, Texas, in 1942. He was the son of an extremely religious couple who ran the local No-Tell Motel. He attended Emory University, where he majored in "beer, with a minor in rock and roll." Said Mac, "I was seventeen and fucking everything that walked. Didn't give a damn about nothing." He took jobs as a ditchdigger, a gas station attendant, and a probation officer. Then, in 1969, he got his big break when Elvis Presley recorded his song "In the Ghetto." At about that same time, Mac also wrote songs for the movie *Norwood*, which starred Kim Darby, Joe Namath, and country music sensation Glen Campbell.

> Glen's a welcome relief. That's why people like him. He's simple, honest, unaffected. You look at him, and you sense immediately that here's one guy who's not going to cause any trouble.
> —Paul Nathan, producer of *Norwood*, 1970

Glen Campbell was born in Billstown, Arkansas, population 450, on April 22, 1936. His father was a cotton-picking preacher,

In the early years of his career, Glen Campbell was shy and virginlike. It wasn't until his later years that he became known for controversial quips like "To me, manual labor is a Spanish phrase."

and Glen himself picked cotton at an early age. When he was fourteen, Glen quit school to join an uncle's touring band. In 1958, he moved to Los Angeles, where over the next several years he became a busy studio sessionman. In 1965, he joined the Beach Boys for a brief period before going solo and scoring smash crossover hits like "Gentle on My Mind" and "By the Time I Get to Phoenix." In 1968, he outsold the Beatles and became the top-selling recording artist in America. That year he also won four Grammy awards and the Country Music Association's Entertainer of the Year Award. Before the end of the decade, he was saddled with nicknames such as "The Farmboy Charmboy" and the "The Hip Hick." He also starred in his own network television variety series and in the feature films *True Grit* and *Norwood.*

Glen had been married to his second wife, former Albuquerque beautician Billie Jean Nunley, since 1959. Mac had been married to his second wife, Sarah Barg, since 1971, when she was eighteen. On September 23, 1975, three days after their sixteenth wedding anniversary, Billie Jean filed for a divorce from Glen. Two weeks later, Sarah Davis filed for a divorce from Mac. Reportedly, everyone in Nashville knew why.

Everyone, that is, except for Mac Davis.

Then came the night of October 13, 1975. It was the night of the biggest social event of the year in Nashville, the Country Music Awards. Friends Glen Campbell and Mac Davis were to be the evening's cohosts. That day at rehearsal, Mac wore a T-shirt that read, "The Glen Campbell Open." The two had played golf together that morning. And Mac still did not know why his beloved wife had left him.

Reportedly, he found out that night. The story that later circulated in Nashville is that Mac found out backstage while Glen was onstage hosting the awards show. When Glen's portion of the program was over, Mac was ushered onto the stage to fulfill his hosting duties. By the time the show was over, someone had warned Glen, who quickly exited the auditorium and returned to Los Angeles. As for Mac, he was spotted the following night at the BMI awards. He was reportedly, and understandably, drunk.

Soon after their respective divorces were finalized in 1976, Glen Campbell married Sarah Davis. Said Glen at the time, "Mac was my friend, and still is as far as I'm concerned, although I can understand how he might be bitter." Mac said of Glen, "I felt for him [following his split from Billie Jean] and tried to be his

Glen's second wife, Billie Jean Nunley, had worked in a bank to support his musical aspirations. After stardom, Glen claimed that she had turned into a jet-setter and an absentee mother. Besides, Glen complained, "She would say, 'That song's no good,' instead of 'That isn't the kind of song I like.' "

"God gave Los Angeles smog
because he didn't want to see what
was going on there."
—Glen Campbell

Mac Davis (pictured here in *North Dallas Forty*): "Baby, baby don't get hooked on
him."

friend. I guess he didn't have the same feeling for me." Meanwhile, Mac consoled himself with Lorna Luft, Judy Garland's *other* daughter. Said Mac, "Lorna is the only woman in my life—and we have a great thing going." And, "Sarah has a new man—and I have a new lady. That's all there is to say." At the time, Lorna was also reported to be dating Burt Reynolds, who was also dating Tammy Wynette.

In 1980, according to *People* magazine, three weeks after the birth of their son Dillon, Sarah Davis Campbell left her husband Glen, charging that Glen had been "running around with other women." Campbell retorted by charging, "Sarah said 'I do' and never did." He also lambasted Sarah's mother and blamed the collapse of his marriage on her: "That woman was conniving, always playing me against Sarah. There can't be two people running a household, especially if one of them ain't supposed to be there in the first place." Reportedly, Glen had requested that his mother-in-law move out of the house and Sarah countered, "If she goes, I go," to which Glen dictated, "No one is to supersede me in my house. Leave." Sarah answered, "But this is my house too," which prompted Glen's declaration, "Yeah, but I am the head thereof." Sarah reportedly received a $3 million dollar settlement, $2 million less than Billie Jean had received a few years earlier. Said Glen of Sarah, "I don't want to cause her problems. She's got enough of them."

And so the saga of Mac and Sarah and Glen came to its conclusion. Some had hoped that Sarah would return to Mac but, alas, Mac just shook his curly head and commented, "I was surprised their marriage lasted as long as it did." And, Glen asserted his innocence in the whole affair: "I didn't steal my best friend's wife. They were already apart, and anyway, Mac and I were never friends. I played golf with him some, is all. People were very rude and stupid concerning the whole thing." And, "God will take his revenge on those liars who wrote those things. Vengeance is mine, said the Lord. And he can think of a lot better things to do to those who lie than I can."

> I gave God a prayer, and He gave me Tanya Tucker.
> —Glen Campbell

> Well, I gave God a prayer, too, and He let Glen find Tanya Tucker!
> —Sarah Davis Campbell

Tanya Tucker:
"Would You Lay with Me?"

"Tanya? She still thinks asphalt is bowel trouble. I mean, the girl is not too bright."
—Glen Campbell on Tanya Tucker

I truly love him. I kinda felt bad that Glen didn't steal *me* from
somebody. Who knows what will happen? Tomorrow, I may run
off with Mac Davis.
—Tanya Tucker

If, after the debacle with ex-wife Sarah, Glen Campbell
thought his dirty bed stains would no longer be laundered in
public, he was monumentally mistaken. The real dirt hadn't even
been flung yet.

When she exploded on the scene at age thirteen with "Delta
Dawn," Tanya Tucker was the little girl dwarfed by that scorching torch of a voice. In a two-year period, she had five number
one hits. Nashville marveled at the novelty of it all but nonetheless predicted her early professional and/or personal demise.
After all, she was growing up at an alarmingly rapid rate. She

138

quit school during her freshman year. She sang songs like "Would You Lay with Me in a Field of Stone" with prodigious authority. She publicly scoffed at Helen Reddy ("I'd blow her right off the stage!"), who had made "Delta Dawn" a major pop hit. She postured, posed, and promoted herself audaciously as the female Elvis. And from the stage at age fifteen, she leered in black leather and cooed to her audience, "I hope my pants didn't rip."

Tanya Tucker was fourteen years old when she met Glen Campbell backstage at the 1973 Country Music Association's award show. As Tanya later recalled, "It was just one of those 'Howdy, how are you doing,' et cetera, meetings." A few years later, they met again, at another CMA awards show, which had by then moved from the Ryman Auditorium to Opryland U.S.A. But it was not until February 1980 that they began to date. Tanya was twenty-one. Glen was a forty-four-old grandfather.

Both of their careers had by then lapsed into a lull. Nevertheless, over the next two years, Glen and Tanya reigned as the top tabloid sensation of the country. They performed together, recorded together, and played together like renegade young lovers. But instead of shying away from the intrusive publicity that generally accompanies a celebrity couple, their love seemed to burn brightest when under the glaring and bemused public spotlight.

Glen was particularly vocal. "I'm dating one of the finest female talents that God lets draw breath," he gushed. And, "This girl is literally the answer to my prayers. I was shattered when my third marriage broke down earlier this year so I went down on my knees and prayed to God. And my prayer was answered in the form of Tanya. Golf is my second love. Tanya is my first. As far as I am concerned, Tanya is the real true love of my life. I want to marry her and have lots of kids."

Tanya was more secular, but no more restrained, in her pronouncements. Of her middle-aged boyfriend's sexual prowess, she crossed her legs and boasted, "He's the horniest man I ever met. Men are supposed to slow down after forty, but it's just the opposite with Glen. I mean, I thought I could handle a lot." This from a young woman who, just a few years before, had told reporters that she would never consider having sex before marriage.

For her twenty-second birthday, Glen threw Tanya a $57,000 bash and invested in a Beverly Hills boutique for her to operate. Tanya meanwhile lavished a $10,000 watch on Glen. Mused Glen sardonically, "My other wives bought me gifts with *my* money. Tanya bought this for me with *her* money. That's the difference.

Tanya: "There are very few singers who are also performers: Frank Sinatra, Elvis Presley, Glen Campbell." Glen: "Shouldn't that be in alphabetical order?"

Glen Campbell, doing his Elvis Presley impersonation.

It means a lot to me. She did it out of love, not out of obligation."

By the end of 1980, they announced their tentative plans to get married. Never one for understatement, Campbell broadcasted, "We haven't decided where the ceremony will take place. It could be on a 747. It's going to be a really big wedding. We even considered getting married on the first space shuttle—but that's a bit way out." And, "Our love is magic, it's a gift from God, and our wedding is going to reflect that." Tanya prophesied, "People ask if we will ever get tired of each other, but I don't think that will ever happen. I don't think anything will ever spoil our happiness."

But before long, they were ready to trade in their happiness, and their magical gift from God, for a newer model. In March 1981, Glen told a Nashville newspaper that they had postponed their plans for marriage. Said Glen, "I'm waiting for her to grow up." The following month, they announced the cancelation of their joint British tour. Soon afterward, it was reported that their relationship was over. Mourned Tanya, "I guess I got too old for him. You're talking about a man twice my age, who's been through three marriages, has five kids, who's been very successful, but he still has this insecurity."

According to *People* magazine, the split had been precipitated by Glen's jealousy. Apparently, Tanya had gone to Le Dome, a Los Angeles restaurant, without him, and he was not pleased. According to several sources, however, they had spent a good deal of their time together drinking and doing cocaine, and the abusive indulgence had finally taken its toll. Campbell himself once acknowledged, "If it hadn't been for Kim [his fourth wife, whom he married in 1982], I'd have ended up like Elvis." And, in February 1988, Tanya entered the Betty Ford Center to treat her addiction to drugs and alcohol. She later acknowledged that her chemical abuse had gotten out of hand in 1980—during the period of her affair with Campbell."

> I'll always love him and I believe he'll always love me. I would lay down my life for Glen Campbell if I could just make him totally happy for one day, but he's not the kind to change his mind. I still love him like my own life. The door is wide open. *He's the most gentle, loving, giving man I've ever met.*
> —Tanya Tucker, 1981

Four years after she made that statement, Tanya Tucker filed a $3 million lawsuit against her former lover, charging "Battery, Mayhem, Assault with a deadly weapon, and Fraud." The case dragged on for several years before it was dismissed or settled out of court. To this day, neither party will discuss the details of the case or the settlement, if indeed there was one.

Of the allegations, Campbell stated, "She's lying. She says I knocked her teeth out. I haven't even seen her in four years. She must need the money." This, of course, is doubtful considering that Tanya's career has accelerated far past Campbell's in recent years.

> The hardest thing to control in this body is that serpent called the tongue. Boy, have you ever said something and wanted to take it back? It's out there, it's gone.
> —Glen Campbell

Whatever the reasons for the dissolution of their flamboyant fling, it is blatantly apparent that they were mismatched from the outset. Tanya Tucker is a woman used to doing things her own way. Glen Campbell is what many would term a Bible-spewing male chauvinist. This is a man who once said, regarding his fourth wife and marriage in general, "There's got to be a captain of this ship and there's got to be a first mate. I was put on this earth as a male and I function and do that for which God

Glen to Tanya: "I'll never do anything to put you down or dishonor you. What I've learned from three marriages is to always fight fair, keep your punches up, never hit below the belt, and always make an argument end. Don't harbor grudges forever—and *never* resort to physical violence."

created me as a male, and she's a female and she does that." He also once declared, "I don't like to cook. I think it's a woman's place to do the cooking. I'll go this far: I'll light the barbecue for my wife if she wants to fix steaks. When it gets right down to it, I can probably fix them better than she does, but I'd rather have her do it." This is also a man who once told a stunned female reporter, "I believe in doing things the way God wants them done. You're a woman. You do what a woman does. I'm a man, and I do what a man does. It's really incredible. Your body is programmed to have kids and to give milk from your breasts. That's all programmed up here [pointing to his head]. This is true. I was reading on it."

There is no doubt that, for a brief period, the Glen Campbell–Tanya Tucker love affair was heated, passionate, and all-encompassing. But it burned on a fuse too short, and the repercussions of its destruction are still being felt. Painfully.

Glen and Tanya were certainly not the first country music duet to take their song lyrics literally. There were, of course, George and Tammy, Johnny and June, and Jim Ed and Helen. Jim Ed Brown and Helen Cornelius scored a number one country hit with the 1976 duet "I Don't Want to Have to Marry You." They had another hit with "Lying in Love with You" and, for a while, they were one of the top duet teams in country music. At the time, they denounced speculation that their onstage gazes were anything more than professional chemistry. However, in February 1979, Jim Ed's wife of nineteen years, Becky, filed for a divorce. Shortly after, Jim Ed and Helen announced the termination of their partnership and Becky withdrew her petition for divorce. However, In January 1980, Helen separated from *her* husband of twenty years. *One month* later, Becky refiled for divorce, and Jim Ed and Helen, after years of backstage denials, finally admitted the nature of their offstage duet and publicly professed their love.

However, by the end of the year, Jim Ed and Helen had separated bitterly. Jim Ed went back to Becky, who withdrew her second petition for divorce, and Helen married her manager, Jerry Garren.

Jim Ed Brown and Helen Cornelius: "I Don't Want to Have to Marry You." They didn't.

Former Duke boys John Schneider and Tom Wopat have both attempted careers in country music Thus far, Schneider has been much more successful.

John Schneider: Too sophisticated for Snailville?

In March 1988, Jim Ed and Helen reunited onstage at the Grand Ole Opry and announced their professional reunion. Apart, neither one of them had been successful. Thus, it seemed appropriate that they should rejoin vocal chords, if not other anatomical parts.

William Lee Golden, the impressively bearded former Oak Ridge Boy, may have married and divorced a former Miss Las Vegas Tourism, but it was John Schneider, the former—and reportedly well-endowed—Duke from Hazzard, who married and divorced a former Miss America.

Big, good-looking and blond, the strapping Schneider has ample measures of sex appeal and savvy. When "The Dukes of Hazzard" was initially being cast, he showed up for his audition with a six-pack of beer and in his best hillbilly affectation, told producers that he hailed from Snailville, Georgia. He got the part and eventually transcended the mediocrity of the material to become a star.

Moreover, he parlayed the fleeting fame of television into an impressive career in country music. His recording career started

When John Schneider returned tc "The Dukes of Hazzard" following a feud with the show's producers, Byron Cherry (r) was left—uh—hanging. Perhaps Cherry, originally from Tennessee, should give Nashville a shot. He already has a *foot* in the door.

with a stutter in 1981 with booming, lachrymose remakes of Elvis Presley's "Now or Never" and "Are You Lonesome Tonight?" In 1984, however, he shrewdly switched musical gears and scored a number one country hit with "I've Been Around Enough to Know." He has scored many hits since and, with undeniable talent, has earned the begrudged acceptance of the Nashville establishment.

In 1982, Schneider met Los Angeles newscaster and 1976 Miss America Tawny Godin Little. Said Schneider, "I thought she was just another pushy reporter." Said Tawny, "He struck me as just another egotistical actor." At the time, Tawny had been dating Burt Reynolds (who *hadn't* been?). In July 1983, John and Tawny were married in a gaudy, grandiose production on the set of "Dukes" in Burbank Studios. At the time, John was quoted as saying, "Tawny means more to me than anything or anyone. We love each other completely." In 1985 they were amicably divorced.

Like his "Dukes" replacement, John Schneider (pictured here emoting in *Eddie Macon's Run*) is amply endowed.

It was Dottie West who embraced Nashville newcomer John Schneider with "He's one of us." But then it's no secret in Nashville that Dottie has a particular penchant for *younger* men.

> I'm sure older guys are great lovers. But I just happen to like young guys. I look through the audience, I'll see a good-looking guy and think, it might sort of be nice.
> —Dottie West

In 1973, the "Country Sunshine Girl," Dottie West, shocked Nashville by abandoning her twenty-year marriage, which had produced four children, to marry her twenty-nine-year-old drummer, Byron Metcalf. She was forty-one at the time. Before their marriage, Metcalf, broke and struggling, was allowed to live in the basement of Dottie's Nashville home. Before long, he packed his belongings and moved upstairs.

Eight years later, the couple divorced. In court, Dottie charged that Metcalf had a drinking problem and an "improper association" with another woman. Further, Dottie's petition read, "On several occasions, while under the influence of alcohol, [Metcalf] has caused embarrassing situations that are damaging to the plaintiff's professional career." It further stated that Metcalf once "went so far as to make threats with a gun, much to [Dottie's] embarrassment and humiliation."

Metcalf retaliated in court that Dottie was "extremely jealous" and that she had had "affairs with other men." His petition further read, "The most humiliating incident for me was when I had gallbladder surgery in 1975 or 1976 and was recuperating at home. [Dottie] falsely accused me of having sex with her daughter Shelly [who would have been seventeen or eighteen at the time]. The accusation was not only sick, it was simply incredible since I was laid up in bed and couldn't even change my dressing." Metcalf further contended, "Her affairs with other men [took] their toll on me. I have reason to believe that she has been unfaithful to me with at least two men." According to Metcalf, one of Dottie's suspected lovers was a twenty-one-year-old boy

"I got me a king-size brass bed, and I just had a mirror put up over it— for the exercise."
—Dottie West

who worked as a dancer in a Dallas nightclub. The other was someone identified only as a man in the music industry.

One man in the music industry that Dottie has been closely aligned with is Larry Gatlin. The two met in 1971, when Gatlin, a twenty-three-year-old unknown, was performing as part of the Jimmy Dean Show at the Imperial Hotel in Las Vegas. Later, in May 1971, Gatlin sent Dottie eight of his songs, two of which she recorded. Then, in 1972, when Dottie formed her own music publishing company, the first songwriter she signed was Larry Gatlin. Years later, Gatlin acknowledged, "If it weren't for Dottie West, I'd probably be a lawyer in Houston." However, Gatlin has denied allegations that he had an affair with Dottie. Quipped Larry, "I love Dottie with all my heart, but not all my loins."

Dottie got her divorce from Metcalf after she agreed to pay him a cash settlement of $55,000 and an additional $10,241 in attorneys' fees. Reasoned Dottie at the time, "I work, he doesn't."

During divorce proceedings from her husband, Allen Frizzell, Dottie's daughter, Shelly (pictured here with former brother-in-law and singing partner David Frizzell) became embattled in a messy child custody case for *her* daughter, Tess.

In 1982, she recorded the scandalously titled "She Can't Get My Love Off the Bed." And the following year, at the age of fifty, she posed for the men's porn magazine *Oui*.

She also remarried. In 1983, Dottie married her third husband, twenty-eight-year-old Alan Winters. Winters, a former road manager and sound engineer, reportedly gave up his job to oversee the maintenance of Dottie's Nashville house and garden. Certainly, no one could accuse Dottie West of marrying for money or power or position, but there are those who believe that she marries for vanity. As Dottie herself remarked at the time of her most recent marriage, "Alan will be a real incentive to stay young." The incentive may have worked, but the marriage didn't. In 1988, fifty-six-year-old Dottie filed for a divorce, charging Winters with cruel and inhuman punishment.

A woman would have to love me a lot to put up with my bullshit.
—Johnny Lee

Johnny Lee and Charlene Tilton were married on February 14, 1982. However, Cupid must have slung his arrow through a vitriolic valentine, because they were divorced two years later amid tales of horror and brutality.

Before he married Charlene, *Urban Cowboy* recording star Johnny Lee, then thirty-eight, had been a lifelong bachelor. Six months after their marriage, Charlene gave birth to their daughter, Cherish. Lee reportedly cut the umbilical cord. Soon after, speculation quickly surfaced that all was not well in the Lee household.

Lee denied the rumors of discord. In May 1983, he told a reporter, "I love my wife. I love how she loves me and makes me feel good when I'm in a slump. I wouldn't know what to do without Charlene and Cherish. I couldn't bear to be without them." Lee also blamed the tabloids for starting the rumors: "A bucket of manure, which is what those papers are, is going to stink for a while. If you leave it alone, a crust will form over the top and it won't stink anymore. But if you stir it up again, it's going to stink again."

Nevertheless, it wasn't the tabloids, foul-smelling or otherwise, that provoked Charlene Tilton to obtain a restraining order against her husband in December 1983. In her request, the diminutive 4'11" "Dallas" star contended that Lee owned many

Johnny Lee (shown here with Bonnie Raitt and John Travolta) was served his divorce papers while onstage at the Palomino Club in Los Angeles.

Following her divorce from Johnny Lee, Charlene Tilton married a Liberace protege, Domenick Allen. In 1987, she was arrested for drunk driving. Later, she was accepted back into the cast of "Dallas," where she resumed her role of Lucy Ewing.

guns and that she was afraid for her life. Further, she claimed that Lee had, during the brief course of their marriage: brutally beaten her black and blue; punched her twenty times with a closed fist; slapped, kicked, and choked her repeatedly; beaten her with a telephone receiver, yanked her pierced earring out of her ear; pounded her head against the wall; and smashed his hand into her face, "trying to push my nose up into my brain," while daughter Cherish screamed hysterically. The worst offense, alleged Charlene, was that Lee, in one of his violent fits, had tied their dog Goldfish to the rear of their car and proceeded to drive at a high speed, pulling the yelping dog by its collar.

However, Lee denied the allegations and charged that it was the church and Charlene's fanatical born-again belief in God that had driven them apart. Lee claimed that Charlene would even do her daily aerobics to gospel music. Said Lee, "I'm an old country boy. I don't feel like I have to stick my arms in the air, and wave, and talk in tongues."

In our church, marriage isn't just for life, it's for eternity.
—Marie Osmond

Marie Osmond does not talk in tongues. The pudgy pubescent—turned *Good Housekeeping* cover girl—turned country music

Back in the 1970s, it seemed as though Donny and Marie Osmond were joined at the gums. At that time, Marie was quoted as saying, "I'll never go on my own. The family is too important to me."

After her second marriage, Marie's country career stalled on the charts. The awful "Everybody's Crazy 'bout My Baby" peaked at number twenty-eight; "Cry Just a Little" peaked at number fifty.

star does not even drink Coca-Cola. She doesn't drink coffee or alcohol, doesn't smoke cigarettes, doesn't snort cocaine. And she would probably never even contemplate the idea of an extramarital dalliance. But she *did*, as America watched with a bemused gaze, commit the cardinal Mormon betrayal. She got a divorce.

Finally, it seemed, there was a blemish on the otherwise flawless Osmond complexion. To some Americans who grew up in the in 1970s (this author included), there has always been something, well, distasteful about the Osmond clan. The Osmonds, with their toothy dispositions, had been thrust onto a pedestal by the media as the symbols of adolescent perfection. They were an image not easy to live up to. They were an image many did not *want* to live up to. Still, they couldn't be denied.

At least the Brady kids could be executed with the flip of a dial, but the Osmonds were everywhere. They grinned on television. They grinned in the movies. They grinned on posters. They grinned on their album covers. They grinned in advertisements for Hawaiian Punch. If you listened hard enough, you could even hear them grinning on the radio. But for many teenagers who struggled through adolescence at that time, it wasn't the kind of grinning that made you happy. It was the kind of grinning that made you feel dislocated. And inadequate. And diabetic.

It was the perfect wedding. They were married on June 23, 1982, before 4,000 guests at the Mormon Tabernacle in Salt Lake City. There were eight attendants and a flower girl; a five-foot-tall cake; and a wedding gown designed by Ret Turner, which featured sixteen-foot trains and reportedly took 300 hours to create.

It was the wedding spectacular of the year, and Marie, the virgin bride, and Steve Craig, her mannequin-handsome groom, grinned for the cameras and basked in the perfection of it all.

I am really in love. I won't ever run home to Mama.
—Marie Osmond

I'll spend the rest of my life taking good care of her.
—Steve Craig

Broken dreams and unfulfilled promises later, Steve Craig left the couple's Provo, Utah, home in June 1984, and moved to Los Angeles. In August, he was called before the Mormon Church for disciplinary action. His membership in the church was placed on probation. The reasons for the nonsecular slap on the hand have never been released to the public. Speculation, of course, has abounded. Most rumored reports contended that Craig had been having an affair. In November, Marie and Steve officially separated. On November 10, Craig was rushed to a Provo hospital after an alleged suicide attempt.

Nothing that lasts for a lifetime can come easy.
—Marie Osmond

With a little bit of luck and a lot of work, Marie and I fully plan to celebrate our golden anniversary together.
—Steve Craig

In May 1985, after a brief reconciliation, Marie filed for a divorce, claiming "great mental distress." She also accused Craig of having treated her "cruelly." Craig filed a response and surprised all by seeking custody of their two-year-old son, Stephen James. Nevertheless, Craig's attorney at the time asserted, "Craig would rather just kiss and make up. He very much would like to not have a divorce and would like to reconcile with her because he loves her and their son very much." Marie countercharged, "I gave him plenty of chances. I never gave him an ultimatum. [His desire for reconciliation] is just not true. I just can't believe that he would think so little of this one [son Stephen] to put him through something like a custody battle."

In early October 1985, Marie and Steve met at 4th District Court in Provo. Although they didn't speak, they did come to an agreement. Marie reportedly got $1 a year and custody of their son. It is not known if Steve Craig received a financial settlement because their divorce, unlike their marriage, has been shrouded in protective secrecy, as though it were a national shame of significant proportions.

Marie's divorce may have marred her religious record, but it did wonders for her country music résumé. Actually, she had had her first country hit, "Paper Roses," when she was thirteen. The song had originally been recorded by Anita Bryant, who had been a country music singer before she became a babbling gay basher. At any rate, following her divorce, Marie was suddenly more *real.* She had suffered. With her album *I Only Wanted You,* she became the first, and thus far only, Osmond to successfully evolve from adolescent idolatry to adult stardom. However, unlike John Schneider, who had to overcome a similar obstacle, Marie has yet to earn the respect of the Nashville community. Quipped one industry critic, "Not that Marie can't sing. She can sing. But so can at least forty-five or fifty contestants in the Miss America Pageant."

> The next guy will be older and established. He won't need me or my money. He'll just need someone to take care of.
> —Marie Osmond

In October 1986, just a few days after her divorce became final, Marie married recording engineer Brian Blosil. The wedding was small (only fifteen invited guests), and the services were conducted by the same clergyman who had orchestrated her marriage to Steve Craig. But Marie Osmond—no longer the virgin bride—picked up her son by another man, clasped her new husband's hand in her own, and happily posed for the cameras anyway.

She was grinning bigger than ever.

7

BIG BALLS IN COWTOWN

D avid Allan Coe, then twenty-four, lathered his mean, tattooed body in the men's communal shower at the Ohio State Penitentiary. He rubbed the bar of soap along the muscles of his arms, chest, and shoulders, thinking perhaps about his girlfriend back in Akron, and what he wanted to do with her when he got *out*. Then, as he worked the soap around to the small of his back, the bar slipped out of his grip and fell to the floor. Coe bent over, butt in the air, to recover the soap as it slid across the tile. As he retrieved it and began to unfold his 6'4" frame, a pair of big, black hands grabbed him by the head. Coe looked up, as his face was shoved, tongue first, into the other man's swollen meat. The inmate growled, "You gonna suck my dick, baby." Coe—who had previously been on the receiving, but not the giving, end of a warm, wet, *male* mouth—went berserk. He grabbed the nearest available weapon, a mop bucket wringer, and battered the black dude's skull. Unfortunately, not only did he beat the erection out of the guy, he also beat the *life* out of him.

That's the way it happened in 1963, more or less, according to *Just for the Record*, the autobiography of controversial country star, ex-biker, ex-pimp, ex-polygamist, ex-con David Allan Coe. At least that's the way, at one time, he wanted everyone to believe it happened. But *is* that the way it happened?

> I'm not going back to prison. Hell, I've got used to pussy and different things.
> —David Allan Coe, *Esquire*, 1976

By the time he got to Nashville at the rear end of 1967, David Allan Coe had spent twenty years in reform schools, state institu-

In 1979, there was widespread rumor that the June Carter–Johnny Cash marriage was in trouble. It *wasn't* because June had embraced another man in the movie, *Country Music Holiday*. One reason for the gossip was that Cash had announced that the Carter Sisters (Jan Howard and Helen and Anita Carter) would no longer be a part of his act. The speculation was that Jan departed at June's request, because Cash had become romantically involved with her. Cash denied it. Said he, "[Jan] and June are the best of friends. Jan would not do such a thing to June."

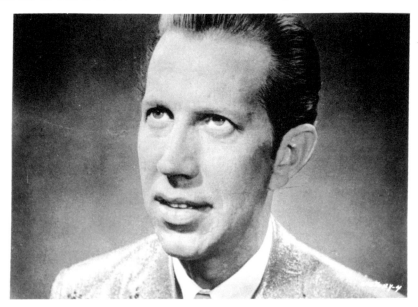

Porter Wagoner and his wife, Ruth Olive Williams, separated in 1965. But it wasn't until twenty-one years later, in 1987, that the sixty-two-year-old Ruth was granted a divorce on grounds of cruel and inhuman treatment.

In 1987, at the age of fifty-three, Conway Twitty (pictured here in *Sex Kittens Go to College*) married his longtime business associate Dee Henry, who is twenty years his junior. Twitty and his wife of twenty-eight years, Mickey, had married and divorced twice—with the final divorce filed in 1984. Reportedly, Mickey received a $10 million settlement.

Linda Thompson (pictured here with Sammy Davis Jr.), former Miss Tennessee and former live-in love of Elvis Presley, is a "Hee Haw" regular. In February 1986, she separated from her husband, 1976 Olympics gold medalist Bruce Jenner.

On December 18, 1969, twenty-seven-year-old Bobbie Gentry of Chickasaw County, married fifty-eight-year-old millionaire, William Harrah of Harrah's Reno and Harrah's Tahoe. They separated three months later. When Gentry burst on the country music scene in 1967 with "Ode to Billy Joe," she was hyped as the southern Streisand.

Following her "Rose Garden" megahit in 1971, Lynn Anderson divorced husband Glenn Sutton ("Rose" producer). In 1978, she flung her honey-blonde hair at the music industry and married millionaire Harold "Spook" Stream. The couple divorced in 1982, with Lynn charging that Stream had repeatedly abused her physically and once attempted to run her over with a car.

tions, and prisons on convictions including car theft, possession of obscene materials, and possession of burglary tools. It was the latter offense that had banished Coe to the Ohio State pen, where he served time from October 22, 1963, until November 2, 1967.

Merle Haggard, Tammy Wynette, and Glen Campbell were the biggest things in country music at the time. Johnny Cash was about to record *At Folsom Prison*, the album that would launch the resurgence of his career. And *Bonnie and Clyde*, with a soundtrack that included country music's Lester Flatt and Earl Scruggs, was the most acclaimed movie of the year. Haggard, of course, had served time in prison, and his burgeoning career capitalized on that status with hit songs like "I'm a Lonesome Fugitive" and "Branded Man." In country music, it was a prosperous, even glamorous, era for cons and ex-cons and would-be cons.

Thus, it is easy to see why David Allan Coe, facing life out of prison, packed up his guitar and headed to Nashville with the suddenly fashionable ex-con stigma all but stamped on his forehead. Surprisingly though, he began his career by recording the *blues*, for record producer Shelby Singleton. His first album, *Penitentiary Blues*, was released in 1968 and included such prison testimonials as "Death Row" and "Cell #33." *Requiem for a Harlequin*, another blues effort, followed. Neither was commercially successful.

In the early 1970s, Coe was signed to Columbia Records and jumped from the blues to country. Nevertheless, he became more famous in Nashville for his flammable flamboyance than his music. He appeared on stage in a rhinestone Nudie suit and a black mask and billed himself "The Mysterious Rhinestone Cowboy." When he wasn't performing, Coe drove around Nashville in a hearse with his name emblazoned on the sides and hung out at Tootsie's Orchid Lounge and other locales the big shots frequented. When, during these rounds, he was confronted by apathetic faces and rejecting nods, Coe threw out his ex-con chest and affected his most menacing leer and intimidated *whomever* into listening to his songs. As a Coe associate later mused, "[David] threatened to wipe the floor with 'em if they didn't."

He was not a popular figure in Nashville.

No matter how talented he was, David Allan Coe was considered to be bad for the country music image. Nashville did not like the 365 tattoos that populated his body (which included an image of the devil on his chest and, reportedly, a spider on his, uh, snake); or the cocksure swagger he flagrantly flaunted in public

Despite only a sixth-grade education, and beneath the badass bravado, David Allen Coe is a sensitive, intelligent writer. Still, one writer couldn't help but dub him a "twenty-nine-year-old wrestler, retired from the ring for a decade."

(Coe described himself to a reporter as "Incomparable. Way ahead of my time, bigger than Bob Dylan"—he also used to wear a T-shirt onstage that read "Damn Near as Big as Texas."); or the way he demeaned women (Coe once remarked of most of the women he had known, "I've just seen the tops of their heads"); or the explicitly salacious songs that he sometimes sang. He recorded two X-rated albums, *Little Susie Shallow Throat*, and *Don't Bite the Dick*, which included such songs as "Pussy Whipped Again," "Cum Stains on the Pillow," "I Was into Whips and Things and She Was into Pain," and "Fuck Anita Bryant."

Even after he wrote two number one mainstream country hits, "Would You Lay with Me in a Field of Stone" for Tanya Tucker and "Take This Job and Shove It" for Johnny Paycheck, David Allan Coe was snubbed, without apology, by the industry. And, despite the fact that his albums sold consistently well, Coe was

160

unable to obtain a hit single because radio programmers, for the most part, refused to play his songs.

In 1977, an article appeared in the *Nashville Banner* under the headline MUSIC ROW SEES "END" OF COE. It read, in part, "David Allan Coe has gone to the bottom and some folks on Music Row are afraid he's trying to take the whole Nashville country music industry down with him. Coe is distributing large posters of himself and his band—men and women—showing their bare buttocks." The article did not detail how dropping one's pants could provoke the collapse of a multimillion-dollar industry, but most of Nashville seemed to agree with it anyway. Country music legend Ernest Tubb reportedly refused to be booked on the same bill with Coe. Vic Willis, president of the Association of Country Entertainers, dictated, "Coe and his band are the epitome of bad taste, bad judgment. Anyone who would involve himself with a picture like this [the butt shot, again] should be locked up. They're not doing country music any favors." Willie Nelson was kinder: "David Allan Coe's as good a songwriter as any of us. But he goes to an extreme. He calls a lot of attention to himself at any cost. David Allan Coe reminds me of a white Muhammad Ali. I think he puts himself down by overpromoting himself. Everything's carnival, circus ballyhoo, the old street hustle." The *Banner* article concluded, rather mean-spiritedly, "He wears a ten-gallon hat, earrings, and has been singing a brand of country music for ten years. Hopefully, this will be his last." It wasn't.

But by far the biggest uproar over David Allan Coe wasn't about his naked butt, or his naked talent, or even the cocaine parties and sex orgies that he allegedly hosted early in his career. It was about that damn mop bucket wringer. Did he or didn't he do *it*?

It was in 1974, during the emergence of the overwhelmingly popular "Outlaw Movement" in country music, that Coe told a writer for *Rolling Stone* that he had killed a man while at Ohio State Penitentiary. Few were shocked. More were impressed. After all, next to David Allan Coe, "Outlaws" Waylon, Willie, Tompall, and the boys were reduced to resembling the Osmond Brothers at a Tabernacle telethon.

Then, in 1975, a television documentary about Coe entitled "The Mysterious Rhinestone Cowboy" was produced. It became the first media source to question the authenticity of Coe's version of The Mop Bucket Killing. Said the program's producer, Mark Birnbaum, "If you look at the film where he talks about the killing, there's a break, a pause. It looks like he's lying. It's my guess that the bigger your crime, the more status you have in prison, and that he began telling this story while in jail, and just continued it when he began his singing career."

> If this is true, I'm obviously surprised, disappointed and somewhat ashamed. David is a very convincing storyteller.
> —Ron Bledsoe, the CBS Records vice president who had signed Coe to the label in 1972

The outlaw backlash had begun. Bill Starnes, Coe's former manager, stated, "It's okay to hype the public, but you can't lie to them. The public's not stupid. The reason David and I didn't make it is because he was always misrepresenting himself." Maybe so, but this is the same Bill Starnes who, on August 11, 1975, had casually described the alleged killing to the *Fort Worth*

After *Rolling Stone* questioned whether or not he was a killer, Coe composed a song dedicated to the magazine's writers. It was called "I'd Like to Kick the Shit Out of You." Said Coe, "Them *Rolling Stone* motherfuckers better be glad the old Rhinestone Cowboy ain't lost his sense of humor, or I might hire me about three gorillas to kick ass. Wouldn't soil my hands on 'em myself."

Star-Telegram as, "Some guy tried to make a sissy out of him, and he killed him with a washing machine wringer."

Then *Rolling Stone* reentered the Hitchcockian spectacle and accused Coe of concocting the whole sordid would-be oral rape and murder for publicity purposes. Coe responded with a carefully worded statement in the *Tennessean*: "There was an inmate killed in the Ohio Penitentiary in December 1963. There were three inmates that were accused of that killing, and I was one of them. The three were placed in L-Block, which was Death Row, and they were threatened with being put in the electric chair and different things in order to make them confess to this crime. One inmate confessed and was tried for the crime. Two inmates did not confess, and I was one of these two."

Around this time, country music writer and magazine editor Martha Hume reported, "He [Coe] very much wanted me to believe that he was indeed a murderer. He told me his standard story of the killing, along with a few more details. He really wanted me to believe it, but at the same he said he was going to deny it. The story is quite, quite confusing. He also mentioned that he'd gotten the money for the bus he owns from Jimmy Hoffa. He said he knew Hoffa personally. No one has been able to verify this."

Publicly, Coe denied that he ever said he had killed anyone and blamed the 1974 *Rolling Stone* article for misquoting him. In 1976, he told *Esquire*, "My manager tells me if I provide any details, then shit, man, I could find myself facing a murder rap. I mean, man, I'm not gonna make any statements that could be interpreted as a confession. I'd be a damn fool to do that." And in 1978, he denied the entire episode: "The whole thing has been blown way out of proportion over the years. The truth of it is this, I did spend time on Death Row while I was in the Ohio State Penitentiary, but I was never convicted of murder, and I didn't kill anybody." This, despite the fact that he had written in his autobiography, *Just for the Record*, "I picked up a mop wringer from a bucket and hit him with it and killed him."

Today, the Ohio State Penitentiary is no longer in operation, and the Case of the Mop Bucket Wringer will, in all probability, never be reopened or solved. Nevertheless, the disturbing commentary that resulted from it remains. David Allan Coe was denounced by society in general, and the country music industry in particular, when the possibility emerged that he was *not*, despite all of his badass braggadocio, a killer. It seems that, in the case of David Allan Coe, imaginative press agentry was a more serious offense than murder.

Coe once claimed to live with twenty-three women at one time. Said he, "Women will start hanging around because they think it's all going to be drugs and sex." Today, however, Coe has become a mellowed family man. Pictured left to right, Carla Dawn, Coe, Tanya Montana, Tyler, and wife Jody Lynn.

Sure it's hurt my career because I'm not a pussy and a yes man. Nevertheless, I'm the motherfucker who has to live with David Allan Coe the rest of his life.
—David Allan Coe

Nashville embraced its urban outlaws, and glamorized the outlaw image, but disowned the genuine article. Willie Nelson was right: David Allan Coe was just too extreme for Nashville to handle. He didn't follow the rules of the game. He didn't ride into town on a white horse and grovel for stardom; he *bolted* into town in a black hearse, or any piece of junk that he could get his hands on, and *demanded* it. And to a degree, in the long run, he has won. He has finally gotten some radio airplay, has had a few hits of his own, and perhaps most impressively, has managed to survive for over twenty years in an industry that has only accepted him begrudgingly, with gritted teeth and pained grimace.

And, who knows, he just *may* have beaten a murder rap. Either that, or he yanked off one hell of a con.

8
ON THE ROAD, AGAIN

I had a premonition it was going to happen. I didn't see how I
could go on riding here and there and not have some sort of an
accident. Any game you play you got to lose sometime. You
can't go on winning forever. I've been traveling for almost thirty
years about 100,000 miles annually, in all sorts of weather.
—Roy Acuff on the July 1965 car crash that nearly took his
life and the lives of two of his band members

The Roy Acuff near-tragedy took place on a slick
highway near Sparta, Tennessee, as Acuff and his
Smoky Mountain Boys headed toward Terell, North
Carolina, to make a personal appearance.
    Country music stars, unlike rock stars or celebri-
ties of other more lucrative media, generally spend most of their
lives on the road. Not in some cushioned first-class cabin on a
major airline, but rather in a car that has probably logged too
much mileage or, if they're lucky, in the back compartment of
their own customized bus (star status in Nashville isn't determined by who has the biggest-selling record but by who has the
biggest, most expensive *bus*).

Unless they're Kenny Rogers, or Dolly Parton, or Willie Nelson,
many country performers are required to perform anywhere
from 200 to 300 *one-nighters* a year. Understandably, then, air
travel is too expensive a proposition. Besides, many of the country music venues are located in small towns, inaccessible by
plane.

And so they travel by car or bus. They load their musical
equipment and their personal belongings into their crowded
vehicles, drive to whatever town they're performing in, sing their
songs, reload their vehicles, and drowsily, sometimes drunkenly,
drive on to the next town. Delusions aside, life on the road is *not* a

Splat, on the road again.

particularly glamorous lifestyle. It can be claustrophobic, debilitating, and horrifying—in ways that even Jack Kerouac, with the most wicked of hangovers, never envisioned. After all, it's not uncommon for a country music performer to spend years traveling from town to town, reading faded road maps like daily newspapers, pouring his heart out on carnival fairgrounds and shitkicker stages, only to crash into a telephone pole, or tree, or car, or other fateful obstruction and, in a blinding flash of fury, spill his blood on the road somewhere in the night.

At the time of his near-fatal car crash, Roy Acuff was sixty-one and country music's oldest *surviving* legend. He suffered injuries including a broken collarbone, a fractured pelvis, and broken ribs. Many of his friends and country compatriots over the years have not been so lucky.

Milton Brown, thirty-two, and his passenger, singer Katherine Prehoditch, were returning home after a performance at the Crystal Springs Dance Pavilion in Texas. It was April 13, 1935.

Brown, a former cop, was leader of the Musical Brownies, a Decca recording group. He was also considered to be the co-founder of western swing and the primary threat to Bob Wills. En route home following that evening's performance, Brown was scorching down the highway, burning rubber on asphalt, doing over 90 m.p.h., when suddenly, one of his car tires exploded. The car did a somersault and crashed at full-speed into a telephone pole. The impact crushed Prehoditch, killing her instantly. Brown was rushed to the local hospital, where he also died.

Shortly after they had the number one song in the country with "I Forgot More than You'll Ever Know," Betty Jack and Skeeter Davis, known as the Davis Sisters (even though they were *not* sisters) were traveling from a performance date in Wheeling, West Virginia, to their home in Cincinnati when the car they were traveling in was struck head-on by another vehicle, driven by a soldier who had fallen asleep at the wheel. Betty Jack, twenty-one, known as "Bee Jay," was killed. It was August 2, 1953. Skeeter was seriously injured, but she later re-formed the duo with Betty Jack's *real* sister, Georgie, before going solo and recording hits like "The End of the World."

In the late 1940s, Roy Acuff was reportedly so afraid of sleeping alone while on the road that one of his band members used to routinely share his room. In 1948, he campaigned to become the governor of Tennessee. His platform was the Bible. He lost.

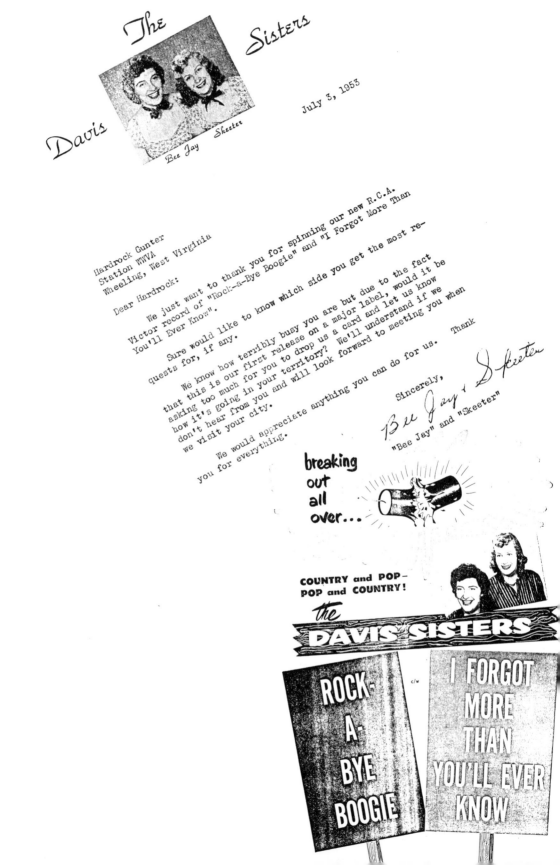

The Davis Sisters

Bee Jay   Skeeter

July 3, 1953

Hardrock Gunter
Station WWVA
Wheeling, West Virginia

Dear Hardrock:

We just want to thank you for spinning our new R.C.A. Victor record of "Rock-a-Bye Boogie" and "I Forgot More Than You'll Ever Know".

Sure would like to know which side you get the most requests for, if any.

We know how terribly busy you are but due to the fact that this is our first release on a major label, would it be asking too much for you to drop us a card and let us know how it's going in your territory? We'll understand if we don't hear from you and will look forward to meeting you when we visit your city.

We would appreciate anything you can do for us. Thank you for everything.

Sincerely,

Bee Jay + Skeeter

"Bee Jay" and "Skeeter"

breaking
out
all
over...

COUNTRY and POP—
POP and COUNTRY!

the DAVIS SISTERS

ROCK-A-BYE BOOGIE   c/w   I FORGOT MORE THAN YOU'LL EVER KNOW

"Blue Suede Shoes" blasted out of the borrowed limousine's radio. It was an early Saturday morning, March 22, 1956. Twenty-four-year-old Carl Perkins yawned and sighed and thought in awe about how far he had come. Just two years earlier, he had been living in a housing project in Jackson, Tennessee, with his wife and two sons. And then came Sam Phillips and Sun Records and rock and roll and "Blue Suede Shoes," which was currently rocking at the top of the charts. Just a few nights before, Carl had performed the song to screaming hysteria in Norfolk, Virginia, and before the next day was over he'd be in New York to do it on "The Perry Como Show" and then "The Ed Sullivan Show." And then after that, who knew?, he might even eclipse Elvis himself as the top act in the country. Not bad for a former cotton-picking southern boy, mused Carl, as he drifted off to sleep and dreamt rock and roll dreams of glory.

Then, at 6:40 A.M., four miles outside of Dover, Delaware, the limousine driven by Carl's manager, David Stewart (a.k.a. Stuart Pinkham), thirty, smashed into a stalled pickup truck, pulverizing it into scraps of so much metal and burning flesh. The driver of the pickup, Tom Phillips, forty-four, was killed. Upon impact, the limo went out of control, hit a guardrail, and careened down an embankment. Carl's brother Jay, twenty-five, broke his neck. Carl, submerged in a sewer of water and mud, was discovered only when one of the survivors accidentally stumbled over him. He went into the hospital unconscious, with a fractured skull, fractured vertebrae, and multiple other injuries.

During the nine months that Carl spent staring at the ceiling from a hospital bed, Elvis Presley appeared on "The Jackie Gleason Show" and sang "Blue Suede Shoes," which he had recorded and which became an even bigger hit than Carl's original version.

Two years later, Jay died from injuries sustained in the accident. It had been a slow death. He died holding Carl's hand. After Jay's death, Elvis's career continued to propel him toward that bathroom in Graceland, while Carl's was still lost somewhere in Delaware, submerged in mud. For the next several years, the only glory Carl was bound for was found in the bottom of a bottle of bourbon.

In 1987, The Academy of Country Music honored Carl with its Lifetime Achievement Award—not really for anything specific he had accomplished but more for what might have been.

By 1960, not only had Johnny Horton, thirty-one, inherited Hank Williams's beautiful young bride, Billie Jean, he had also

The glory days.

staked his claim as the top act in country music. Just a year earlier, Horton had scored a mega-hit with "The Battle of New Orleans," which went number one on both the country *and* pop charts. He followed that with his 1960 million-seller "North to Alaska."

On Friday night, November 4, 1960, Horton performed at the Skyline Club in Austin. Following the performance, Horton, his manager, Tillman Franks, forty, and his guitar player, Herald Tomlinson, thirty, loaded into Horton's white Cadillac. They were headed back toward Shreveport, Louisiana. Outside of Milano, Texas, at about 1:30 on Saturday morning, a 1958 Ford Ranchero barreled head-on into the Cadillac, crushing it into a hulk of twisted debris. Ambulances rushed Horton, his two companions, and the driver of the Ford, nineteen-year-old Texas A&M student James Evans Davis, to St. Edward's Hospital in Cameron, Texas. Horton was dead on arrival. The three others survived. At the scene of the accident, investigator Gilbert Smith removed two bottles of beer and a partially empty bottle of liquor from Davis's Ford.

Johnny Horton left behind him his widow, two young daughters, and enough recorded material to keep his name on the country charts throughout the 1960s. His friend Johnny Cash escorted his body from Texas to Nashville and delivered the eulogy at his funeral.

1963 was not a good year for country music. On March 6, the shredded remains of Patsy Cline, Cowboy Copas, and Hawkshaw Hawkins were found scattered in trees outside of Camden, Tennessee. Two days later, a memorial service for Cline was held in Nashville.

Jack Anglin, the forty-six-year-old tenor half of the successful duo Johnny and Jack got into his car with the intention of attending the service. He had, after all, performed at the same Kansas City benefit earlier in the week that Cline, Copas, and Hawkins had performed at. However, instead of returning to Nashville via small chartered plane as *they* had, Anglin had taken a commercial flight. And he was grateful that he had.

Perhaps that was what Jack Anglin was thinking about on that rainy Thursday afternoon—how some are chosen to die and some are not—when his car careened out of control, plunged off a fifteen-foot embankment, and smashed into a tree. When officers arrived at the scene, Anglin was still breathing. By the time he was delivered to Madison Hospital, however, he was dead from a fractured skull.

That day, WSM Radio in Nashville had been playing only the songs of Cline, Copas, and Hawkins. When they learned of Jack Anglin's tragic and ironic death, they promptly added the songs of Johnny and Jack to their exclusive playlist.

A few days later, Nashville wearily donned its mourning clothes again and attended the Jack Anglin funeral. Honorary pallbearer at the service was country music superstar Jim Reeves, who had succeeded Johnny Horton as the hottest performer in the industry. Just over a year later, Reeves would attend another funeral—in a box.

Ira Louvin was considered by some to have had one of the greatest voices ever to be recorded in country music. The Louvin Brothers, featuring Ira and younger brother Charlie, became popular with their close harmony duets. They scored several hit records, including "When I Stop Dreaming," and became regular members of the Grand Ole Opry in 1955.

By the early 1960s, however, the hits had become sparse for the Louvins, and after a feud the two brothers dissolved their partnership and went their separate ways. Charlie continued to score hits and remained a member of the Opry. Ira, unfortunately, did neither. He was having personal problems. During an argument at his Nashville home, his second wife, Faye, shot him six times in

Brothers Ira (left) and Charlie Louvin: Sibling rivalry?

the arm, chest, and shoulder. When he got out of the hospital, Ira divorced Faye and formed his own show with his third wife, Florence (who sang under the name Anne Young). Together, they went out on the road.

It was a Saturday, June 19, 1965. Father's Day. Ira and Florence had just completed a date in Kansas City and were en route to Henegar, Alabama, Ira's birthplace. They were driven in a 1963 Chevrolet hardtop by one of their musicians, Billy Barksdale, thirty-one, and his wife Adelle, twenty-nine.

Near Williamsburg, Missouri, at about 4:40 A.M. on Sunday, Tommy Franklin, a fifty-three-year-old janitor driving a 1964 Dodge coach, accidentally swerved into the wrong lane. He may have had too much to drink. Five pints of liquor and several cans of beer were later found in his car. When Barksdale saw the approaching Dodge, he slammed on his brakes and tried to swerve out of the way. At the last second, Franklin attempted to get back into his own lane. The two cars met on the centerline. Head first.

The Missouri highway was red with blood. When police arrived at the scene, they found the worst traffic accident ever recorded in the area. The cars were crumpled like metal accordions. The bodies were severed and splattered all over the road. Barksdale was found with his face crushed, his pants split, his knee caps shattered, and his foot still lodged on the brake. Billy and Adelle Barksdale, Louvin, Franklin, and Luther Daniels (a passenger in the Franklin vehicle), fifty-one, were all dead at the scene. Florence Louvin had a severe skull fracture but was still alive. She was rushed to a nearby hospital in Fulton and then to the University of Missouri Medical Center, where she was pronounced dead on arrival.

At their rainy, open-casket funeral, Ira and Florence Louvin were buried in a common grave as Bill Monroe sang "Where No Man Stands Alone."

Four days later, Ira's brother, Charlie, performed in Kansas City. He stopped on the stretch of highway that had been his brother's death spot. Debris from the wreckage was still in evidence. And the asphalt was still stained with his brother's blood.

And the road continued to be littered with talent.

Clarence White didn't even have a chance to get into his car. It was July 14, 1973, and Clarence, a bluegrass guitarist and former member of the Byrds, had just completed a performance in Palmdale, California. With the help of his brothers, Roland and

Red Sovine: Dead end.

Eric, he was outside the club loading an electric amplifier into a van, when he was struck by a speeding car. Clarence was thrown about seventy-five feet before he crashed onto the pavement. He never regained consciousness. He was twenty-nine. The driver of the killer car, Yoko Ito, was booked on suspicion of felony drunk driving and manslaughter.

Red Sovine was best known for his truck-driving songs like "Phantom 309" and "Teddy Bear." It seems only appropriate, though inarguably unfortunate, then, that he was killed in a Nashville car crash. On April 4, 1980, Sovine, driving his 1979 Ford van, inadvertently sped through a red light at the intersection of Lealand and Battery lanes. The van smashed into another car and careened into a tree several hundred feet down the road. Sovine, sixty-two, suffered a lacerated spleen and liver and later died from massive abdominal bleeding.

Barbara Mandrell was not en route from a performance gig; she was returning to her Hendersonville, Tennessee, mansion following a shopping expedition when it happened. Her children, fourteen-year-old Matthew and eight-year-old Jamie, needed new school clothes, and Barbara had taken them to the Rivergate Shopping Mall. After buying the clothes, Barbara stopped by The Antique Shop to see if there was anything *she* wanted. When she finished her browsing, Barbara and her children loaded into her 1982 silver Jaguar. Matthew got into the front seat on the passenger side, and Jamie sat in the back directly behind her mother. Barbara fastened her seat belt, a practice she didn't ordinarily exercise, and instructed her kids to do the same.

It was September 11, 1984.

Mark White, nineteen, was a student at the University of Tennessee in Knoxville, where he was about to become a sophomore. While in high school, he had been a member of the basketball team and the newspaper staff and was named to the *Who's Who of American High School Students.* Nevertheless, he had been turned down for a college scholarship due to medical reasons which involved an ear injury. Thus, because his family didn't have much money, Mark took a job at the Tri-Tech Corporation to put himself through school.

On September 11, 1984, Mark performed his usual monotonous duties at Tri-Tech—sandblasting, painting welding fixtures, and cleaning up equipment debris. He left work at 3:30 P.M., returned home, cleaned up, had a conversation with his mother at the kitchen table, and left the house at 6:00 P.M. From there, Mark drove to the local sporting goods store, where he purchased some archery equipment. He then got into his 1981 red Subaru, placed his new crossbow on the backseat, and headed back home.

He *didn't* fasten his seat belt.

It was almost 6:30 P.M.

Barbara Mandrell has always been cute and pixieish on the outside, armed with a steely ambition on the inside—somewhat resembling Dolly Parton, but less mysterious and more transparent. Part of her appeal has always been the little girl with the husky-throated voice who manhandled all those stage instruments with such plucky virtuosity. Audiences shook their heads in amazement and never failed to comment on how "sweet" she was. Whether in gingham or sequins, she symbolized clean old-fashioned fun, country style. She was a hard worker, not afraid of sweat, and she enthusiastically espoused the good-golly-oh-gosh drivel so treasured by the Bible-Belt constituency. Along with her sisters, Louise and Irlene, Barbara was country music's version of the Osmond Brothers. She even named her band "The Do-Rights," and fans always depended on their Barbara to do exactly that. For her unabashed *lovability,* Barbara was awarded with two consecutive Entertainer of the Year awards by the Country Music Association (in 1980 and 1981—the first artist to be awarded that distinction twice) as well as a Hendersonville mansion, a forty-five-foot yacht, two Rolls-Royces, and, of course, that 1982 silver Jaguar.

Barbara was eastbound on U.S. Highway 31E. Mark White was

The sequined sisters of prime-time television, the Mandrells.

Plucky Barbara: Hair-do with a hard-e

Barbara Mandrell, smiling for her supper.

Barbara Mandrell: Queen of the Do-Rights.

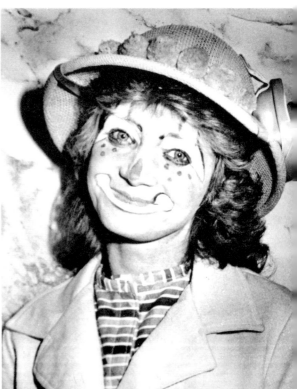

"You could tell there was a real impact. Her windshield was shattered and the hood was bashed in and pressed all the way up to the roof. It looked as though the driver must have really gotten hurt."
—A witness to the Mandrell accident

westbound on the same highway. At about 6:30 P.M., in front of the Victory Baptist Church between Tyne Bay Drive and the Johnny Cash Parkway, and for reasons never determined, Mark White's Subaru crossed the centerline. The eastbound car directly in front of Barbara spotted the oncoming Subaru and alertly swerved to the right to avoid a collision. Unfortunately for Barbara and her children, it was too late for her to execute a similar maneuver. All she saw was a big hulk of moving red metal staring her in the face.

It wasn't a pretty sight. Metal crushed metal with complete disregard for the human flesh trapped inside. When the police arrived at the scene, radio knobs and other pieces of the Jaguar's dashboard were imbedded in Barbara's chest. Matthew was lying injured in the nearby grass. Jamie was sitting stunned on the side of the roadway. Barbara was still breathing.

When two worlds collide: What remains of Barbara Mandrell's Jaguar is on the left; Mark White's Subaru is on the right.

It was obvious that the driver of the other car was dead. There was no question in anybody's mind about that.
—A witness

Mark White had been pinned under the Subaru. There was a two-inch laceration on his right eyebrow, excessive bleeding from both of his ears, reddish-white foam coming out of his nose, a five-inch laceration across the bottom of his chin, and severe lacerations on his neck, chest, right wrist, and forearm. There was an abrasion on the inside of his right leg near his groin, a severe laceration below his left kneecap, and a deformity of the left foot near his toes. He was *not* breathing. Hydraulic metal cutters were required to rip his body out of the wreckage.

178

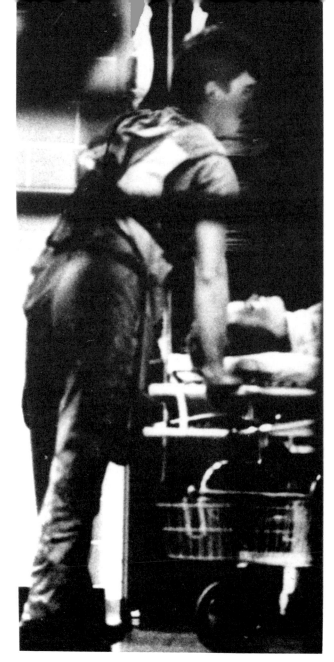

Barbara Mandrell is wheeled into surgery at Baptist Hospital in Nashville.

He was pronounced dead on arrival at Hendersonville Hospital. His crossbow was retrieved from the backseat of what was left of his Subaru, as was a blue-colored pamphlet that had been found on the front seat. It was titled "About Facing Death as a Christian."

> She wasn't even coherent when she arrived. She couldn't even recognize her father. She looked like she had been in a real bad car wreck. She had blood on her clothes, but you couldn't see any bone sticking out.
> —A witness

Barbara was rushed to Baptist Hospital in Nashville, where she spent the next nineteen days. She had a severe concussion, a broken right leg, a badly injured knee, and a shattered bone in her right ankle. In a three-hour operation, surgeons removed glass from her right knee before setting a broken thigh bone. A foot-long steel rod stretching from her hip to her knee was inserted into her right leg.

Over the next several weeks, Barbara lost her memory and drifted in and out of consciousness. Meanwhile, Ronald Reagan and Jimmy Carter telephoned her hospital room and home. She was sent 450 floral arrangements and received more mail than any other individual person in Nashville history. Before the tragedy, Barbara Mandrell had been widely admired. After it, she became one of the most beloved entertainers in the entire country. For a while.

Investigators of the accident were perplexed. There appeared to be no cause for the tragedy that injured Barbara Mandrell and killed a nineteen-year-old boy. Alcohol, drugs, and speeding had all been ruled out. And Mark White, up until the second of impact, had no blemishes on his driving record.

But it was not Mark White or his family who got the overwhelming sympathy of the public and press. It was Barbara Mandrell. On January 3, 1985, Barbara called a press conference at Nashville's Opryland Hotel. In her first public appearance since the accident, she hobbled into the room on crutches, cried, and told the roomful of reporters, "I thank God I'm alive" and, "It's very painful. The only thing I can compare it to is having my babies" and, "I've cried a lot. I'm still pretty emotional." She also explained that the reason she decided to call the press conference was "because I've been treated so wonderfully in my twenty-five years in show business." And then she proceeded to promote her CBS television special that was set to air later that week. Said Barbara, "This one is not just saying it's special; it *is* a special. This is a super show. I'm proud of it."

A month later, Barbara and her husband, Ken Dudney, announced that she was pregnant. In May 1985, she returned to the studio to record her album *Get to the Heart*. It was released that August. In September, Barbara gave birth to their third child, Nathaniel Mandrell Dudney.

But the Barbara-bashing backlash was already in motion, and nothing, not even motherhood, could dull its jagged edge. It was an old story. In Barbara Mandrell, America had created another idol. Then, when it became painfully apparent that the idol was only human after all, former followers stood in line to watch the public execution.

"It's a miracle I still have my legs."
—Barbara Mandrell

It began on September 4, 1985, when it was publicly announced that Barbara had filed a lawsuit against Mark White, the teenager who didn't live to become a college sophomore, and his family. The suit claimed "negligence" and sought $8 million in projected earnings that Barbara allegedly lost while recuperating from the accident, an additional $2 million for her pain and suffering, $200,000 for her son, who was injured in the accident, $100,000 for her daughter, and $25,000 for Ken Dudney, "for the loss of the services [which were not specified], companionship, consortium and society of his wife."

It was not a great public relations move.

Even though most of the settlement, if any, would be paid by the Whites' insurance company, not by the White family, it was interpreted by the public as being an action against the bereaved White family. The Whites publicly confessed to being "scared to death" of the Mandrell suit because, technically, they could have been held liable for the damages.

The lawsuit reportedly provoked a rash of hate mail with Barbara Mandrell's address boldly printed with poison pens, a succession of obscene phone calls, and a flurry of snickering Barbara Mandrell jokes like, "Oh, her Rolls-Royce was hurt? Too bad. She'll just have to use one of the other cars, or the helicopter, or the yacht. . . ." One Nashville newspaper reported, "Armies of fans are deserting her now, despite their one-time faithfulness and undying love and devotion." Another reporter asked, "What's Nashville's most popular new sport? Barbara Bashing. It's so easy to play. All you have to do is say something nasty about Barbara Mandrell."

Brave little soldier that she has always been, Barbara announced that she was going back out on tour. She told reporters, "I knew how much the fans loved me, but I never realized how much I loved the fans. I miss them so much." And she explained to a writer for *McCalls*, "You know why I did this tour? For my fans. They're the *neatest* people." It seemed to some that Barbara Mandrell wasn't so much going out on tour as she was trying to make amends with the fickle fans who had deserted her.

She also taped public service announcements for radio and television, urging people to fasten their seat belts. She hosted the opening ceremonies of the Seventh International Summer Special Olympics to benefit the nation's handicapped. She invited *Ladies Home Journal* into her home to photograph her baby, Nathaniel's, nursery. She starred in a television movie entitled, ironically, *A Question of Guilt,* and she was the subject of a lachrymose "This Is Your Life" television tribute, complete with the requisite tears, targeted directly at the easily tugged American heartstrings.

Despite the bold public face, however, there are indications that the tragic crash, the multimillion-dollar lawsuit, and the vicious public backlash have stripped some of the once infectious verve out of Barbara Mandrell. For months after the accident, she kept her demolished Jaguar in storage, like some token reminder of death. After she got out of the hospital and was able to walk, she took her children, Matt and Jamie, to where the car was stored and told them, "Let's stare at this and let's memorize it so every night we can thank Jesus we're alive, because we don't have the right to be." Barbara's sister Louise was quoted as saying, "I love my sister as much today as I did before the accident, but it's like loving another sister. I prefer the old Barbara. It's all so different now. She's still bossy like she used to be, but she's so serious and withdrawn. She's not the happy sister I used to know." Barbara herself acknowledged, "I used to be one person, now I'm another."

In January 1986, Barbara filed suit against MCA, her record label, for $1.2 million, seeking to terminate her contract. She has since signed with Capitol Records, but her career has not yet recovered from the Barbara-bashing backlash. In 1984, she had *four* Top 5 country singles and two Top 10 albums. Since she filed her lawsuit against the White family, however, she has not had a single top five record and her albums have not even made the Top 20, much less the Top 10.

It has been a painful fall from grace for the former country music princess of prime time. Her lawsuit against the Mark White family has not yet been settled, and, for many, it seems that Barbara Mandrell's previously delectable sweetness has taken on a decidedly acerbic aftertaste.

9
HONKY TONK LAMENT

It was at the Exit/In nightclub in Nashville. Late 1979. The audience was jammed with illustrious members of the country music fraternity who had gone on that night to witness the comeback of a legend they called "The Last Country Singer." The lights dimmed. And even then it was too bright for George Jones, who stepped out onto the desolate stage. He squinted his eyes, glazed with ambiguity, and searched for a friendly face in the audience. But all he could see with his distorted vision was a roomful of well-dressed judges, each armed with a contemptuous grin and a wooden gavel. He wasn't on stage. He was on trial. A trial by his peers. His mind swirled, like a warm glass of whiskey on a hot August night. He closed his eyes, squeezed tight, and then reopened them.

If ever there was a walking, talking *nightmare*, George Jones was it. On that night at the Exit/In, the dream was particularly horrifying, as it wrapped itself around his neck and choked his pallid flesh with vindictive glee. He was one breath away from death, and he looked it. When he opened his mouth to sing, nothing came out. George thought he was losing his mind. He clasped his head in his hands and tried to keep everything— blood, brains, and booze—from spilling out right there on the stage. He held on tight. He then raised his head and said to his audience, "My friend Donald Duck is going to take over this show because Donald Duck can do what George Jones can't." He then proceeded to sing the songs of George Jones in the dialect of Donald Duck. The audience was amused at first. And then it became painfully apparent that it wasn't a joke. George Jones, *the* George Jones, the greatest singer in the history of the music, had collapsed before their very eyes, his voice taken over by a demon in the guise of a duck.

He was carried off the stage, reportedly in a straitjacket.

183

Nashville was not particularly shaken. After all, for several years George Jones had been a tragedy waiting to happen. As writer Bob Allen brilliantly analogized in the *Tennesean,* "It's like watching a badly battered prizefighter with blood in his eyes stagger around the ring, trying to keep his feet." What *was* surprising was that it wasn't the bottle—which he publicly grieved over in songs like "If Drinking Don't Kill Me, Her Memory Will" and "Still Doin' Time in a Honky Tonk Prison"—that was George's primary nemesis. It was cocaine.

> It wasn't drinking that bothered him so much, like most people think. It was powder. White powder. And his friends, or those who was supposed to be his friends, were the ones giving it to him, even though they could see it was killing him.
> —Pee Wee Johnson, a Jones friend

George Jones reportedly became addicted to cocaine in 1977. Those in Nashville who knew closed their eyes as George squandered away his talent—a national treasure—his life, and his money. That year, he was sued for $75,000 by a Nashville couple who claimed that he had signed papers to purchase their house. In December, he was sued for another $20,000 by an Iowa corporation which had given him an earlier loan. By 1978, The Possum Holler, the nightclub he had opened the day after his divorce from Tammy, began to fail. In August, he was court-ordered to pay two women $11,800 in damages. The women, Joyce Jones (no relation) and Sonja Northern, claimed that George had physically assaulted them. The incident had taken place in November 1976 at the apartment of Billy Willheit, a Jones business associate. Mrs. Jones contended that George "physically and forcibly embraced" her, forced her to drink vodka, and then, when she objected, poured vodka all over her clothing. The suit further charged that "the defendant, without cause, began to shout obscenities and expletives" at Mrs. Jones and then "viciously, intentionally and maliciously struck [her] in the face with his hand, whereupon [she] raced out of said apartment into the presence of her children." Then, when Mrs. Northern got up to follow, Jones "picked up a briefcase and threw it at her, striking her in the back of the head, causing her severe pain and bodily injury." George Jones, known in Nashville as "The Possum," and "No Show Jones," characteristically did not show up in court. However, Billy Willheit spoke up in his defense and claimed that the argument ensued when the two women declared that they "didn't particularly care for country music."

On September 1, 1978, a Nashville judge called for George Jones's arrest after he failed to pay ex-wife Tammy Wynette $36,000 in back child support. Jones's manager at the time, Shug Baggott, decried, "At this point, George Jones doesn't have any assets to speak of except his voice. But we have made a lot of arrangements and done some major restructuring of his career, and I can guarantee you that Tammy will be paid in full by the end of next week." George himself commented bitterly, "[Tammy] knew I was getting a $60,000 check from CBS Records the same day she filed. I can only guess they wanted some press for Tammy or some bad press for me." Also in September, George was ordered to pay $13,554.35 to a Nashville furniture store for goods that he had purchased several years earlier.

> I think your mind gets messed up, you get too much hate in there, and you gotta get it out.
> —George Jones

On September 17, 1978, George was arrested in Florence, Alabama, for attempting to murder his best friend, songwriter Earl "Peanut" Montgomery. The incident occurred several nights before on the riverbank of Cypress Creek. It was about 1:00 A.M. Montgomery pulled his Trans Am up alongside George's vehicle, window to window. It was a hot southern night, and the air was thick with whiskey, religious fervor, and hostility. Montgomery, who had reportedly quit drinking in favor of God, stuck his head out the car window to make a particular point to his friend and was greeted by the barrel of a .38 Smith & Wesson. George, sweating with pangs of betrayal, gripped the gun in his clammy hand and slurred, "See if your God can save you now!" And then he pulled the trigger. Somehow the bullet missed and lodged into the car door's frame, just an inch below the base of Montgomery's neck. It wasn't the first time that George had brandished a gun in the face of a loved one. Nashville is full of stories of George and his gun. One particularly colorful incident involved Tammy Wynette. Reportedly, George had arrived home one night and passed out in a drunken stupor. Then, as Tammy attempted to unzip his trousers, George shot out of bed, whipped out a loaded pistol, and fired at her.

On October 4, 1978, as she returned to her car parked in the Green Hills Mall parking lot, Tammy Wynette was reportedly abducted and beaten by a man wearing a stocking over his face (see Chapter 4). That day, George Jones failed to show up in court and was ordered to pay a concert promoter nearly $30,000 for missing a performance in Virginia. Speculation stormed through Nashville that George had somehow been involved in Tammy's kidnapping. They had not been on good terms since Tammy had married George Richey just a few months before. Reportedly, Richey, husband number five, had told Jones, husband number three, "We don't want you callin' here no more, and we don't want you around here no more." Nevertheless, the case has never been solved and George Jones was not arrested in connection with it.

In December, George filed for bankruptcy, listing $1.5 million in debts. He remorsefully claimed, "I gave up everything I had to two ex-wives—the last two I was married to."

On December 26, 1978, George was arrested and jailed in Alabama on charges of assault and battery. His fiancée, Linda Welborn, contended that George had hit her in the face with his hand, shoved her across the table, and threatened other action against her. George told reporters, "I am sorry for what happened. But I took her and her three-year-old son in when they had nothing, gave her a home, a car, fine clothes, and jewelry. Being a fool, I left her with the furniture, the car, and some money to start over again." A month later, like Peanut Montgomery before her, Welborn dropped the charges and reconciled with Jones. Years later, Welborn filed a bizarre lawsuit for divorce against Jones, despite the fact that they had never been married.

> I've always listened to other people, and I've been took by a lot of people. I've been took by just about everybody I've been associated with in my twenty-one years of professional music business. But I can assure you I'm associated with some very fine people right now, and there's no way I can be took.
> —George Jones, 1975

> He was all right until he got with that son of a bitch, Shug Baggott.
> —Shorty Lavender, a Jones friend

Country music fans *wanted* to believe that the decline of George Jones was directly attributable to the dissolution of his marriage to Tammy Wynette. Others closer to the situation, however, seemed to believe that George's downfall was the result of another relationship. In 1975, Shug Baggott Jr. became George Jones's manager. George signed full power of attorney over to Baggott. Between 1977 and 1978, a period in which Baggott managed George's business affairs, George earned a reported $2 million dollars in revenue. However, he could only account for $30,000 of it. And he was broke. He couldn't even pay the $500 rent he owed on his Nashville apartment, which caused his landlord to take out a warrant for his arrest. Nashville whispered that George Jones had been cramming those hefty royalty checks up his possum nose. This theory was given added credence in August 1979, when Shug Baggott Jr. was indicted by a federal grand jury. The indictment read, in part, "Alcy Benjamin Baggott, Jr. would and did organize, supervise, manage and conduct a cocaine distribution network for the purpose of distributing and transporting cocaine." Shug pleaded guilty to two counts of possession of cocaine with intent to distribute and later served a federal prison term. George later charged, "Shug got me started on it [cocaine] to keep me messed up. Just the way he got me drunk all the time . . . he's a crook. He robbed me blind."

By the end of the decade, after the Baggott arrest, George Jones was on the verge of death. One Music Row executive sadly surmised, "He's not eating. He only takes the cocaine. Some of us think this is George's last go-round." And a Nashville record producer told reporter Susan Thomas, "I remember one time we were sitting around the studio late one night after a show and George came in stoned out of his mind. I'll never forget it because George had this plastic bag full of cocaine with a soda straw sticking out of it. Every few minutes, he would take snort."

In December 1979, following his infamous onstage Donald Duck impersonation, George was committed to the psychiatric ward of Hillcrest Hospital in Birmingham, Alabama. The $10,000 treatment was paid for by ten of George's friends in the music industry, including Johnny Cash and Waylon Jennings, each of whom donated $1,000.

When George emerged from treatment in January 1980, he told reporters, "I don't drink anymore. I know I've said that before. But I guess I finally woke up." However, within a short time, it was obvious to those in the music business that George was back on the bottle and back on coke.

Nevertheless, at age forty-nine, he found his career suddenly exploding out of the respectably durable category, which it had been banished to, and into the superstar territory, where one's worth is appraised by record company executives with meat-market relish. Early in 1980, George reunited with Tammy Wynette (whose own career had faltered dramatically since their professional split, and has yet to recover) and recorded "Two Story House," which went to number two on the charts. Then George had the biggest hit of his career. It was called "He Stopped Loving Her Today."

Nevertheless, within the next few years, he was broke once again.

One of the major reasons for Jones's extreme financial depression was that he continued to miss scheduled performances, seemingly more often than he made them. In December 1980, the Exit/In, scene of George's mental breakdown a year before, sponsored "The Nashville Loves George Jones Night." It sold out. The entire city wanted to backslap George for the sudden acceleration of his career. At the last minute, however, George canceled. In June 1981, an Ohio promoter filed a $10.2 million suit against him for missing a performance. In October, he failed to show up for a special engagement on the Grand Ole Opry. In early 1982, he failed to appear at a Jackson, Tennessee, concert with Johnny Paycheck and Donna Fargo, and police had to subdue spectators who rushed the box office when they learned that George would not be performing. In April, he missed another engagement on the Opry. In May, he didn't show up for a performance in his own hometown of Florence, Alabama. During August, he missed sold-out concerts in Tullahoma, Tennessee, and Odessa, Texas. After one concert that he *did* make, a country sheriff confiscated his wristwatch and diamond rings—right off his hand and fingers—to fulfill a $25,000 judgment that had been brought against him in Virginia in 1982. Before a scheduled concert in Denver, George's manager at the time had to post a $2,000 bond, insuring that the increasingly-difficult-to-book Jones would perform as scheduled. He missed the show, lost the $2,000, and, was dealt yet another "no show" lawsuit. In May 1983, George was sued again, this time by the owner of the Armadillo Palace in Athens, Georgia. The owner, Marion Cartwright, charged that George walked off the stage in the middle of his act, as soon as his agent received George's $10,000 performance fee. Cartwright told reporters, "George was doing a good show. I don't understand. He just took his guitar and took off, almost running. We thought at first he was doing an encore. But then he went out the side door and took off in a van." Reportedly, the enraged Cartwright then chased after George's van—armed with a hunting rifle. At another concert, in Fredericksburg, Texas, a group of irate fans who presumably felt that they had not gotten their money's worth grabbed George's microphone, forced George and his band to the back of the stage, and proceeded to auction off the band's instruments.

I have $237, they tell me, in my bank account. For a Male Vocalist of the Year, a man who's won the awards I'm supposed to have won, and achieved what I was supposed to achieve, I have nothing in my name. I have nothing but this pair of blue jeans and this shirt and one of my suits that I had in the cleaners. They [his management company] won't let me have my car, they won't let me have my clothes, they won't let me have my furniture. They won't let me have anything. I went to Texas last week and tried to work one or two of the dates and they lied again, and stuck the money in their pockets and wouldn't give me one cent.
—George Jones to a reporter

George shuffled and reshuffled his managers, making a lame attempt at solvency, but it was obvious to all that money was not the worst of his problems. He was deteriorating physically. His weight dropped from 145 to 98 pounds. His gums bled from malnutrition. As Jones later reflected, "I just didn't care anymore. It was real scary. I'd been about five years in virtually another world. It's hard to explain how I felt. Imagine yourself going to bed at night and staying in the darkness for five years."

In July 1981, George was hospitalized in Beaumont, Texas, for what was termed "exhaustion." Later that year, headlines screamed, GEORGE JONES SERIOUSLY ILL! George's interim manager at the time, Wayne Oliver, did not disclose the nature of George's illness. But by then everybody knew.

On March 29, 1982, Nancy Sepulveda, George's girlfriend, was stopped by a patrol car in Jackson, Mississippi, for speeding. As he was writing out a ticket, the patrolman noticed white powder on the floormats beside George's feet. He called the Bureau of Narcotics. A narcotics-sniffing dog was brought in, and it reacted positively to the powder. The Jackson Police subsequently identified the substance as cocaine. George was arrested and released on bail. *The following day*, George was driving down a north Mississippi road when his 1981 Lincoln slid down a 300-foot stretch of gravel roadway, flipped over several times, and landed in a ditch. His car was totaled, he suffered minor facial lacerations, and he was arrested again—this time for drunken driving.

A few days later, George's family had him committed to Hillcrest Hospital in Alabama. Two weeks after he was released, however, he was back on drugs. On May 25, 1982, he was arrested again, this time in Nashville. He had been weaving down Interstate 65 in his silver Cadillac, with a cardboard facsimile of a license plate that read "Possum #3" showcased in his rear

George Jones motions in a Nashville court with one hand, and cups his balls with the other. He pled guilty to 1982 drunk driving charges and was given a thirty-day suspended sentence and had his license suspended for six months.

window. According to Officer Tom Campsey, George's speech was slurred, his eyes were bloodshot, he reeked of alcohol, and there was a half-empty fifth of Jack Daniels lying on the front seat. After he unsuccessfully attempted to touch his nose with his finger, George wailed to Officer Campsey, "I'm drunk. Take me to jail!" Campsey obliged, but not before George attacked David Goins, a local television cameraman who had witnessed George's arrest. For the drunk-driving charge, George received a thirty-day suspended sentence and was ordered to pay $737.50 in fines and court costs. George paid by check.

A week later, the check bounced. George's bank account, at the First National Bank in Mussel Shoals, Alabama, had been closed *after* the check was written. George's friend, Pee Wee Johnson, came to his aid and paid off the fine. Around this time, George was slapped with another lawsuit, by the Commerce Union Bank, which claimed that he owed nearly $100,000 for nonpayment of old loans. Meanwhile, regarding George's Mississippi canine cocaine bust, Judge Breland Hilburn waived a prison sentence and/or a $30,000 fine in lieu of a free George Jones concert.

Naturally, George and his attorney readily agreed to the legal bribe. Later that year, the case was dismissed.

But the chemical abuse continued. George showed up an hour late at a concert in San Antonio. When he did arrive, he staggered onto the stage and told his audience, "I'm drunk, but I love y'all." Five hundred people walked out. The rest stayed to boo. George's boozing and other addictions had gotten so notorious, so *accepted* in the Nashville music community, that the major industry publication *Country Music* magazine openly suggested that George should do a series of endorsements for a major whiskey company. The proposed ads, according to the publication, would feature George—in front of the battered Cadillac which had been overturned in a Mississippi ditch—with a bottle of "80-proof painkiller" in his hand. The accompanying caption would have read, "I Never Leave Home Without It."

> I think the world of George. When he's straight, there's not a more kind-hearted person in the world. There's just a little problem with . . . with his problems.
> —Gerald Murray, George's fourth manager in less than a year

George's "problems"—no matter how often they were condemned to the furthest regions of his mind—resurfaced with decisive resiliency, seemingly hell-bent on killing him. Once, according to *Country Music* magazine, in a paranoid, self-destructive drama of pathetic proportions, George picked up a pillow, drew a face on it, set it upon the couch, and blew it away with his pistol. He then telephoned his friends and excitedly informed them, "The king is dead! The king is dead!"

> I was about as crazy and messed up as you can get. I was doing all kinds of drugs—marijuana, cocaine, booze, you name it, and I was doing it.
> —George Jones

His drinking intensified. Said one friend, "Even when he vomited, he wouldn't turn loose of that bottle. He'd hold on to it. And, unless you got it away from him and hid it, he'd get up and wipe his mouth off, and keep right on drinking." And to an interviewer Jones confided, "They were going to get me." When pressed as to who "they" were, Jones mentioned his former manager Shug Baggott Jr. and his other drug suppliers.

Then, in 1982, he met Nancy Sepulveda, a divorced factory worker and avowed George Jones fan from Shreveport, Louisiana. Reportedly during the first year of their relationship, while George was heavily involved with drugs, he would routinely beat Nancy, kick her off his tour bus, and then leave her alone in strange towns with no money. Once, while in one of his common states of drug-induced paranoid delusions, George disappeared and had one of his attorneys send Nancy a letter instructing her to vacate his house—and his life. Nancy was devastated. A friend of hers was quoted as saying, "She just cried and cried and cried. I've never seen anybody so upset. She just kept sayin', 'I don't wanta live without that man! I just wanta cook buck-eye peas and cornbread for him. That's all I wanta do. I don't care if we have to live in an old shack!' "

George and Nancy were married on March 4, 1983. He reentered an alcohol and drug rehabilitation program, and for several years he seemed to find a quiet corner of comfort in his new domesticity. In 1986, he announced, "In the last four years I've been straight. I see the light of life and I enjoy it a lot more." He put on weight and, surprisingly, managed to fulfill most of his scheduled performances. Perhaps after all those years of chemical warfare, all he really needed was the love of a good woman. Nashville marveled at the country simplicity of it all.

In August 1987, George's close friend, Pee Wee Johnson, was

George Jones, the man with the life-scarred face, was never one to wisely invest his money. Nashville legend has it that he once flushed thousands of dollars down the toilet in a drunken and/or drug-induced rage.

arrested in Jacksonville, North Carolina, and charged with misdemeanor death. The bus that he was driving, and in which George and Nancy had been passengers, struck a motorcycle and killed its driver. Later that month, George himself was hospitalized at University Hospital in Birmingham for "exhaustion," a kidney infection, bronchitis, and prostate problems. Against doctors' orders, George checked out of the hospital prematurely. With Nancy at his side, he had driven as far as Monroe, Louisiana, when he suddenly keeled over in pain. He was dying. Finally, after so many practice attempts and dress rehearsals, he was ready to crawl into that casket—built so many years before—descend into that hole, and let Nashville cry its false tears and sing his praises.

But he didn't die. Again. He had just fallen off the proverbial wagon. Again. Nancy chartered a jet from a gas station and had him transported back to the hospital, where he made more promises to start a new life without drugs or alcohol. Again.

George Jones has squandered so much of his life and shed so much of his blood over the vast southern countryside that it is amazing he has the resources to persevere. Never before has someone so short cast so long and troubled a shadow. But then he *is* the cat on a hot tin roof, scratching his way through what may or may not be his final incarnation. Nashville watches and waits with bated breath as the battered boxer staggers around the ring, fiercely determined to go a few more rounds. Not because he enjoys the taste of his own blood but, rather, because he still thinks he can win the fight.

10
CON ARTISTS

The biggest thing about prison, man, is the tension. You never know from one minute to the next when some motherfucker is gonna lose his mind and try to fuck you or start stabbin' people for no reason at all.
—David Allan Coe, *Esquire*, 1976

The stench of urine. The indignity of open toilets. The violation and degradation of homosexual rape. The piercing explosions of violence that cut across the steel-encased night. The suicides. The murders.

To the country music publicity mill, there is something vaguely glamorous about prison—and the men who have, at one point in their lives, toyed with the law and spent captive time trapped behind closed bars. However, no one has yet to identify exactly what that *something* is. Perhaps, to some twisted psyches, prison life somehow makes a man *more* of a man, and therefore more appealing. Or perhaps it is the dueling contradiction of a poetic soul trapped in the cumbersome body of a 7-Eleven armed robber. Or maybe it is just that country music fans like their stars to have suffered.

Whatever the reason, for the past three decades Nashville has churned out publicity releases that have propagated the idea of the ex-con as hero: the more time served, the better the publicity. Even if a star spent only a week, or a day, or an *hour* in jail, the news was bound to find its way into a country music fan magazine. When it was learned that shortly before his death, a drunken Hank Williams had spent a brief, sobering stretch behind iron, it only added to his legend. Many others have been lured by the jailbait ole Hank left behind. George Jones once spent five days in the can for being behind on child support payments to his first wife. On the liner notes for his album

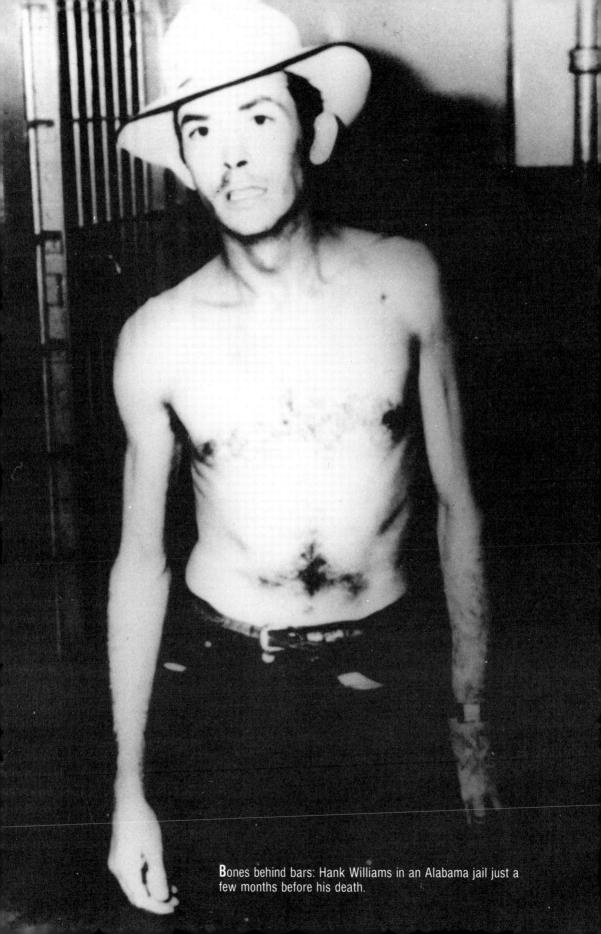

Bones behind bars: Hank Williams in an Alabama jail just a few months before his death.

Johnny Cash at Folsom Prison, Cash related, "I have been behind bars a few times—sometimes of my own volition, sometimes involuntarily. Each time, I felt the same feeling of kinship with my fellow prisoners." Cash received so much publicity from statements like this and from his Folsom and San Quentin albums that it belied the fact that he has spent only a day or two in jail. One can't help but ponder just how much "kinship" he cultivated in such a short visit. In 1971, Jerry Lee Lewis, spent a night in a Fort Worth jail for having missed a performance in Dallas in *1959.* Drawled Jerry Lee, "Ah was jes checkin' the place out. They did the whole shot on me—had me get outta ma clothes, inspected me, had me bend ovah, kick my legs up, gave me some overalls, locked me in the slammer, and then asked me for ma autograph." Kris Kristofferson spent a night in a Los Angeles jail for shooting up some chemical or another. And even Randy Travis, country music's genteel favorite son and maverick of modesty, has had run-ins with the law on his record. Said Travis, "I'd been on probation several times—probably six or seven years, actually."

But it was Merle Haggard who was the first to take his prison record straight to the country music bank.

All Merle wanted to do was emulate the life of Jimmie Rodgers. Merle lived in Bakersfield doing battle with boredom until his mid-teens, and then drifted across the vast wastelands of the Southwest, where he worked on farms, drove potato trucks, hopped freight trains, hitchhiked, and hoboed. His fiddle-playing father had died of a brain tumor when Merle was nine. His mother, good woman and Church of Christ member that she was, was not equipped to corral her young son with the wild, wayward *longing* in his eyes.

While in search of that lonesome whistle blow heard intermittently in the distance, Merle got himself entangled on the wrong side of the sharply divided social tracks. With casual, strictly-for-kicks crimes like petty theft and fraud on his juvenile report card, he was banished to play out his adolescence in the Fred C. Nelles School for Boys in Whittier, California, and later in the Preston School of Industry near Stockton.

He was introduced to adulthood at the Ventura County Jail, where he spent nine months in captivity for taking a stolen car out for a joyride through a vanishing youth. He was eighteen years old. Then, on Christmas Eve 1957, at the age of twenty, Merle was arrested for the attempted burglary of a Bakersfield

"Being behind bars was almost beginning to be a way of life. I didn't like it, but I didn't like life on the outside either."
—Merle Haggard

bar. He was sentenced to six months to fifteen years in San Quentin—*San Quentin.* The name alone carries an aura of power and is spoken in tones of hushed reverence. Merle only ended up serving two years and nine months of actual time, but for a twenty-three-year-old with journeying on his mind, it was a lifetime.

He could no longer travel the countryside and get lost in the landscape. His body was bound in a box. But even his jailers could not hold captive his mind—which he set free to drift inward. If anyone ever grew *up* in prison, it was Haggard.

Upon his release in mid-1960, Merle returned to the only home base he knew, Bakersfield. He got a job digging ditches, driving a truck, and laying wire, for which he was paid $80 a week. He was too old for delinquency and, with a wife and two kids (and more on the way), too grounded for vagrancy. Besides, during his term at San Quentin, he had met Johnny Cash and had had the opportunity to see him perform. With a song, Cash was able to transport his audience to a place where men were more than numbers. Merle was impressed. By the time he was allocated his thin slice of freedom, Bakersfield's own Buck Owens had become one of the top stars in country music, and Bakersfield itself was gaining distinction as "Nashville West." Sufficiently inspired, Merle got himself a night job playing guitar and singing songs at a local bar.

Unlike others who have swapped their convict numbers for a place on the country charts, Merle Haggard has always been discreet about his tenure in captivity. He is also undeniably one of the most brilliantly gifted singer/songwriters ever to emerge from country music, and, if justice had been served, he would have become a star even without the dubious, yet curiously attractive, ex-con status. Nevertheless, there is little doubt that his early career in music was propelled by his prison background. His first number one hit was "I'm a Lonesome Fugitive" in 1966. He followed that with other autobiographical prison tales of pathos and woe like "Branded Man" and "Mama Tried."

Merle Haggard has since diversified his work, stayed atop the country charts for nearly twenty-five years, and scored more Top 10 singles than any other artist in the history of the genre. He has traveled the great breadth of his country and in his music, the equally profound expanse of his heart and mind. He is today a man without chains.

The ex-con and the outlaw. "Okie From Muskogee" established Merle Haggard as a redneck with clout. President Nixon wrote him a letter of congratulations. George Wallace asked him for a political endorsement. And Ronald Reagan, then the governor of California, gave him a full pardon.

"You know, the biggest hooker in the world is a housewife. The only difference between a hooker and a housewife is the hooker does *it* with a lot of people. A wife only hooks for you, but she takes more money than a hooker would."
—Freddy Fender, espousing his brand of ex-con wisdom

It was Friday the 13th in May 1960. Baldemar Huerta, alias Freddy Fender, was singing onstage in a honky tonk in Baton Rouge when he was arrested by local vice cops for possession of marijuana. America had survived the panty-staining onslaught of rock and roll and was yet to experience its first collective acid trip, and marijuana was still regarded as a communist plot or a felonious crime against decency. For the next three years, Freddy Fender was banished to Louisiana State Penitentiary at Angola. As he later recalled, "Prison for me was like a burial cemetery." And as he concisely described to writer Bob Allen, "[Solitary] was a bare concrete floor with a pipe running down through a hole, and the edge of the hole was where you shit." He further related that human life in prison was so tenuous that the inmates often slept with Sears & Roebuck catalogs strapped to their chests to guard against stabbings. During his stay at Angola, Fender received a knife scar on the side of his neck as a permanent remembrance.

Jerry Jeff Walker.

Fender was released from prison in 1963 and pardoned by then Louisiana state governor, Jimmie Davis (a former country music personality who had written "You Are My Sunshine"), but it was not until 1975 that he hit the national charts with "Before the Next Teardrop Falls." He followed that with an updated version of "Wasted Days and Wasted Nights" (which had been a minor regional hit for him in 1960) and was touted as the King of Tex-Mex country rock.

However, by 1981, Fender's career was in eclipse, leaving him in financial recession. He was estranged from his producer, estranged from his wife of twenty-three years, and hounded by the Internal Revenue Service.

Not only did Huey P. Meaux, Freddy Fenders's longtime producer, nibble at the jailbait, he also allegedly escorted it to Nashville. In 1968, Meaux was arrested and jailed for transporting an underage nymphet to a disc jockey convention in Nashville. Meaux, "The Crazy Cajun," allegedly hired the teenage prostitute to serve as a promotion at the convention. He received a fourteen-month sentence for his efforts.

Jerry Jeff Walker, the singer/songwriter who once greeted a writer for *Playboy* with, "Hey, you pussy, you don't know enough about country music to write it on my balls," reportedly wrote, or was inspired to write, "Mr. Bojangles" while spending a night in a New Orleans jail in 1966. He had been charged with unnecessarily rowdy conduct.

Paul English, Willie Nelson's longtime drummer and close friend, served nearly a year at the Ellis County prison in Texas. Quipped English, "I committed some burglaries in my time, but not the one they got me for."

Singer/songwriter Glen Sherley did ten years time at the Vacaville Institution in California for armed robbery. During that time, Sherley partnered with a fellow inmate and wrote a few songs. His name was Spade Cooley. As fate would have it, Sherley was present at Folsom Prison in early 1968 when Johnny Cash gave a performance there. At the concert, Cash sang a song called "Greystone Chapel," which had been written by inmate Sherley. When Sherley was released from prison in 1971— largely through the efforts of Cash (with an assist by Cash's friend, the Reverend Billy Graham, who reportedly telephoned then–California governor Ronald Reagan)—he was invited to join the Johnny Cash performance troupe. John and June Carter Cash greeted Sherley at Nashville's Metro Airport. At that time, Cash forecasted stardom for his bedazzled protégé. Seven years later, Sherley, forty-two, was shot to death on the porch of his California home. Said police, "It looks like suicide." For Glen Sherley, it would seem, freedom was just another word for something left to lose—his life.

After Glen Sherley's release from prison, a Nashville-based group, spearheaded by David Allan Coe and Paul Richey, formed a songwriting publishing company called Alias, Inc. It was designed to help prison inmates get their songs recorded in Nashville. The deal was that if his song was recorded, an inmate would be paid $50 and additional royalties, depending on sales. The deal also entailed the possibility that inmates would be briefly released from confinement so that they could go to Nashville to "demo" their songs on record. There were additional plans for country music luminaries to conduct songwriting seminars behind prison walls. Said one prison official, "We think we have some boys out there who have talent, but there has been no way for them to get notice." A short time later, the entire proposal was shelved, leaving a lot of prison inmates—who had been furiously scribbling down their song ideas—disgruntled.

Johnny Rodriguez, the Tex-Mex heartthrob who catapulted onto the country music charts in 1972, had been imprisoned four times before he reached the age of eighteen. His most serious offense, however, had been stealing a trio of goats, slashing their throats, and hosting a barbecue. Rodriguez was imprisoned in a local jail near Bracketville, Texas, in 1969. He later beat the rap, reportedly by singing and playing guitar for the arresting officer, Joaquin Jackson, who subsequently became the conduit for Rodriguez's entry into the music business.

Lee Stoller, who produced *One Day at a Time*, an album that is promoted as the biggest-selling gospel album of all time, for his wife, country-gospel singer Christy Lane, was jailed in 1982 for convictions on extortion and bribery charges. He served one year of a three-year sentence. While locked up, Stoller penned his wife's biography.

It was after a performance in downtown Dallas on New Year's Eve 1987. Steve Earle, one of the hottest new acts in the industry, was involved in a fight, reportedly with one of his road crew members, in the hallway of the West End Market Place. Police officers Lonnie Allen and Walter Orzechwski were summoned to the scene. Orzechwski ordered Earle and his sparring partner to leave the premises. Earle reportedly refused. A fight ensued. Allegedly Earle struck policeman Allen in the head with his fist and then kicked him in the balls. A woman with Earle reportedly grabbed one of the cops by the hair and yanked. Policeman Allen, presumably gripping his groin with one hand, employed with the other what is called in cop vernacular "a lateral vascular neck restraint" on the popular singer. Orzechwski then hand-cuffed Earle, who had fallen to the ground unconscious, and loaded him into the squad car.

Even country music's maverick of modesty, Randy Travis, has been frisked by the cold hand of the law.

Steve Earle, down and dirty in Dallas.

Steve Earle was subsequently booked, fingerprinted, and photographed. He was described in police reports as a white male, age thirty-two, 6'0", 160 pounds, with brown eyes and brown hair. He was charged with aggravated assault and disorderly conduct and spent the next twelve hours in jail before he was released on bail.

Earle's manager, Will Botwin, publicly termed the incident an "unprovoked attack" on his client. Earle pled not guilty, and later filed a civil suit, claiming that he had been beaten and choked by one of the policemen.

There have been others, of course, who have stood at one time or another in the country music prison line-up, but none have had as much trouble with the law as the little guy with the big black Stetson, Johnny Paycheck.

11
TAKE THIS JAIL
AND SHOVE IT!

According to one of his songs, he is the only hell his mama ever raised. But, oh what a blaze of wrath and tortured damnation he grew up to be. Donald Lytle, a.k.a. Donny Young, a.k.a. Johnny Paycheck, is small in stature (5'5") but big on bravado—all steel balls, a pair of Charles Manson–like wildfire eyes, and a big black Stetson. He lives by his own rules and swaggers through life with one hand clenched and the other hand performing tricks with his gun.

Larry Wise, thirty-seven, didn't realize what he was getting himself into at the North High Lounge Barroom on December 19, 1985. Johnny Paycheck, forty-seven, had returned home to Ohio for Christmas vacation. The wall clock, with its requisite neon beer advertisement, read just after 11:30 P.M. Wise and Paycheck were embroiled in a heated exchange. The topic of debate, reportedly, was the virtues of deer and turtle meat. Paycheck, perhaps incensed at what he perceived to be a mocking of his poor boy cultural heritage, turned to Wise and reportedly retorted, "Do you see me as some sort of a country hick?" Then, according to Ernest Turner, the lounge owner, Paycheck declared to Wise, "I don't like you. I'm going to mess you up." Turner walked around the bar and approached the two men, but by the time he reached them, it was too late. Paycheck allegedly whipped out his .22 caliber handgun, raised it to Wise's head, and pulled the trigger. As Turner later exclaimed, "Mr. Paycheck had done shot Mr. Wise." Wise ran out of the bar and onto the street, blood spilling from his head. Paycheck followed.

It was not the first time that the seething hell within Johnny Paycheck had reared its ugly head and exercised its serpent tongue.

While a youth in the navy, Paycheck attempted to kill a supe-

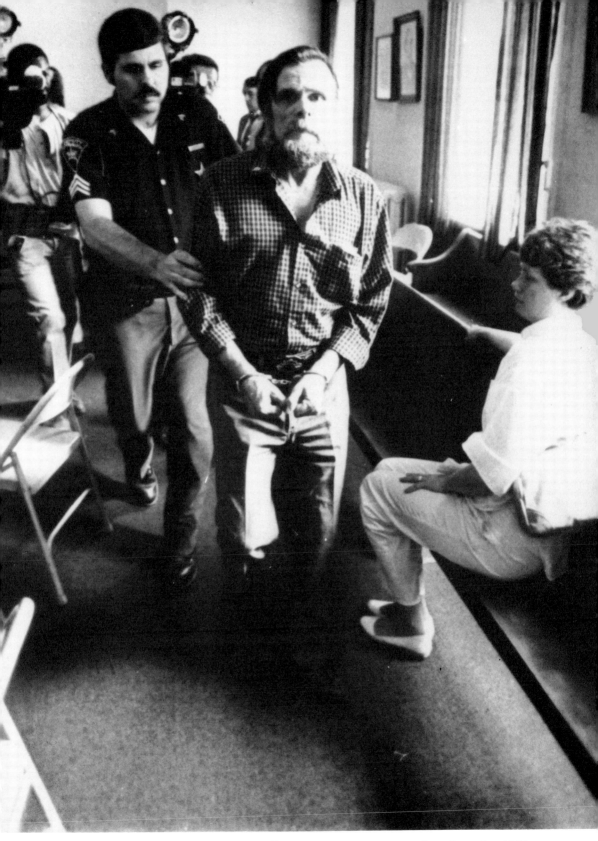

Paycheck, welcomed back to Ohio, December 1985.

rior officer by pummeling him in the head, fist to skull. He was charged with thirty-two counts of assault and sentenced to eighteen years of hard labor at the Naval Disciplinary Command in Portsmouth, New Hampshire. His sentence was later reduced to two years, but not before Paycheck attempted to escape from the maximum security unit by exiting, with a saw, through the shower room ceiling.

> Shit, the sixties was my time and I was drinkin' and shootin' up a storm. I was headed for a fall but good. I fell. Right into the friggin' gutter. I found myself in places—man, I never knew how I ever got there. I was in Los Angeles one time—dyin'.
> —Johnny Paycheck

He arrived in Nashville in 1959 and became a member of the George Jones band, the Jones Boys. Later, he played bass and sang background vocals for Faron Young, Porter Wagoner, and Ray Price. In 1966, he charted his first Top 10 solo record with "The Lovin' Machine." He also wrote Tammy Wynette's debut recording, "Apartment #9," which hit the charts that same year. However, by 1967, a heavy dose of alcoholism had thwarted Paycheck's fledgling career.

In 1968, he was arrested for burglarizing a Nashville home. He had allegedly taken some antique furniture and was fined $50. By the end of the decade, Paycheck packed away his whiskey-stained reputation and moved from Nashville to Los Angeles, where he was reduced to working the local bar circuit.

With his body withered down to a hundred pounds and his life drifting in and out of fleabag motels and southern California skid-row gutters, Paycheck was a borderline bum and country music has-been before the age of thirty. However, as he teetered at the precipice of shattered promise, Paycheck was rescued by the same charging white knight who had saved Tammy Wynette from the beauty shop doldrums. Billy Sherrill flew Paycheck back to Nashville and gave him a hit-bound single to record. It was called "Don't Take Her, She's All I Got."

It was about this time, in 1971, that Paycheck was given the dubious nickname "Johnny Badcheck." He was convicted of passing a bad $100 check at a Holiday Inn in Nashville and was sentenced to eleven months and twenty-nine days in prison and three years of probation. When "She's All I Got" hit the charts a short time later, his sentence was suspended.

His problems were not.

In 1976, he filed for bankruptcy. That same year, Vivian

"Yes, I do cocaine, but cocaine isn't a killer drug and neither is alcohol. Cocaine and alcohol are okay, upfront drugs."
—Johnny Paycheck, 1984

Johnny Paycheck and David Allan Coe, the formidable forces behind "Take This Job and Shove It," which became a major motion picture.

Richards filed a paternity suit against him, for which he later spent a night in a Canadian jail. One of his business associates at the time, Nick Palladino, dismissed the charge as "probably some woman out to make a quick buck." In 1978, Paycheck had the biggest hit of his career. "Take This Job and Shove It," written by David Allan Coe, became a monster hit and the working man's anthem. In eight years, Paycheck had gone from the skid rows of Los Angeles to the top of the national music charts. Unfortunately, he had also gone back to the bottle and, like his friend George Jones, had begun to develop a consuming passion for that pile of white powder with the empty power.

In January 1979, Nashville trustee Glenn Ferguson filed a lawsuit against Paycheck that spawned a series of allegations and countersuits. The two had met in 1972, when Ferguson wielded his local political power to help Paycheck avoid prison after he had been convicted of passing the bad check. Subsequently, Paycheck asked Ferguson to become his manager. In 1975, Ferguson lent Paycheck over $16,000. He also held a $60,000 mortgage on Paycheck's home. Reportedly, the two became very close, and their relationship thrived until Paycheck scored with the overwhelming success of "Take This Job and Shove It."

In his initial lawsuit, Ferguson sought the return of a $10,000 gold chain that Paycheck had allegedly borrowed, signed a promissory note for, and had not returned. Two weeks prior to filing his suit, Ferguson sent Paycheck a letter that read, "I would appreciate your sending me $10,000 for that gold chain you lost. It has been since October of 1978 that the chain disappeared and evidently you have not found it. If I do not get some response from you about this particular problem, I am putting that note out for collection and seeking judgment against you. I would feel much better about our future negotiations if you would act in good faith about this matter and get it out of the way."

Paycheck counterfiled, claiming that Ferguson owed him money. Paycheck charged that Ferguson had mismanaged his career and his money. Said Paycheck, "In those six years (1972–1978), I've made about $2 million. But where's my money?" In response, Ferguson filed an amended complaint, which prompted Paycheck to file an amendment to his countersuit. In his amended complaint, Paycheck charged that Ferguson, an elected official of the city of Nashville, had used his office to conduct Paycheck's business. Paycheck further contended that Ferguson had interfered in his personal life by telling Paycheck's wife that he had been "running around with other women" and had urged her to divorce him. Paycheck also alleged that Ferguson had threatened to ruin his career and that he had been forced to move from Nashville to Florida because of other unspecified threats made by Ferguson. Said Paycheck, "Glenn Ferguson's trying to destroy me."

Ferguson responded by attributing the problem to Paycheck's drug abuse. Said Ferguson, "This is typical Paycheck. Paycheck has had a serious problem for the last several months and everybody in the music industry knows it." He also blamed outside forces: "[Paycheck] was receiving advice from a variety of other people, both in Nashville and elsewhere, some of whom included persons interested in taking advantage of him and disposing of me as his manager. Some of these people obviously thought they saw an opportunity to ruin my political career and they were willing to sacrifice Johnny Paycheck's career by initiating irresponsible discovery proceedings."

On October 14, 1980, the suits were dismissed amid secrecy. There were reports that Paycheck had agreed to pay Ferguson a small amount of money, but it is not known whether or not Ferguson ever got back his gold chain.

On April 8, 1981, Helen Espinoza, a Frontier Airlines flight attendant on Flight #435 from Denver to Casper, Wyoming, asked her passenger, in her best plastic stewardess lingo, to kindly fasten his seat belt before takeoff. Her passenger, Johnny Paycheck, refused. Espinoza informed the pilot, who announced over the speakers that the plane would not depart until all passengers had buckled up. Paycheck retorted, loud enough so that Espinoza could hear, "Tell that bitch I have my seat belt on." At that point, Paycheck's traveling companion and band member James Murphy reportedly grabbed Espinoza by the arm, shook her, and verbally leered, "Sit here with me, so we can have some fun."

Helen Espinoza subsequently filed a lawsuit against Paycheck and his companion and was awarded a settlement of $175,000 in October 1983.

April 8, 1981, was not a good day for Johnny Paycheck. Nor was it a good night. Following his performance in Casper, Paycheck went home with a woman from his audience, presumably for a few rounds of horizontal humping between cotton sheets and consenting adults. He ended up staying at her house for the next two days. Apparently he overstayed his welcome. In December 1981, the woman filed felony statutory rape charges against Paycheck, claiming that while in her home Paycheck had forced her *twelve-year-old daughter* to have sexual intercourse with him—twice. The woman contended that she had waited so long to file her complaint because she had received several mysterious, threatening phone calls and "feared [Paycheck's] power as a star."

In July 1982, the case was plea-bargained down from statutory rape (which held a penalty of ten years in prison) to misdemeanor sexual assault, because "critical witnesses [presumably, the girl] indicated a strong reluctance to testify." Paycheck pleaded "no contest" to the fourth-degree sexual assault charges, was fined $1,000, and placed on one year of probation. The girl's mother also filed a $3 million civil suit against Paycheck.

It was about $3 million more than Johnny Paycheck had. In April 1982, he was sued by the Internal Revenue Service for $103,000 in back taxes. In July, he was sued by the state of Tennessee for $1,600 in back taxes. Around that same time, he was sued for $10,000 by a Midwest promoter who claimed that Paycheck had given an offensive performance. He was also arrested in Raleigh, North Carolina, for not having paid a $26,000 judgment after failing to appear at a Greensboro concert in 1979.

The $3 million civil suit was subsequently dropped because, according to Dallas Laird, the girl's attorney, "We checked his assets situation out, and it didn't look like we would be able to collect anything. He has a large federal tax lien." In October 1982, Paycheck again filed for bankruptcy, just minutes before his property, which had been seized by the IRS, was scheduled to be auctioned off.

Reportedly because of the charges of statutory rape, Paycheck lost his contract with CBS Records. Paycheck adamantly denied this with, "Don't ever believe CBS dropped me. I walked out. I couldn't stand the back-stabbing stench there anymore. They didn't drop me for shit. I dropped them." As for the alleged incident with the twelve-year-old girl, Paycheck's manager at the time, Tony Conway, maintained that the girl's mother "was just somebody trying to get some money." Paycheck himself claimed that the whole affair was the result of a drug deal gone bad.

> I'll try anything once to see if I like it. And if I like it, I'll stick with it, no matter what anybody says, I won't do something that will hurt somebody else, but I'll do what I damn well please. If something makes me feel good, I'll do it.
> —Johnny Paycheck, *The Tennessean*, September 10, 1984

Back at the North High Lounge in Hillsboro, Ohio, Paycheck's bark was worse than his bullet. Larry Wise, the local resident

"They [the country music industry] can take their shit and keep it. I've never kissed an ass or licked a boot and I won't ever compromise what I believe in for nobody. I won't live by their rules. I'll do whatever I damn well please."
—Johnny Paycheck

who ran out of the bar leaving a trail of blood behind him, received only a grazing blow to the head and was not seriously injured. Nevertheless, Paycheck was arrested and charged with felonious assault, carrying a concealed weapon, and tampering with evidence by disposing of the weapon. He pleaded innocent, claiming "I was a victim of circumstances. It was an accident."

In May 1986, Paycheck entered the Hillsboro courthouse, located a half-block from the North High Lounge and was found guilty of aggravated assault and tampering with evidence. He was sentenced by Judge Darrell Hottle to nine and a half years in prison.

Paycheck appealed the decision, and while free and awaiting the new court ruling, attempted to temper the hell that his mama had raised and improve his public persona. He joined Nancy Reagan's "Just Say No" antidrug campaign, signed a new recording contract, and recorded a gospel album with defrocked evangelist John Wesley Fletcher, the man who precipitated the fall from grace of Jim and Tammy Faye Bakker. He also attempted some uncharacteristic quiet reflection. Said Paycheck in his first Nashville interview since he was released on appeal, "This will probably be my last time around. They [the fans] have taken me back every time so far, but you only stay young for so long."

Nevertheless, as he awaits the determination of his residency for the next nine or so years, Johnny Paycheck, pinned to the mat by the weight of the world but not down for the count, is already plotting his future career moves. An enterprising record company official for Mercury Records said hopefully, "If he goes to prison, we'll record a prison album with him in prison."

12
BABYLON BITCHING

I t was all over a swimming pool, shaped in the image of a guitar. During the 1950s and 1960s, Webb Pierce was one of the biggest stars in country music. However, by the early 1970s, his record sales had, pardon the pun, *dipped* considerably.

And then he had an idea. In 1974, tour buses began to arrive at the Pierce residence, located on North Curtiswood Lane, a narrow two-lane street in the wealthy Nashville suburb known as Hillbilly Hollywood. Webb greeted the Kodak-carrying tourists with a smile, a handshake, a peck on the cheek, and a dose of manufactured drivel. He escorted them on a "tour" of his unusually shaped pool, which had cost him $35,000 to construct. He signed autographs and for the nominal fee of five dollars, sold copies of his record albums. It was the best tour package deal in town. Within a short time, the Webb Pierce swimming pool became the second-biggest tourist attraction in Nashville, second only to the gaudily opulent million-dollar enterprise known as Opryland.

The residential résumé of Hillbilly Hollywood, more formally known as the city of Oak Hill, also claimed Minnie Pearl, Jerry Reed, and Harold Ragsdale, among others. Ragsdale, a.k.a. Ray Stevens, best known for his hits, "Ahab the Arab," "Gitarzan," "The Streak," and "Everything Is Beautiful" lived on North Curtiswood Lane directly across the street from Webb Pierce and his aquatic hole in the ground.

In 1975, in order to accommodate the busloads of visitors to his home, Webb Pierce obtained a city permit to pave over a portion of his front yard to construct a bus ramp. Ray Stevens, understandably agitated by the daily influx of gawking strangers parading about his neighborhood, filed a lawsuit to block Pierce's ramp. Stevens claimed that not only would the ramp

WebbPierceandtheneighborhoodnuisance.

become a neighborhood nuisance, it would also alter the area from a residential to a commercial zone. Pierce responded in the press with, "If Mr. Stevens wants to be a hermit, let him go live on a mountain somewhere." Pierce won the lawsuit, and the ramp was constructed.

However, as Ray Stevens predicted, the ramp served as an open invitation to the Nashville tourist industry. On Wednesday, August 11, 1976, 790 tourists bombarded Pierce's property, arriving via six large passenger buses and fifty smaller vans. That Saturday, 2,520 people invaded the musical pool, conveyed by fifty-one buses, fifty-seven vans, and nine cars. Curtiswood Lane, the exclusive, private fraternity of the stars, had become a jungle of noise, exhaust, honking bus drivers, and little old camera-clicking ladies from Peoria.

Subsequently, the city of Oak Hill filed a lawsuit against Webb Pierce, charging that the activities at his home were commercial and not for charity, as he had contended. This time, the court ruled against Pierce and enjoined him from using his home as a tourist attraction. Today, tour buses still drive down North Curtiswood Lane, but they are not allowed to stop at or enter the Webb Pierce home. Presumably, neither is Ray Stevens.

> He was walkin' toward me and I felt someway, somehow, that there was somethin' we had in common, you know? And just immediately, we went over to talk to Luther Perkins, he was just working on the other side, and we just became like blood brothers on the spot, before he ever left the building.
> —Marshall Grant on his first meeting with Johnny Cash, in a Memphis garage, 1954

Johnny Cash and Marshall Grant used to be the best of friends. With Luther Perkins, they formed a band, Johnny Cash and the Tennessee Two, in 1954. Together they recorded "Cry, Cry, Cry," "Hey Porter," "Folsom Prison Blues," and "I Walk the Line," among others. And by the late 1950s, Johnny Cash had become a star.

As his famous friend slid into the deathly decline of drink, drugs, and debauchery (see Chapter 3), it was Marshall Grant who played protector and nursemaid. Once, in Toronto, Marshall found Johnny in his tour bus, unconscious from an apparent drug overdose. Reportedly, Marshall saved his friend's life with mouth-to-mouth resuscitation. In 1967, with the help of Marshall, June Carter, and others, Johnny Cash was able to overcome his addiction to pills.

In March 1980, after a twenty-six year friendship (and amid rumors that Cash was back on pills), Marshall Grant received a letter from Johnny Cash informing him that his services were no longer required and that their partnership had been dissolved. Grant, still reeling from the sting of the letter, filed a lawsuit against Cash on December 31, 1980. Grant's complaint charged Cash with breach of contract and slander, among other things, and sought several million dollars in relief. According to Grant, during the term of their partnership Cash had not disbursed the profits from the group's recordings. Court documents further alleged, "As Defendant began to abuse drugs, he would become angry and at times violent when questioned about these monies."

Grant also contended that he and Perkins had co-composed many of Cash's hits without credit or payment.

The battle between the two former friends, separated by a love for the dollar, has been waged in the U.S. District Court of Tennessee for over seven years without a settlement. As their attorneys get wealthier with each legal motion, one can't help but wonder whatever happened to those two friends who, during the hungry years on the road, used to sleep together in the same motel room bed. Whatever happened to those two boys, bonded by love for music, who locked gazes, shook hands, and swapped dreams in the back of an auto mechanic's garage in Memphis?

Hank Williams had two wives who slugged it out in court after his death (see Chapter 2). He also had two children. One of them became famous before he stopped wetting his pants. The other didn't even know who her father was until she turned twenty-seven. Today they are both in court, fighting over their dead father's immensely profitable record royalties.

> Once Cathy's in the pot as a beneficiary, she'll receive several
> hundred thousand dollars a year until she's eighty-two.
> —Keith Adkinson, Cathy Stone's attorney

Shortly before his death, Hank Williams Sr. was having an affair with a twenty-nine-year-old Nashville woman named Bobbie Jett. There were, of course, several problems, as there frequently were when Hank mixed his women—with his women. Hank was reportedly still in love with his recently divorced wife, Audrey. He had also gotten involved with a young Louisiana beauty, Billie Jean Jones Eshlimar. And Bobbie Jett had gotten pregnant. Naturally, it wouldn't have looked too good in the press if it was released that ole Hank had impregnated a woman out of wedlock, especially when he was fixin' to marry himself another one. Thus Hank drove Bobbie to his mother's boardinghouse in Montgomery, Alabama and on October 15, 1952, reportedly signed a prebirth custody agreement. Three days later, Hank married Billie Jean. Less than three months later, he was dead.

On January, 6, 1953, two days after the circus of mourning that was the Hank Williams funeral, a baby girl, Antha Belle Jett, was born in St. Margaret's Hospital in Montgomery. That baby girl, as it was later proven, was Cathy Stone. Cathy was then adopted by Hank's mother, Lilly Stone. When Lilly died a couple of years later, Hank's sister, Irene, turned Cathy over to the state of Alabama, and she was placed with a foster family. In 1956, she was adopted by a couple from Mobile, Alabama, and it was not until she turned twenty-one and received a small $2,000 inheritance from the Lilly Stone estate that she had an inkling of her famous parentage. And it was not until 1980 that she *knew* she was the daughter of Hank Williams. It was then that Cathy learned of the Alabama prebirth contract between Bobbie Jett and Hank Williams Sr.

> It was the first time that I knew for sure, one, that he was my father and, two, that he wanted me. The main thing is, he wanted to raise me, he wanted to provide for me, and he wanted me to be his. Now that I know who I am and that my father wanted me, I want a share of what is mine.
> —Cathy Stone

Naturally, Hank Sr.'s beneficiaries, including his song publishing company, Acuff-Rose, his widow, Billie Jean Williams Horton, and his son, Hank Williams, Jr.—all of whom have made a fortune off of the continuing Williams appeal—have been none too pleased about these recent "Dynasty" subplot-like developments. It's not that they dispute Cathy Stone's claim that she is the "love child" that Hank Williams fathered; it is her claim to a share of his royalties, worth millions, that has them perturbed.

In October 1987, a Montgomery judge ruled that Cathy Stone was indeed Hank Williams's biological, illegitimate daughter but because she had been twice adopted, she had no legal right to a portion of his estate. However, this matter has yet to be fully resolved. Another lawsuit, filed in New York, is still pending, and Cathy Stone's attorney promises to appeal the Montgomery ruling.

In the meantime, Cathy Stone married her attorney, Keith Adkinson, and changed her professional name to Jett Williams. She has also trained under the auspices of record producer Owen Bradley, who once played piano for her father and who was instrumental in the careers of Patsy Cline and Loretta Lynn, among others. It seems that Cathy Stone Adkinson, much to the chagrin of Nashville, wants to become a country music singing star—just like her father.

It doesn't take Elsa Manchester to suggest that siblings Cathy Stone and Hank Williams Jr. should not be invited to the same family reunion. For, despite sweet-smiled claims to the contrary, Nashville is anything but one big happy family. The pink-cheeked hospitality, all wrapped up in a warm southern drawl, is

often laced with back-stabbing arsenic and good ole boy hostility. Litigation is the recreation in vogue, and money is the unwa-
vering bottom line.

So, before drawing up that guest list and hosting that big
Nashville party, consider the following:

Willie Nelson and Ray Price. When Willie and Ray were Nashville neighbors, one of Ray's fighting cocks continually molested
Willie's laying hens. When Ray did not respond to his protests,
Willie loaded up his shotgun and reportedly wasted the offending cock.

Loretta Lynn and the Wilburn Bothers. Early in her career,
Loretta was managed by the enterprising Wilburn Brothers. By
1970, however, their relationship had deteriorated, and Loretta
hired herself a new manager, David Skepner. Nevertheless, the
Wilburns had a contract that gave them a percentage of Loretta's publishing rights, which they would not relinquish. As a
result, Loretta, for the most part, stopped recording songs that
she had a-written.

Tanya Tucker's father and Tanya Tucker's road manager. In
October 1981, Tanya's father, Beau Tucker, was arrested in Nevada after threatening Tanya's road manager, Steven
Wallach, with a pocket knife. The incident occurred after Wallach took an advance of $6,550 to pay salaries and petty cash
expenses to the cast and crew of Tanya's show. Tucker thought
that Wallach had taken the money for himself.

Buck Owens and Kinky Friedman. Former country singer
Kinky Friedman had too much humor for Nashville. Nashville
smiled, but with a rigidly locked jaw. Perhaps it was because it
has always been difficult to discern when Kinky was joking and
when he was not. After all, this is a man who named his band
"The Texas Jewboys" and referred to them as "boy chicks"; who
referred (in *Gallery*) to women as "slits" to be "hosed," and who
reportedly claimed, "I can't see any point in relating to a woman
except sexually; I don't think women have it in them to make
good friends. I don't think they even have it in them to make
good people a lot of times"; and whose catalog of music has
included such songs as "They Ain't Making Jews like Jesus
Anymore," "Get Your Biscuits in the Oven and Your Buns in the
Bed," and "Men's Room L.A.," which was about a man in a public
restroom with a dilemma: whether to use or not to use a photo of
Jesus as toilet paper, as the roll had run out. It was reportedly
another song, "Asshole from El Paso" (a take-off on Merle Haggard's "Okie from Muskogee"), that provoked the feud between
Kinky Friedman and Buck Owens. Explained Kinky in 1980: "I

Kinky Friedman, country music's former singing satirist, once quipped that his cowboy boots were made from the foreskin of a brontosaurus. By 1987, he gave up music and became an author. Said Kinky, "Now that I don't want to sing, I get offers all the time. But, I'm happy doing what I'm doing. I don't have to deal with as many assholes."

contended that Buck was a humorless, constipated prig—un-American, unmelodic, and unpleasant—a fascist insect who devours amendments. Hell, even Kris Kristofferson could sing better than him. During our litigations, Buck threatened to call in the FCC, the Ku Klux Klan, the Oral Roberts Crusade Singers, and the Bakersfield Kiwanis Club. I threatened to call the ACLU, the JDL [Jewish Defense League], Truman Capote, and my lawyer, Sonny Corleone."

Bill Monroe and Lester Flatt. Bill Monroe, the father of blue-grass, was Lester Flatt's mentor and inspiration. However, when Flatt quit Monroe's band and teamed up with Earl Scruggs, Monroe harbored a heavy grudge. By 1955, Flatt & Scruggs had become stars in their own right and were granted membership into the Grand Ole Opry. Backstage, Flatt approached his old boss and attempted to strike up a conversation. Monroe, who has a reputation for his stony dignity, ignored him. For the next fifteen years, Monroe and Flatt worked the Opry on the same nights, and for that fifteen years they did not speak. In 1971, Flatt, the scorned prodigal son, surprised everyone by showing up on stage with Monroe at a bluegrass festival, reportedly ending the long-standing riff.

Skeeter Davis and the Grand Ole Opry. On December 8, 1973, a group of religious fanatics was arrested at a Nashville shopping mall for harassing Christmas shoppers. That night, Skeeter (who refused to work in nightclubs because, as she explained, "If Jesus returned, and I know He will, I wouldn't want Him to find me in a nightclub"), went on the Opry and, instead of singing her scheduled country number, sang "Amazing Grace." She also criticized the Nashville Police Department for arresting friends of Jesus. Subsequently Opry management suspended Skeeter for an indefinite disciplinary period. Upon hearing the news, twenty of the religious fanatics picketed outside the Opry and announced, "The devil runs Nashville!" Skeeter, then forty-one, disappeared. Reports surfaced that she had run off to Africa to sing for a Christ is the Answer Crusade.

Roy Orbison and Wesley Rose. In 1982, Orbison filed a $50 million suit against his manager, Nashville power Wesley Rose. Orbison alleged that Rose had mismanaged his career for twenty-four years. In 1985, the Nashville law firm representing Orbison turned the tables by suing Orbison for $150,000 in unpaid fees.

Waylon Jennings and Tompall Glaser. Outlaw compatriots Waylon and Tompall were at one time the very best of friends.

Forgotten by Nashville: Troy Hess, ambitious tyke or boy puppet?

Mickey Gilley (pictured here with Bonnie Raitt and John Travolta) was more famous for the club that bore his name than he was for his music. Now, he's giving up the club.

The biggest honky-tonk in the world (50,000 square feet) is located in Pasadena, Texas. Mickey Gilley claims it needs a facelift. It might just be needing a name change as well.

However, after the overwhelming success of the Outlaw Movement, which they had pioneered, Waylon and Tompall feuded over who had done what and eventually ceased speaking to one another altogether.

Hank Williams Jr. and his road manager. In June 1981, James Blachman, Hank Jr.'s ex-road manager of three years, was arrested for the attempted blackmail of his former boss. Blachman, who had been fired the month before, allegedly made a series of phone calls to Hank Jr., threatening to use incriminating information against him unless he was given $3,500 and a mobile home with air conditioning and a septic tank.

Mickey Gilley and Gilley's. In 1971, the relatively unknown singer Mickey Gilley approached nightclub owner Sherwood Cryer and asked to borrow money. Cryer gave Gilley a job as the featured entertainer in a Texas club known as Shelly's. When Cryer became Gilley's manager, he renamed his club Gilley's. In 1980, after the release of the movie *Urban Cowboy*, Mickey Gilley, the club with his name, and a ball-breaking mechanical bucking bull all became famous. Said Gilley at the time, "I wish I had a dozen of 'em around the United States that would pull the people that this one's pulling right now, because I could laugh myself all the way to the bank." However, in 1984 Gilley fired Cryer as his manager, and in 1987 he filed a lawsuit to disassociate himself from the club. Gilley claimed that Cryer had not accounted for the club's profits and owed him money. He further explained that he wanted his name removed from the club because its condition had deteriorated. Said Cryer in response, "I don't know what's wrong with that boy. He's acting flaky. Ever since his fiftieth birthday he's acted funny. I'd say he's just got about his raisin'."

Jimmy and Don Dean. Jimmy Dean, the sausage entrepreneur,

Singing entrepreneur Jimmy Dean spends his time pitching his sausage on national television. His sausage (company) is now the largest in the United States. When he is not pitching his pork, Jimmy vacations aboard his yacht, *Big Bad John*. Ah, the pleasures that a good sausage can bring . . . .

There was everything but harmony between William Lee Golden (center) and the rest of the Oak Ridge Boys.

and the writer and singer of the million-selling "Big Bad John," has been in and out of court with his brother Don over the past decade. In July 1987, a New Orleans appeals court overturned a verdict that had ordered Jimmy to pay $500,000 to Don. Don had initiated the suit, charging that he had suffered emotional harm due to remarks made by Jimmy.

William Lee Golden and the Oak Ridge Boys. Bearded baritone William Lee Golden was the longest surviving member of the Oak Ridge Boys. Until 1987, that is. In 1986, Duane Allen, Joe Bonall, Richard Sterban, and William Lee Golden called a press conference to announce that, contrary to rumors, there was no dissension within the group. A few months later, in March 1987, the other three members voted to oust Golden. Said Duane Allen of Golden, "He hated everybody in the group." For a while, the joke in Nashville was that Golden was to be replaced by David Lee Roth, who had been voted out of the heavy metal rock band

Van Halen. However, it was Steve Sanders who was given the job as the replacement Oak. In May 1987, William Lee Golden, forty-eight, filed a lawsuit against his former musical partners to the tune of $40 million dollars.

Dolly Parton and Redd Foxx. On his television variety program in 1977, Redd Foxx quipped to his viewers that Dolly Parton had imprinted her breasts in cement in the forecourt of Hollywood's Graumann's Chinese Theatre. He further suggested that the imprints were so large that series regular midget Billy Barty could get lost in them. Either amused or offended, Dolly wired Foxx with the following statement: "Imprints of these or any other parts of my anatomy are not currently in the forecourt. I would be the first to admit that I am well-endowed, but I seriously doubt that even your show's little person, Billy Barty, could be lost in such alleged imprints. I hesitate to add to your current woes, but I feel that in this case you owe me two equally ample apologies."

Other performers blast the Nashville establishment as a whole. Outlaw Tompall Glaser claimed, "I'm just sick of the whole damn prostituted mess and I'm tired of being quiet about it. People should know what goes on in Nashville." Waylon Jennings agreed, explaining to *Penthouse*: "Not only do they dictate what is country music and what is not country music; then, they get into dictating lifestyles, man, telling people how they should live and act. If you wanted to be in the country music business, then you did it their way. I always felt this way: if they didn't like the way I was as a person, then they could keep the hell away from me."

13
THEY CALL HIM "KILLER"

I'm the toughest son of a bitch that ever shat out of a mean ass.
—Jerry Lee Lewis

He is the salacious leer in the dark corner of country music. He is the sweating passion and hot pumping fury and unrestrained sexual aggression of rock and roll. He is heaven and hell, preacher and sinner, truth and deception, love and lust—all wrapped into one torturously conflicting, difficult to touch, and impossible to contain great ball of fire. He is the southern fried white boy, the piano playing badass from Ferriday, Louisiana, that they call the Killer.

Elvis made the young girls scream and cry, but Jerry Lee made them cream their crinolines. The piano was his instrument, and he pounded it with relentless abandon. He pumped and writhed and whipped his Samson-like hair out of his face. In 1957, there was a whole lotta shakin' goin' on in the world, and Jerry Lee Lewis was the responsible culprit. He was a man possessed by his music, the music of the devil.

I don't give a damn about it. I wanted to get married. I got married. They don't like it, they can kiss my butt.
—Jerry Lee Lewis

"They" didn't kiss his butt. They booted it out of England by making him the whipping boy of rock and roll. On December 12, 1957, Jerry Lee Lewis married Myra Gale Brown, his thirteen-year-old cousin. In May 1958, Mr. and Mrs. Lewis arrived in London to launch Jerry Lee's British tour. Then an enterprising scribe for the *Daily Mirror* reported that Myra was just out of the seventh grade and was only thirteen. Hell blazed afire and

Before the British: Hot pumping fury.

unleashed a torrent of destruction that scorched across conti-
nents. The press screamed about the child bride and the lascivious lech. The *Daily Mirror* reported with sadistic glee, "The
passports of American rock 'n' roll singer Jerry Lee Lewis and
his thirteen-year-old 'bride' Myra were examined by a hotel
security officer yesterday—AT THE REQUEST OF THE PO-
LICE." The *Daily Sketch* blared, POLICE TO ACT IN CASE OF MRS.
"ROCK" AGED 13. Jerry Lee was booed off the stage. Former fans
tightened the noose that had been strung around his neck and
hissed, "Baby-snatcher!" The tour was aborted. Top 40 radio
stations back in America banned him. His career was over before
he reached the age of twenty-three.

And so he was shot down in the late spring of his youth, and he
never really recovered. At first, Jerry Lee didn't know what was
happening. And then, when the ugliness of it all sunk in, he
swallowed hard whatever innocence he had left. After all, he
seethed, who were *they* to judge *him*, when only God should have
that right? He took a long, deep, slow drag on his cigarette, ran
his fingers through his wavy and untamed hair, and curled up
his mouth into a killer snarl.

The infant genre that he had fueled with unprecedented, hot-blooded fervor, turned its pompous, moralistic, Pat Boone–like back on him, and for the next ten years, Jerry Lee lurked in the shadows of his own wake. He continued to play clubs, but they were dingy cubbyholes, not worthy of his glittering brilliance. It was not until 1968, when he was embraced by *country* fans, that his career rekindled with some semblance of its former glory. But he was not particularly appreciative of his revived popularity. Nor was he amenable to bowing down in homage to the country music traditions and institutions. In fact, when he made his debut on the sacred Opry in 1972, he performed his old *rock and roll* hits and expounded sacrilegiously to the conservative, die-hard country audience clad in its collective polyester, "I am a rock 'n' rollin', country 'n' western, rhythm 'n' blues singin' *mothafucker!*"

But then, Jerry Lee Lewis was never one for conformity or vocal discretion. He has lived by one rigid set of laws—his own. He has paid homage to no one or nothing, except his music, his meat, and occasionally, his God. On his first experience with the Opry management, which occurred before Sun Records and subsequent stardom, he lambasted, "I auditioned for those idiots and they came down and asked me if I could play a guitar. I said I could. And they said, 'Well, now, you change your act to a guitar and you might make it.' I said, 'You can take your guitar and ram it up your ass.' "

He has been equally outspoken about his musical contemporaries. On Elvis Presley: "He was a weakling, man." On Buddy Holly: "He couldn't fart a hit." On the Beatles: "I don't like the Beatles. I think they stink, man. I never did like 'em." On the Rolling Stones: "Worst bunch of shit I ever heard." On Waylon Jennings and Willie Nelson: "I don't like hillbilly shit." And on Jerry Lee Lewis: "There's only been four of us. Al Jolson, Jimmie Rodgers, Hank Williams, and Jerry Lee Lewis." He also once barked to Leon Russell, "Hey, Leon, you the one that married that nigger?"; to a magazine critic, "The next motherfucker that gives me a bad write-up, I'm gonna hunt down and blow his fuckin' head off"; and to his audience, "I hope you all have heart attacks." When one writer asked him what he enjoyed doing other than performing, he replied, simply and unequivocally, "Fuck."

> If you ever leave me again, I'll throw acid in your face. If you
> ever leave me, I'll throw you in the river. Leave me, an' I'll kill ya.
> —Jerry Lee Lewis to Myra Gale Lewis
> *Great Balls of Fire*, Myra Lewis

The former child bride had grown weary of playing house. On November 9, 1970, after thirteen years of marriage, twenty-six-year-old Myra Gale filed for a divorce claiming that she had been subjected to "every type of physical and mental abuse imaginable." Once, according to Myra, when Jerry Lee's supper was not ready at 3:00 A.M., he battered her face black and blue and told their seven-year-old daughter, Phoebe, "Look, Phoebe, your mama's gone crazy. She's hittin' herself in the face." Myra also cited infidelity in her list of grievances. As Jerry Lee later acknowledged, "One of my wives had a detective on me and he caught me with twenty-five women. Not all at once—just twenty-five different times."

A month after Myra obtained her divorce, Jerry Lee was sued by a Tennessee woman who claimed that he had been physically abusive to her in a nightclub. The woman claimed, among other things, that Jerry Lee tried to drag her bodily across an electric organ.

He didn't need to force his fourth wife to the altar. Her name was Jaren Elizabeth Gunn, twenty-nine, and she was pregnant with his child. Nevertheless, the wedded couple lived in domestic bliss for only a brief period, if any period at all. Two weeks after their marriage, they separated. For the next eleven years, their frightening farce of a marriage was reduced to a series of combative retreats and advances. For the most part, Jaren lived in Memphis while Jerry Lee lived in Mississippi, reportedly with his young girlfriend, Charlotte Bumpus.

Just a few days before his death, Jerry Lee Lewis Jr. appeared on a "Midnight Special" television show as the drummer in his father's band. In his troubled young life, Jerry Lee Jr. had checked in and out of mental hospitals and drug addiction wards, and according to his father's biographer, Nich Tosches, he once insisted that a little boy and girl from Ferriday were living in his belly. On November 13, 1973, Jerry Lee Jr. was killed when the jeep that his father had given him for his nineteenth birthday overturned. He was Jerry Lee's second son to die young and under tragic circumstances. The first, Steve Allen Lewis, had drowned in 1962 at the age of three in his father's Memphis swimming pool.

> I never hit anybody—unless I want to.
> —Jerry Lee Lewis

In September 1975, Jerry Lee growled under hot breath and a steel gaze, "Look down the barrel of this." He then raised a .357

Magnum, and fired into the chest of his bass player, Norman "Butch" Owens. Owens, hands clutched to his chest, stumbled into Jaren's living room and much to her horror, bled red all over her white carpet. Lewis avoided jail, but a federal jury later awarded Owens $125,000 in damages. That same year, a Memphis woman filed suit against Jerry Lee, claiming that he had "brutally and savagely attacked" her with a fiddle bow. In 1976, the man they call the Killer drove up to the Memphis gates of Graceland, the Southern Camelot, waved his gun through the thick night air, and demanded to see the man they called the King. It was 4:00 A.M. Jerry Lee was down at the gate. Elvis was up behind one of the windows. Between them were the years of rivalry and animosity and the armed palace guards. In *his* view, Jerry Lee was Mozart to Elvis's Salieri. Elvis may have found the favor of the people (and *retained* it), but it was he, Jerry Lee, who was the man who deserved to be king. And so he brandished a gun and demanded entry into the fortress—perhaps to claim the title that was rightfully his or perhaps just in intoxicated outrage. Either way, the King refused to grant him an audience, and Jerry Lee was picked up and admonished by the Memphis police. He then explained to the patronizing face of the world, "Elvis called me up that night 'cause I was playing in town. He said he wanted to see me 'cause he was depressed." A year later, Elvis was dead in his palatial toilet. Jerry Lee did not mourn, at least not in public. "I was glad," he said. "Just another one outta the way."

"I don't know much about medicine or brain damage, and I'm not saying he's got it, but there's a switch in there that violently flies off. It's frightening and it's pitiful."
—Carl Perkins on Jerry Lee Lewis

Jerry Lee was too busy dying a slow death of his own. In February 1976, he entered the hospital for "treatment of influenza and a nasal problem." The following year, he was rushed to an emergency ward, suffering from what was termed "respiratory distress." However, as was suspected at the time and as was later confirmed, The Killer was addicted to drugs, and his *mental* health was doing a perilous high-wire act between heaven and hell. Dr. David Knott of the Memphis Mental Health Institute, who treated Jerry Lee in 1976 and testified in court in 1981, was later quoted as saying that Lewis "exhibited severe agitation, wide mood swings, delusions and hallucinations. [There was] a definite paranoid trend to his thinking." According to Knott, Jerry Lee had been addicted to drugs since the early 1960s, and Tennessee Assistant District Attorney General Jewett Miller contended that Dr. George Nichopoulos (who had also been Elvis's doctor), had written Lewis 680 prescriptions for amphetamines during a *four-month* period in 1975. In September 1979, Jerry Lee was arrested on charges of narcotics possession. Police, acting on a tip from the Internal Revenue Service (which Jerry Lee has been baiting and battling for years), had discovered marijuana and cocaine in his home. On June 30, 1981, he was rushed from his Mississippi ranch to the Memphis Methodist Hospital, where he underwent the first of two emergency operations for a perforated stomach. He was close to death. In fact, premature reports of his death were recorded in various newspapers across the country.

But it wasn't he who was buried. In June 1979, Jerry Lee filed for a divorce from Jaren, alleging "habitual, cruel and inhuman treatment." In September 1980, following yet another in a series of reconciliations, Jaren filed for a divorce against Jerry Lee, proclaiming, "This time I really want out. I just want *out.* I just want to live my own life and be a normal person." It wasn't the first time that Jaren took her emotionally suspect marriage to court. In December 1973, shortly after the death of Jerry Lee Jr., and again in April 1975, she had filed divorce complaints which alleged that her volatile husband had threatened her with bodily harm.

Jaren also obtained a court order prohibiting Jerry Lee from "coming around her, threatening her, assaulting, molesting, or harming her" or their eight-year-old daughter, Lori Lee. Jaren also caused a scandal by applying for food stamps. According to Jaren, Jerry Lee had paid nothing to support her or their daughter since December 1979. She further lamented that she had been forced to move out of the Memphis home owned by Jerry Lee because the phone and utilities had been cut off.

Jaren's court documents alleged, "The Defendant has an extremely violent temper, especially when he becomes intoxicated with alcohol and/or drugs, and he has choked your Plaintiff on numerous occasions, has beaten her up, knocked her down the stairs, and threatened her very life . . . one month ago, when your Plaintiff called the Defendant for financial assistance for herself and the parties' minor child, Defendant went into a rage and stated that she should not worry about any support because 'you are not going to be around very long anyway, and if you don't get off my back and leave me alone, you will end up in the bottom of the lake at the farm with chains around you.' "

There were no chains found around Jaren Lewis on June 8, 1982—shortly before she was to receive her final divorce settlement—when she was found at the bottom of a backyard Memphis swimming pool. Dead.

Mary Kathy Jones of San Antonio lived with Jerry Lee for a three-year period during and after his marriage to Jaren. She told Geraldo Rivera on "20/20" that when she confronted her lover with the news that she was leaving him, he threatened "that if I stayed in town that he'd put me in a mental institution or put me in jail, and I'd never see daylight." According to Jones, he also once broke her nose and shot a gun at her through a bedroom door.

Shawn Michelle Stephens was twenty-three when she met Jerry Lee Lewis in her hometown of Detroit in February 1981. Their first date was set up by her girlfriend, Pam Brewer, a girlfriend of Jerry Lee's manager, J. W. Whitten. After Jaren's death, Jerry Lee reportedly pressed Shawn to marry him, which she eventually did on June 7, 1983. When a friend asked her why she agreed to marry Jerry Lee, Shawn reportedly retorted, "Because he has a big dick and a lot of money."

During the short course of their marriage, Shawn Lewis was presumably given a lot of both. The marriage lasted seventy-seven days. According to *Rolling Stone*, on August 23, 1983, Shawn Lewis telephoned her mother at 3:30 in the morning and told her that she was leaving Jerry Lee. The following day, Shawn was dead. She was found in bed in the Jerry Lee Lewis Mississippi home that featured a swimming pool shaped in the image of a piano. Sonny Daniels, the first ambulance attendant on the scene, took mental note of two bright red claw scratches on the back of Jerry Lee's hand. Jack McCauley, a deputy sheriff, arrived at the scene and noted blood stains on Jerry Lee's bathrobe. There was also blood on Shawn Lewis's hand, in her fingernails, in her hair, on her clothes and bra located in another room, on a lamp, and on the carpet.

"I've never hit a woman in my life."—Jerry Lee Lewis to Geraldo Rivera

And then the blood disappeared. The private autopsy, paid for by Jerry Lee, contended, "No foul play. It's pulmonary edema. Fluid in the lungs. Due to causes unknown." Drug tests showed an overdose of methadone. The local newspaper headlines announced, LEWIS' WIFE KILLED HERSELF, OFFICIAL FEELS. There was no further investigation, and Jerry Lee Lewis was never charged with any wrongdoing in connection with the deaths of either Jaren Elizabeth Lewis or Shawn Michelle Lewis. Still, as his own manager, J. W. Whitten, acknowledged to Pulitzer Prize–winning writer Richard Ben Cramer, "Listen, they'll never bust him in DeSoto County. That's like bustin' Elvis in Memphis. Never. Never. And you can quote me on that."

Eight months after the death of Shawn Michelle Lewis, Jerry Lee married his sixth bride, a twenty-two-year-old aspiring country music singer named Kerrie Lynn McCarver. Her mother, Sarah McCarver, was quoted as saying of Jerry Lee's questionable marital history, "I don't dwell on someone's past. The future is ahead for them, and if they have happiness, I'm all for it." Shortly after Christmas 1985, Jerry Lee filed for a divorce. Following a brief reconciliation, Kerrie Lynn filed for a divorce in early 1986. She claimed that her husband had bloodied her nose during an argument about his interest in other women. She further stated that he had a "quick and violent

231

temper, and that he has cursed, threatened and struck her on occasions too numerous to mention." Jerry Lee responded to the allegations by smashing his Rolls-Royce into her car while it was parked at a Memphis nightclub. Nevertheless, in January 1987, Kerrie Lynn gave birth to their first child, Jerry Lee Lewis III, and withdrew her petition for divorce. At least for the time being. . . .

Still, there are those who believe that Jerry Lee lost the love of his life when he lost Myra Gale—the thirteen-year old woman-child who unknowingly precipitated his abysmal decline. Perhaps, to Jerry Lee, Myra represented his biggest hope for salvation. Perhaps that is why, in late 1970 after Myra filed for her divorce, Jerry Lee publicly denounced his music and claimed that he had turned to God. Said Jerry Lee, "I guess my wife just put up with a lot of unnecessary drinking and stuff, which I don't blame her at all . . . but I have hopes of a reconciliation. I don't know. If God's for us, who can be against us? Therefore, I figure—I don't know—but that I'll get the old lady back some-day."

He never did get her back. And his allegiance to God was only a transient proposition. He has buried two sons and two wives, made a lot of music, and survived a cesspool of condemnation. Today, at age fifty-three, the man they call the Killer is still scorching across his keyboard and rocking to his own frenetic beat. When asked by writer Robert Palmer in 1987 if he had mellowed with the years, Jerry Lee replied, "Ninety percent. Everything on me shrunk, except my dick." When asked what he intended to do when he got too old for sex, he curled up the corner of his mouth into a killer snarl and drawled, "Ain't no way Jerry Lee is gonna get too old to fuck."

And you can't doubt him for a second.

14
THEY FELL TO PIECES

She was at the height of success. She pressed her head, full of the promise of tomorrow (and aching with a slight case of the flu), against the window of the single-engine Piper Commanche plane, but all she could see was an ominous gray, with danger on its periphery. Somewhere down below was a vast, perceptibly infinite landscape, and it was hers, or it seemed to be. Funny how fame and youth can deceive one so about mortality. She thought about her husband. She thought about her babies back in Nashville and how she couldn't wait to get back to them. And she thought about her own early beginnings in Winchester, West Virginia, and about the past two years of acceleration and ascendency. She closed her eyes and then, with the low, steady hum of the plane as a lullaby, got lost for a moment in her sweet dreams of stardom. . . .

The rumor in Nashville was that Patsy Cline, thirty, had slept her way to the top of the *Billboard* charts—speculative bitching, propagated by far lesser talents "eat up" with jealousy, and decidedly *not* true. So she *may* have had a few moist indiscretions notched between her parted white thighs. And she *may* have had a pair of ironclad balls tucked beneath her frilly cowgirl regalia. And she *may* have been brassy and ambitious in ways that other, more *proper* women of the 1950s and early 1960s weren't supposed to be. But so what? She was (and is), without exception, the most outstanding female vocal talent to ever wrap her pretty, painted mouth around a mournful country ballad. By 1963, with hits like "Walkin' After Midnight," "Crazy," and "I Fall to Pieces," Patsy Cline was the biggest attraction of The Grand Ole Opry. She was also the Country Music Association's Entertainer of the Year. And just before 7:00 P.M. on March 5, 1963, she was on an airplane, en route to becoming the intoxicating stuff legends (and country songs) are made of.

The Piper Comanche was piloted by Randy Hughes, thirty-five, Patsy Cline's manager, friend, and alleged former lover. His father-in-law, Cowboy Copas, fifty, was a passenger, as was Hawkshaw Hawkins, forty-one. Both were Grand Ole Opry stars in their own right. Copas's career had declined by 1951; however, his recording of "Alabam" in 1960 signaled something of a comeback. As for Hawkins, his song "Lonesome 7-7203" had

In June 1961, Pasty was involved in a head-on collision in Nashville that killed a young woman. Patsy, listed in critical condition, suffered from face and head cuts and a dislocated hip. "I Fall to Pieces" was the number two song on the country charts at the time.

entered the charts only two days before. It would go on, unbeknownst to him, to become the number one song in the country. Hawkins sat in the seat next to Hughes, Copas sat behind Hawkins, and Patsy sat behind Hughes.

They were returning home to Nashville from a benefit performance in Kansas City, which had been produced to raise funds for the family of disc jockey Cactus Jack Call. Call, a popular figure in country music, had been killed in a car crash a short time before.

At 12:30 P.M. on March 5, the four travelers checked out of the Town House Hotel in Kansas City. At 2:00 P.M. the plane departed. At about 5:00 P.M., the plane landed in Dyersburg, Tennessee, to

(l–r) Ferlin Husky, Patsy Cline, Faron Young (who had a close friendship and, reportedly, a few sexual outings with Patsy), and Jerry Reed.

refuel. The other passengers headed to the restaurant for a cup of coffee while Hughes had a meeting with the airport manager, Bill Braese. Braese warned Hughes of a misty rain and a developing danger in the wind. He suggested that the famous foursome spend the night in Dyersburg. Hughes declined. He telephoned his wife in Nashville to say he would be home soon. Hawkins also telephoned his wife, country star Jean Shepard, to say he'd be home soon. Hughes paid for the twenty-seven gallons of gasoline, and at 6:07 P.M., the Piper Comanche roared its guns and climbed back into the unfriendly skies.

Darkness fell. Shortly before 7:00 P.M., farmer Sam Webb saw the lights of a small airplane circling the sky above his house in Camden, Tennessee. The plane, he said, sounded like it was "revving up its motor, going fast and slow like it was trying to climb." Other area residents told of hearing a plane with definite engine trouble, which they likened to the sound of a car losing its muffler. The small plane, like the human lives locked inside of it, was taking one last, desperate gasp for breath. Sam Webb lost sight of the plane, and a few moments later heard what sounded like something hitting the brush of nearby trees.

After the plane was four hours overdue in Nashville, an all-

Scattered among the debris of the wreckage was one of Patsy's bras and a can of hairspray.

Sweet dreams of stardom.

night search party got under way. At 6:00 A.M., in a scrub hollow three-and-a-half miles west of Camden, cotton farmer W. J. Hollingsworth and his son, Jeners, located the scraps of wreckage. The area was wooded, full of hollows, hills, and swamps. Pieces of green and yellow metal were scattered everywhere. Pieces of shredded human flesh were spread across the landscape, on the ground, and in the trees. When asked if all four bodies had been located, a civil defense official at the site responded, "There's not enough to count. They're all in small pieces." The bodies, strewn some 250 feet from where the plane had apparently sliced into an oak tree, were so mutilated that the only way male identities could be determined was from their billfolds, which had remained intact.

The days of aftermath and mourning were typical of country music. Less than twenty-four hours after the crash, a record company announced the release of the new single by Cowboy Copas entitled "Goodbye Kisses." Hawkshaw Hawkins did not live to see his "Lonesome 7-7203" top the charts, nor was he there for the birth of his second child, who was born three weeks after his death. His widow, Jean Shepard, whose own career had been in a lull prior to the crash, suddenly started having a rash of hits. A week after the funeral, singer Rusty Adams recorded a single called "Angels from the Opry" that was released a few weeks later. And Patsy continued to score hits with "Sweet Dreams," "Faded Love," and others.

As for the Kansas City benefit for Cactus Jack Call, which lured the top talent in Nashville—and which, in essence, resulted in the deaths of Patsy Cline, Randy Hughes, Cowboy Copas, and Hawkshaw Hawkins—it raised a paltry $3,000 dollars. It was a very expensive benefit.

We were burying 'em around here like animals for a while.
—Roy Acuff

It was a stormy Friday afternoon in Nashville on July 31, 1964. At 5:00 P.M., the single-engine plane disappeared from the radar screen. The last message that "Gentleman" Jim Reeves, thirty-nine, communicated to the aeronautics tower of Nashville's Beery Field Airport was that he was encountering a heavy rain.

Jim Reeves, the biggest country music singer of his time.

The Jim Reeves search party consisted of 700 volunteers, twelve planes, two helicopters, and a boat. They are pictured here viewing the sheet-covered bodies of Reeves and his piano player, Dean Manuel.

It had been twelve years before when Hank Williams—engaged in a concerted effort at self-depredation—failed to show up for his scheduled performance on the Louisiana Hayride. Unknown singer Jim Reeves, a Shreveport-area disc jockey and former pitcher with the St. Louis Cardinals, was asked to pinch-hit. A record company executive was, of course, in the audience that night, and Reeves was signed to a recording contract. As a result, he had a 1953 hit with a song called "Mexican Joe." It was to be the first of forty-six Top 10 hits for Jim Reeves. He joined the Opry in 1955, and in 1959 scored a major success with "'He'll Have to Go." By 1964, he was considered by many to be the top act in all of country music.

> What I dislike most is the traveling. The main trouble and danger, maybe, with tours—is getting there and back.
> —Jim Reeves, May 1964

Reeves and his piano player, Dean Manuel, thirty, were returning to Nashville from Batesville, Arkansas, where they had been investigating the purchase of some investment property. Just after 5:00 P.M., as pilot Reeves made his approach to land at the Nashville airport—through a vindictive summer rain—the plane crashed into the densely wooded area near Brentwood, the affluent Nashville suburb of the stars. One of its residents, singer Marty Robbins, stepped outside to rinse his hair in the violent downfall. Like a child of mischief, he reveled in the rain, unaware of the imminent bloodshed, the bloodshed of a friend. And then he heard the sick buzz of a plane. And then he heard the crash. And then he yelled, to no one in particular, "Somebody's been killed out there!"

A massive search party ensued. Marty Robbins, Chet Atkins, Eddy Arnold, and Ernest Tubb joined in the search that included 700 volunteers, twelve planes, two helicopters, and a boat. However, it wasn't until two days later that the wreckage and bodies were located amid the thick and devastated foliage.

Through the efforts of his enterprising widow, Mary, Jim Reeves continued to score hits through the 1960s and 1970s. In fact, he has scored six posthumous number one hits—more than he had achieved while alive. And, in the early 1980s, through electronic wizardry, he "dueted" with singer Deborah Allen ("Take Me in Your Arms and Hold Me," "Oh, How I Miss You Tonight") and with Patsy Cline ("Have You Ever Been Lonely?"). The latter marked the first time in history that two voices were summoned back from their graves, manipulated in a recording studio, and released for public consumption. All for a few dollars more.

By 1966, after "Ozzie and Harriet" had been mercifully axed from prime time, and his pop records ceased to hit the charts, Ricky-turned-Rick Nelson veered his perpetually adolescent good looks to country music. The albums *Bright Lights and Country Music* and *Country Fever* resulted. In the early 1970s, he scored a Top 10 crossover hit with the autobiographical lament "Garden Party." However, despite the fact that he was gaining increased respect from country-rock aficionados and continuing to appease his other fans with revival shows of the rock and roll variety, it was to be his last substantive success.

On Monday, December 30, 1985, Rick Nelson, forty-five, per-

Ricky Nelson, America's
Wonder Bread heartthrob.

formed at P.J's Lounge in Guntersville, Alabama. Ironically, his
final song that night, and what became the performance finale of
his life, was Buddy Holly's rockin' "Rave On." Holly (who, by the
way, got his start in country music) had lost his young life
twenty-six years before in a single-engine Beech Bonanza over
the winter night skies of Mason City, Iowa. It was a crash that
also snatched the young lives of Ritchie Valens and J. P. Richardson and could have very easily killed twenty-one-year-old Holly
protégé Waylon Jennings, as well. Jennings, in the fateful story
that has often been told, gave up his seat in the small chartered
plane to Richardson and spent the night traveling by bus to
Morehead, North Dakota. The following morning, as he walked
into the hotel lobby, he was greeted by news of the crash
splashed across the front page of the local papers. Reflected
Jennings years later, "It just seemed like such a waste of lives. I
felt responsible, like God had cheated somebody. I was pretty
young, and it took me a while to get back on the right track. No
more than a day goes by, I don't think of him [Holly] still."

On Tuesday, Rick Nelson boarded his forty-three-year-old
DC-3, which had once belonged to Jerry Lee Lewis, and hoped
for the best. The plane was not in good condition, and at least one
band member reportedly threatened to quit the act because of it.
Nevertheless, on this particular journey Rick Nelson was accompanied by the five members of his Stone Canyon Band and his
fiancée, Helen Blair. The pilot was Brad Rank and his copilot was
Kenneth Ferguson. They were en route to a New Year's Eve
performance in Dallas.

Near the Texas border, Rank radioed the Dallas–Fort Worth

The Rick Nelson crash: an explosive tail end.

airport and reported with alarm that smoke had infiltrated the cockpit. He then attempted to make an emergency landing onto a highway, but a moving car obstructed the runway, and Rank, desperate, was forced to settle the plane in a cow pasture near De Kalb, Texas, clipping electrical power lines along the way. It was about 5:15 P.M.

The plane landed intact. And then it burned. The pilots were able to make an escape landing through an emergency hatch in the cockpit. The seven passengers burned to death. Their skeletal remains were found in the front of the cabin, huddled near the cockpit door.

A rash of lawsuits and charges of cocaine usage on the plane have since erupted. Reportedly, cocaine, both metabolized and unmetabolized, was found in Rick Nelson's blood and urine samples, as was marijuana and the painkiller Darvon. At his funeral services, Jesuit Father Frank Parrish sermonized, to unintentional comic effect, "I think of him in heaven, playing his instrument, while all the heavenly beings gather around him—just like the teenagers on earth."

Even after his good looks had charred to ash, even at his own funeral, Rick (or was it Ricky?) Nelson still couldn't shed the despised image of an overaged teenager.

15

THE YOUNG
BABY SPANKER

Six-year-old Nora Jo Catlett of Clarksburg, West Virginia, collected celebrity autographs. Thus, when it was advertised that a troupe of country music stars would be performing at the Nathan Goff Armory, her father, Joseph Catlett Jr., purchased advance tickets from the local volunteer fire department. On September 17, 1972, the night of the show, Nora Jo was instructed by her mother, Janette, to stand in the front row but *not* to approach the stage. Thus, when the performers finished their sets and exited the stage, Nora Jo was advantageously positioned to collect her treasured autographs.

Faron Young's hit single at the time was titled "This Little Girl of Mine." Thus, when he spotted little Nora Jo standing at his feet, he whistled, called her a pretty baby, and invited her to join him onstage. After all, he knew an audience-sapping device when he saw it. He could already hear the little old ladies gushing through their time-worn dentures. But there was a problem. Nora Jo, recalling her mother's words of warning, declined the star's invitation. Naturally, this did not please the star. After Nora Jo continued to ignore his advances, Faron reportedly muttered a few words, walked offstage, grabbed Nora Jo, turned her over, and repeatedly whacked her across the butt, much to the shock of the audience and the alarm of her parents. He then returned to the stage and announced to the crowd that he would no longer perform.

But the scandal had only just begun.

Faron Young, "The Singing Sheriff," was born in Shreveport, Louisiana, on February 5, 1932. He was raised on a dairy farm ("I had to get up every morning at four to milk the cows"), and in a family so poor that he didn't have a birthday cake until he was five years old.

FARON YOUNG
sings
THIS LITTLE GIRL OF MINE
FEATURING: WHATEVER'S LEFT * PLAY NOW, PAY LATER *
FOREVER WAS THE NAME OF OUR SUNSHINE * TO GET TO YOU

STEREO SR 61364

Faron Young's recording of "This Little Girl of Mine" has taken on humorous significance since the scandal of the Nora Jo Catlett affair.

In 1959, he scored his first number one hit with "Sweet Dreams," subsequently tallied a total of thirty-six Top 10 singles, and has become a successful Nashville entrepreneur. He is known for his lascivious tongue, an affinity for the bottle, reported incessant womanizing and a penchant for exercising his trigger finger. In 1972, he gunned down the light fixtures of a Nashville bar called The Clubhouse. In 1987, his wife of thirty-four years, Hilda Young, obtained a divorce, claiming that he had threatened her and their sixteen-year-old daughter with a loaded pistol. Her complaint further alleged that, much to her dismay, Faron repeatedly fired his gun into their kitchen ceiling. She further charged that "on numerous occasions during the marriage of the parties, while in an intoxicated state, the Defendant struck and physically abused" her. Among the jointly owned marital assets cited by Hilda were two buses, a speedboat, and a prize bull. She did not, as can be best ascertained, seek custody of the bull.

SONGS · COMEDY · DANCING · and PLENTY of Good Ole COUNTRY MUSIC!!

Country Music JUBILEE

STAR STUDDED ROAD SHOW

CAST OF OVER 100 FROM THE GRAND OLE OPRY

on our GIANT WIDE SCREEN in EASTMANCOLOR

FARON YOUNG

RELEASED BY CITATION FILMS, INC

In June 1970, Faron Young, who once said, "I'm not an alcoholic, I'm a drunk," was involved in a head-on collision car crash in Nashville. Young suffered a cut through the middle of his tongue, and was arrested by the police for reckless driving.

Following the West Virginia performance on September 17, 1972, Nora Jo was taken to a physician, while her father marched to the local justice of the peace and swore out a warrant for the Sheriff's arrest. By then, Young had fled the county. Nevertheless, his bus was tracked and stopped in neighboring Wood County, where he was arrested. Young pleaded guilty to the charges of assault and battery and paid $35 in fines and court costs.

Just less than a year later, Nora Jo's parents filed a civil suit against Faron Young. The complaint charged Young with striking Nora Jo "15–20 strokes of his hand on her legs and buttocks." The assault, according to the court documents, was "willful, malicious, and unlawful." And according to Catlett, "Faron Young's handprints as well as bruises were left all over her small-framed body." The suit sought $200,000 in damages.

In his defense, Faron's road manager, Louis Redding, contended that Faron had struck Nora Jo only because she had pulled his hair, pulled his microphone cord, and stuck her tongue out at him. Faron claimed that he had raised the back of Nora Jo's dress and only "lightly spanked" her because, as he explained, she had slapped him first and had spat in his face.

The case of the Faron Young–Nora Jo Catlett baby spanking was not settled until almost two years later. The Catlett family was awarded $3,400, only a fraction of what they had sought. After attorney's fees were deducted, they were given $2,266.67. It wasn't an overwhelming sum of money but nonetheless, it was better than an autograph.

16
VICTIMS

The players of country music are, for some inexplicable reason, cursed by the cruel chill of tragedy. It is as if the drama of their music, in some way, makes an extended impression on their personal lives. Or is it merely that the drama of their personal lives is extended into their music? Either way, the eventual results are the same: poignant, volatile, lamentable, tragic, and often highly theatrical.

Texas Ruby Owens, "The Sophie Tucker of Folk Singers" and radio's original cowgirl, was born in Wise County, Texas, on June 4, 1908. In 1937, Ruby paired her sultry-throated vocals with Curly Fox's fiddle bow. Two years later, they were married. Together, they enjoyed a long, successful reign on the Opry. In 1948, they moved to Houston for several years before returning to Nashville and the Opry in 1955. On the night of March 29, 1963, just a few weeks after the tragedies that killed Opry stars Patsy Cline, Cowboy Copas, Hawkshaw Hawkins, and Jack Anglin, Curly returned home from a Friday Opry performance to find his home—and his beloved Ruby—swathed in ash and flames. Curly moved out of Nashville and retired in Illinois.

Luther Perkins, Johnny Cash's guitarist and a founding member of Johnny Cash and the Tennessee Two, went to bed with a burning cigarette in his hand on the night of August 3, 1969. He woke up to a house full of fire. Two days later, he was dead.

"Flat-Top Pickin' Sam McGee," was born on May 1, 1894, in Franklin, Tennessee. Along with his younger brother, Kirk, Sam was a member of Uncle Dave Macon's Fruit Jar Drinkers Band and joined the Grand Ole Opry in 1925, less than a month after it

Texas Ruby (pictured with unidentified man and Curly Fox): Southern Fried Cowgirl.

first went on the air. Although it has been disputed by others, Sam claimed to be the first musician to employ an electric guitar on the Opry stage. And in 1971, at the age of seventy-seven, Sam was honored as the oldest living member of the Opry. Four years later, he was run over by a tractor on his 400-acre farm and was crushed to death.

Guitar great Merle Watson once committed the cardinal country sin by publicly admitting, "I don't especially like country music too much." He cited the southern rock band the Allman Brothers as his preferred musical interest. It was a treasonous sentiment that didn't go unpunished. Early in the morning of October 23, 1985, at the Watson family Appalachian homestead near Lenoir, North Carolina, Merle accidentally cut himself with a table saw and rode, via tractor, to a neighbor's house for treatment. On the way home, the tractor overturned and slid down an embankment. Merle was trapped, pinned under a blade. The entire community ran to his rescue and struggled to release him from the piercing grip of the tractor blade. They failed. Merle Watson was pronounced dead at the scene at 4:15 A.M.

Between 1957 and 1960, Jimmie Rodgers (not to be confused with *the* Jimmie Rodgers of "The Singing Brakeman" fame) had twelve Top 40 *pop* singles, including "Honeycomb," "Kisses Sweeter than Wine," and "Oh, Oh, I'm Falling in Love Again." A six-year dry stretch followed, and in 1966–67, he embarked on a successful comeback. However, following a Los Angeles Christmas party in December 1967, his career plans were thwarted when he was beaten to a near-dead pulp. As he drove home, he was tailed by a driver in another car. The other driver pulled up behind him and motioned for him to pull over on the side of the road. Obliging with the Christmas spirit, Rodgers stopped his car. He should have known better in L.A. The guy got out of his car. Rodgers rolled down his window. He didn't even see the bar as it came crashing into his face. As Rodgers later recalled, "I don't know what transpired because I was unconscious." He was left for dead in his car on the side of the road. Several hours later, he was discovered sprawled across his front seat, with his skull caved in, his right arm broken, and the skin stripped away from one of his legs. He spent the next year in the hospital and underwent brain surgery three times. His assailant, believed to have been an off-duty cop, was never found. In 1985, Jimmie Rodgers returned to Nashville—where he had started his career—with hopes of yet another comeback. This time, in country music.

A few days before Christmas 1981, three bandanna-clad Jamaican terrorists burst into the Johnny Cash estate in Montego Bay. It was 7:30 P.M. Edith Montague, the family housekeeper, was delivering the nightly grace. Also seated at the dinner table were Johnny and June Carter Cash, their eleven-year-old son, John Carter Cash, his friend, Doug Caldwell, Reba Hancock Hussey (Cash's sister), and her husband, Chuck Hussey. Without warning, the three uninvited guests charged into the room bearing a knife, a hatchet, and a .38-caliber pistol. "What do you want?" asked Cash, standing up. "Everything," countered one of the guests, "or the boy [Caldwell] dies."

As later told by Reba Hussey, "They pulled the rings right off our fingers. I had a necklace on and I tried to take it off, but the latch was stuck. I was going to break it, but they wouldn't let me. There were very careful not to damage the jewelry. They pushed [and] shoved, asking all the time if we wanted to die. We were thinking we were going to die at any minute. We were told not to look at them. They kept asking, 'Do you want do die, mon? Keep you head down, mon.' " Cash was ordered to lie face-down on the floor with his hands behind his head. June Carter faked a heart attack, to no avail.

After the impolite intruders concluded ransacking the Cash home, they corralled the group, which included three servants, into a fourteen-by-fourteen-foot concrete room known as the dungeon wine cellar and ordered them to remain there for two hours. However, Cash and Hussey were able to tear apart the

That's June Carter behind those painted eyebrows. When attacked by a trio of Jamaican terrorists, June faked a heart attack.

mahogany door with a scrap of metal and had the victimized group freed in forty-five minutes. The terrorists had fled in June Carter's British Land Rover. They had taken $50,000 in jewelry and cash. Four hours after it had begun, the nightmare was over. By then, tempers were hot and dinner was cold, and the Christmas spirit was in the grubby hands of three bandannaed would-be wise men from Jamaica.

In August, 1986, a would-be robber fired a pistol into the stomach of singer/songwriter Paul Davis, thirty-eight, at the Hall of Fame Motor Inn in Nashville. Davis was hospitalized in critical condition and survived. A few weeks later, his duet with Marie Osmond, "You're Still New to Me," went to number one on the country charts.

On November 27, 1973, James Widner, Hank Snow's leading guitarist, was robbed and murdered at a Nashville Holiday Inn. As for Snow, he had been terrorized as a child by an abusive stepfather.

Country comic Pat Buttram, best known for being Gene Autry's cowboy sidekick and "Mr. Haney" on television's "Petticoat Junction," was dealt a near-fatal blow in 1950 when a small brass cannon exploded—in his arms.

Bobbie Gentry: Vegas rhinoplasty.

On a night in October 1972, Bobbie Gentry, still tepid after the swamp saga success of "Ode to Billy Joe," was headlining at the Desert Inn in Las Vegas. During one of her innumerable rapid costume changes, Bobbie ran backstage and smashed face-first into a speaker and broke her nose. She reportedly finished her show before being escorted to a local hospital.

Ronee Blakely, forty-one-year-old singer and the actress who superbly evoked the Loretta Lynn–like country-queen-in-distress in Robert Altman's *Nashville*, filed suit against the city of Los Angeles in late 1987 for $1 million. In her complaint, Ronee explained that she did not appreciate it when a Los Angeles traffic enforcement officer "drove his vehicle" over her foot. Ronee claimed that she had suffered "serious and disabling personal injury, and emotional upset and distress." The incident occurred on February 5, 1987, near the corner of Sunset Boulevard and Crescent Heights. The traffic cop in question reportedly cited Ronee with two tickets in a twenty-minute period. An unfriendly "discussion" ensued, ending when the officer threatened to drive his vehicle over her foot—and then did.

The clutching shadow of sorrow has no boundaries and lurks unassuming on the city streets of Nashville. Is it just coincidence that Elvis Presley, Jerry Lee Lewis, Carl Perkins and Johnny Cash—country boys who found Sam Phillips and the Sun—all lost a brother under tragic circumstances? Jessie Garon Presley, Elvis's twin, was dead at birth. Elmo Lewis Jr. was killed at the age of eight by a drunk in a flatbed truck. Jay Perkins broke his neck in the Delaware car accident that crushed his brother's dreams of rock and roll glory. Jay suffered for two years before he died. And Jack Cash was only fourteen when he fell upon an electric circular table saw that shredded his stomach. He lived for eleven days more.

Roy Orbison, perhaps the greatest vocalist of them all, was another Sun recording artist with roots deeply imbedded in country music. In 1966, his wife, Claudette, was killed in a motorcycle accident. Roy had been driving a short distance in front of her and unfortunately, witnessed her death. Two years later, two of three sons, ages ten and six, were killed when the Orbison home in Nashville exploded in a barrage of flames.

Bill Anderson, who had many hits during the 1960s and 1970s, is still a fixture on country music television as the host of The Nashville Network's game show "Fandango." One night in October 1984, Anderson's wife, Becky, was driving home when she was plowed into by a drunken driver with a license to kill. Becky survived, but she sustained serious head injuries and brain damage.

Before she achieved success as a country singer, Lacy J. Dalton, then known as Jill Byrem, lived on food stamps and once worked as a topless dancer for two weeks. In 1971, her husband (who also managed her band) had a freak swimming pool accident, colliding with another swimmer. He was paralyzed and died three years later, leaving Lacy to raise their young son by herself.

Jan Howard, born Lula Grace Johnson on a Friday the 13th in

1932, was once considered a contender for the title of "Queen of Country Music." According to her autobiography, *Sunshine and Shadow*, Jan's first husband was a drunken, philandering wife beater, who once threatened to cut her throat with a butcher knife. Another, happier marriage was annulled when her husband discovered that he wasn't legally divorced from his previous wife—whom he went back to. She later married then-struggling songwriter Harlan Howard, who has since become one of the most successful writers in country music history.

Once, according to Jan, Harlan allegedly placed her in a private sanitarium. Another time, Jan wrote, upon catching him with a prostitute in a downtown Nashville motel, she inhaled an entire bottle of Seconal. Then, she wrote, after ten years of marriage, Harlan, the man who wrote "I Fall to Pieces" among many, many others, unceremoniously dumped her.

Jan has been dealt more tragedy (and lived to tell about it) than any other country performer, including the "Heroine of Heartbreak" herself, Tammy Wynette. Jan had three unsuccessful marriages. One of her daughters died in infancy. Another baby girl died in delivery. In 1968, two weeks after she had written and recorded her song "My Son," her son Jimmy, twenty-one, was killed in a mine-field explosion in Vietnam. In 1973, her youngest son, David, a cast member of Opryland U.S.A., killed himself with her .25 caliber pistol. Jan found the body in the upstairs bedroom of their Nashville home. Jan subsequently went into semiretirement. Who can blame her?

Even country music's favorite Strait man is not immune to tragedy.

In March 1970, Ferlin Husky's seventeen-year-old son, Danny, was killed in a head-on collision near Cadiz, Kentucky. At the time, Danny was a drummer in his father's band.

In 1976, Bobby Bare's fifteen-year-old daughter, Cari, died of heart failure. Cari had sung on her father's album, *Singing' in the Kitchen.*

In July 1985, Eddie Rabbit's infant son, Timothy Edward, died less than two days after undergoing a liver transplant.

In June 1986, George Strait's thirteen-year-old daughter, Jennifer, was killed in a car crash in San Marcos, Texas.

In August 1986, Ricky Skaggs's seven-year-old son, Andrew, was riding in the passenger seat of a car driven by Brenda Skaggs, Ricky's ex-wife, on a Roanoke, Virginia, highway. As Brenda attempted to change lanes, truck driver Edward Duehring Jr., thirty-seven, stuck a .38 caliber handgun out the window and shot Andrew in the face. Andrew survived, luckily, and Duehring later claimed that he had been using drugs to stay awake and that the drugs had caused him to hallucinate that unfriendly forces were following him.

And the list, unfortunately, goes on.

It all started, perhaps, with Mary Magdalene Garland, more commonly known as Aunt Molly Jackson. She was born in Clay County, Kentucky, in 1880. When she was six, her mother died of starvation. At the age of ten, she was jailed for her involvement in organizing a union. Later, her brother, husband, and son all died in coal pit accidents. Her father and another brother were blinded in mining accidents. Years later, she became a country music singer.

With her background, what else would she have done?

17
REDNECKS
AREN'T BLACK

Do y'all know why God created Adam as a white man? Ever try
to steal a rib from a nigger?
—Glen Campbell, making a lame attempt at a joke, to his
   audience in Atlantic City

It's no secret that the country music industry is borderline racist. And Nashville itself, buried deep in the muck of the Bible Belt, is far from being the most liberal-minded metropolis. A *recent* poll, published in the *Wall Street Journal*, reported that 24 percent of Nashville men and 28 percent of Nashville women believe that interracial marriage should be *outlawed*. As for Music Row, suffice it to say that *not one* black has been elected to the Country Music Hall of Fame and only a pathetic pittance of performers with color have been accepted into the decidedly white-breaded bosom of the industry.

Deford Bailey, the "Harmonica Wizard," was the first musician to perform on the Grand Ole Opry. And on September 28, 1928, he became one of the first artists to record in Nashville when he performed eight numbers for Victor Records. Nevertheless, he was considered to be no more than the Opry's novelty mascot. While touring, Bailey frequently had to pretend that he was Uncle Dave Macon's personal servant in order to obtain food and lodging. It was a demeaning guise but one that he was familiar with wearing. At the age of three, he had been afflicted by infantile paralysis. Not only was he black, he was also stunted. He was 4'10", weighed less than a hundred pounds, and had a deformed cavity of a chest. But, oh, could he ever blow a roomful of blues out of a mouthpiece. Nevertheless, in 1941, after fifteen years with the Opry, Deford Bailey was fired. Boss man George Hay contended that Bailey was ousted because he was lazy, "like

The Ku Klux Klan was formed in Pulaski, Tennessee, just south of Nashville, in 1865. In 1986, after moving into an all-white Nashville community, a black family found a ten-foot-high wooden cross burning in its front yard at 3:00 A.M. on a Sunday. Earlier, it had found a white sign in their yard. It read, "KKK."

some members of his race." Exiled, Bailey abandoned his music, professionally at least, and was later reduced to shining shoes at a stand on 12th Avenue South in Nashville. In 1982, at the age of eighty-two, Deford Bailey died an embittered man.

Linda Martell has the distinction of being the first black female singer to *guest* (she was not invited to be a regular member) on the Opry. Her first single release, "Color Him Father," hit number twenty-two on the *Billboard* charts in 1969; however, subsequent recordings were less successful, and she resigned herself to being only a colorful mark in country music history.

O. B. McClinton, "the Chocolate Cowboy," had several country hits in the early 1970s, and in 1984 scored with a song entitled "Honky Tonk Tan." In 1976, McClinton publicly campaigned to, in his words, "de-taboo" use of the word *nigger*. He recorded a song called "Black Speck, Nigger, Sang Like a Redneck." Said McClinton, "I'm going to crusade so that someday the niggers, the polacks, kikes, gooks, whites, anybody can laugh their names off. If you've got clothing in the closet that stinks, take it out and air it out." In September 1986, McClinton was diagnosed as having cancer. Reba McEntire, Ricky Skaggs, Waylon Jennings, and a few other individuals rallied behind him with a benefit concert that raised $41,000 to defray his medical expenses. A year later, he was dead in Nashville.

Between 1974 and 1979, Ruby Falls, born Bertha Dorsey, scored nine hits on the country charts. However, as the hits ceased, Ruby renounced the music industry and reportedly got a job with a computer firm. She later died of a brain hemorrhage at the age of forty.

I'm the Jackie Robinson of country and western music.
—Charley Pride

"I'm blushing, only you can't tell."
—Charley Pride

Red Sovine and Willie Nelson were among those who helped Charley Pride early in his career. And on the televised Country Music Association's awards show in the early 1970s, Loretta Lynn innocently caused a rather inane controversy by warmly and *openly* hugging Charley.

In essence, there has been *one* black country music star—the black man with the white voice, Charley Pride. There was simply no way to deny him. Some thought, and even dared to utter, that he had the best country voice since Hank Williams himself. Still, when he first started out in Nashville, it was within a tense ring of fear. RCA, his record label, deliberately refrained from publicizing his color and opted not to distribute his publicity photographs. Company executive Chet Atkins later admitted, "I worried about it a lot because I didn't know a heck of a lot about the people in Mississippi and Alabama, and was afraid that some of the record stations might block our records if we sent out Charley's single without some sort of explanation, and they'd later discover he was black and they had been tricked. But, in the end, we let it go on its own merits and, if it were a hit, then we didn't owe anybody any apologies." The song was "Just Between You and Me," and in 1966 it became a hit.

A short time later, Charley was scheduled to perform live in front of a large crowd for the first time. However, the audience, who was familiar with his hit single, did *not* know that he was black. Upon his introduction, he was given the customary enthusiastic response—until he stepped out onto the stage. As the applause hushed, Charley stepped into the light and quipped, "I realize this is kind of unique—me coming out here on a country show wearing this permanent tan."

It was at that time that Willie Nelson escorted Charley on a performance tour of the South. In Louisiana, Charley was not allowed into the motel and was forced to sleep in Willie's room. Then, at a performance now legendary in the annals of country music, Willie introduced his young protégé. As Charley approached him onstage, Willie surprised him with a kiss, square on the mouth. It wasn't a kiss of passion. It was a kiss of approval.

In 1971, "Country Charley Pride" was named the Country Music Association's Entertainer of the Year. In the early 1970s, he scored a hot streak of five number ones in a row. Now he has had nearly thirty number one hits, more than fifty Top 10 hits, and the distinction of being RCA's all-time biggest-selling recording artist next to Elvis Presley. By 1984, his estate was estimated at $30 million dollars. Not bad for a former cotton-picking, baseball-playing black boy from Sledge, Mississippi. He might be the only black star in country music, but at least his talent has been extremely well rewarded.

Stringbean: He wore a long, forlorn expression. . . .

18
"HEE HAW" HORROR— THE STRINGBEAN MURDERS

I t was like any other Saturday night in Nashville. Almost. On November 10, 1973, cousins John and Doug Brown, ages twenty-four and twenty-three, parked their Buick not far from the home of David and Estelle Akeman. They raised the hood to give the impression that they had experienced mechanical difficulties and were forced to abandon the car. And then they walked, with premeditated steps, the rest of the distance to the house. It was situated in a wooded, isolated area between Ridgetop and Goodlettsville, Tennessee. It wasn't a house, really. It was more like a shack. A red three-room shack. It was dilapidated and small, hardly befitting a star of the Grand Ole Opry and a regular cast member of television's "Hee Haw."

David Akeman, fifty-seven, better known as Stringbean, had been on the Opry since 1942. He was well known for his banjo picking, his homespun humor, and his rather unconventional appearance. He exaggerated his 6'2", string-thin frame by typically wearing a long, forlorn expression, a long, dresslike shirt that hung down well past his thighs, and a pair of stunted trousers that fastened at the knee. He was lovable and unflappable, and not unlike a scarecrow in his stage persona.

That Saturday night, some 3,000 tourists jammed into the church-pew bleachers of the Ryman Auditorium to see the first of two shows at the Grand Ole Opry. Little did they know that they soon would witness the tragic curtain call of a beloved comic. The first show started at 7:00 P.M. Stringbean was introduced to the audience by Tex Ritter, the singing cowboy (who would be dead himself only a few weeks later when he journeyed to the Metro jail in Nashville to arrange bail for one of his band members and suffered a fatal heart attack on the spot). At the Opry, Stringbean delivered his one-liners with customary deft-

"He just shot her in the back of her head, like a dog. Then he went back to the cabin carrying her bag and grinning."
—An informant on John Brown's murder of Estelle Akeman

ness and sang two songs "Y'All Come," and "I'm Going to the Grand Old Opry and Make Myself a Name."

John and Doug Brown broke into the house through the window of the back door. And then they began their search. The had heard that Stringbean stashed a lot of cash in his house and on his person. Specifically, they had been told that $20,000 was hidden somewhere in the shack, and they were determined not to leave without it. When their search yielded only a chainsaw and some guns, they decided in exasperation to wait for Stringbean to come home—and get their money in person. They confiscated a few beers from String's refrigerator. They smoked a few cigarettes. They turned the radio dial to WSM, reclined on Stringbean's furniture, and listened to his performance on the Grand Ole Opry. And they waited.

Following the second show, Stringbean changed into his bib overalls, packed his costume into his duffel bag, zipped up his banjo case, and headed out to his car in the parking lot. It was a brand-new green Cadillac. String lived in country simplicity, but he traveled in city style—it was just one of his quirks. He got into the passenger side of the car. His wife, Estelle, sat behind the steering wheel as she always did. It was approaching 11:00 P.M. as

Stringbean, gunned down in his country shack.

Estelle maneuvered the car out of the lot. It usually took about thirty minutes to get back home.

Estelle drove up the driveway and let Stringbean out. He walked to the front door, fumbled for his key, and turned the knob. As he stepped inside the house and set down his banjo, he was confronted by an unfriendly face with hot-flushed liquor on his breath and money on his mind. It was Doug Brown. An argument ensued. String reached for the gun in the duffel bag that carried his costume. But it was too late. Doug's cousin, John, bolted out of hiding, aimed his gun at Stringbean's chest, and fired. String fell to the floor.

Outside, Estelle, who had been parking the car, heard the gunfire and fled as fast as her fifty-nine-year-old legs would take her. It was a race for life or death. John Brown chased after her. He had already killed one person and was hungry for more. He caught up with her on the front-yard lawn, about forty yards from the house. Estelle fell to the ground, Brown pointed his gun. Estelle got up on her hands and knees and begged for her life. Brown fired three times. Estelle fell, face-first, onto the grass.

The final curtain?

At 6:40 the following morning, Opry star Grandpa Jones arrived at the house to pick Stringbean up for their scheduled hunting expedition. He didn't know that the prey had already been slaughtered. The first thing he saw, as he drove up the driveway, was Estelle's body sprawled out on the front yard, her right hand clutching a fistful of grass. Closer inspection revealed that a bullet had lodged in her brain. Jones then found Stringbean, spread out on the floor beside the wood-burning fireplace. His familiar spectacles were on the floor beside him. There was a gun in one of his hands, blood on his overalls, and a bullet in his chest.

The subsequent investigation, conducted by detectives Sherman Nickens, Thomas Jacobs, Dave Roberts, and Bobby Green, was among the most intense ever undertaken by the Nashville police department. They scanned the dark corners of an entire city. One of their earliest and easiest determinations was that the killers had not obtained what they had sought. Three thousand one hundred and eighty dollars was found in the bib pocket of Stringbean's overalls, and $2,150 was found in a tobacco pouch stuffed into Estelle's bra. All that the killers got away with was $250, one of Stringbean's costumes, the murder weapon, a chainsaw, and Stringbean's guns. It was the latter two items that gave the detectives the physical evidence that they needed to solve their case. John and Doug Brown were charged with double murder in the first degree. Doug's brothers, Charlie and Roy Brown, were charged as accessories.

The trial began on November 5, 1974, amid heated public speculation. An Opry star had been gunned down in cold blood, and his public demanded justice. Roy Acuff campaigned for the reinstatement of capital punishment, while John Brown's attorney attempted to get his client off the jagged-edged hook by claiming insanity. To support this contention, Brown's father was called in to testify that, as a boy, John had yanked the wings off birds, and severed the tails off cats. The testimony, however, illustrated more sadism than insanity and was dismissed. On November 9, 1974, almost a year to the day after the slayings, John and Doug Brown were convicted of two counts of murder in the first degree. They were sentenced to life in prison.

That night, the Opry performances went on as scheduled. The grim memory of that macabre Saturday night when the Opry was jolted out of its conservative complacency was all but lost amid the flurry of saccharine frivolity. But, ole Stringbean was not entirely forgotten. He was still being seen, in some areas, on the television reruns of "Hee Haw."

Nothing like a dead cast member to boost the ratings.

For his funeral, String was buried in a blue suit and tie instead of his preferred attire. Roy Acuff, Bill Anderson, Bill Monroe, Porter Wagoner, and Tex Ritter, among others, attended his funeral. All of the Grand Ole Opry members were made honorary pallbearers.

19
THEY DIED TOO YOUNG

T he hero climbed atop his horse, and as the music swelled to a sentimental crescendo, he rode off into the cowboy sunset and never looked back. . . .

It's a familiar finale in our culture. Live fast and make a dramatic exit off into the horizon—and you'll never be forgotten. Actually, it all started with that sheiklike tango dancer with the slicked-back hair and the big Italian sausage. His name was Rudolph Valentino and he died at the age of thirty-one from blood poisoning, or a wounded male ego, or some such nonsense. Ever since, other stars, male and female, have followed in his funeral procession and waltzed off to their graves while they were still young enough to dance.

Early death is certainly not just a Hollywood tradition, though at times one is given that impression. Country music has had more than its share, sadly, of those who died too young. Of course, some have been more missed than others. Hank Williams, who died at the age of twenty-nine, most notably comes to mind. He compressed incomparable brilliance into such a short span that one can't help but wonder, *What if.* . . . What if he had lived a life of normal duration? What if his talent had more time to develop? *What if.* . . .

Before there was Hank Williams, there was Jimmie Rodgers. Rodgers, the wailing, yodeling "Singing Brakeman" was born the son of a railroad section foreman in 1897. His mother died of tuberculosis when he was four, and Jimmie himself was always ill as a child. At the age of fourteen, he quit school and, like his father, got a job on the railroad. For years an amateur singer, Jimmie recorded his first solo tracks, "Sleep Baby Sleep" and "Soldier's Sweetheart" in 1927. A million-seller, "Blue Yodel" (now known as "T for Texas"), followed, as did other million-sellers, despite the fact that the country had been crippled by economic depression. By the early 1930s, he had established himself as the first major commercial star of country music. He has since been dubbed "the Father" of the genre (as opposed to "the King") and in 1961 became the first person elected to the Country Music Hall of Fame. Certainly, along with Hank Williams, he has had more impact on the music than any other individual in history.

But in 1933, Jimmie Rodgers was just a hillbilly singer, albeit a well-known hillbilly singer, who had a penchant for wailing the blues and, unfortunately, a devastatingly wracking cough. By May he was critically ill with an incessant fever and had languished down to haggard flesh and protruding bone. Nevertheless, he arrived in New York City on May 14 for a recording session at Victor's Studios at 153 East 24th Street. He had lost all else, but he still had that voice.

The session of twelve songs took just over a week to record. For Jimmie Rodgers they were days of debilitating pain, pain that he had accepted and befriended as it became familiar. Death was imminent. And everyone there, including Rodgers himself, was acquiescent to that fact. He collapsed frequently, and a cot had to be erected for him in the studio. Occasionally his neck and back had to be propped up with pillows so that his mouth could reach the microphone. It was a wrenching sight. Still he persevered, driven by the desire to have his final voice on record.

When the sessions were completed, Jimmie decided to take an extra day in New York. He wanted to go to Coney Island. It was his death wish. Escorted by a hired nurse, he ate a hot dog, drank a beer, and perhaps shared a last laugh. Enroute back to his hotel room, Jimmie collapsed. That night, he suffered from massive tubercular hemorrhaging. Before daybreak, he slipped into a coma and soon succumbed, drowning in his own blood.

His body was transported via train back to his hometown of Meridian, Mississippi. As the train pulled into the mourner-mobbed Union Station, it moaned a lonesome whistle blow that echoed throughout the southern landscape. It was a poignant tribute and an appropriate finale for Jimmie Rodgers, the man who sang the hillbilly blues. He was thirty-five years old.

Harry Choates

THE FIDDLE KING OF CAJUN SWING

HIS ORIGINAL
1946-1949 RECORDINGS

GOLD STAR RECORDING CO. HOUSTON TEXAS

Gold Star

KING of the HILLBILLIES

1313-A

LOUISIANA
STRING BAND

BASILE WALTZ

HARRY CHOATES
and his fiddle

FULL RANGE

Harry Choates (left), the prodigal fiddler, who was an alcoholic at the age of twelve.

Harry Choates, "the Cajun Fiddler," was born near Rayne, Louisiana, on December 26, 1922. In 1946, his recording of "Jole Blon" became the biggest-selling Cajun song ever produced and the unofficial Cajun national anthem. At the age of twenty-four, Choates was one of the preeminent men in his field. But, like that of many prodigies, his genius was shadowed by a lurking self-destruction. He chased too many women and had been a heavy drinker since the age of twelve. By 1950 a pathetic drunk, he abandoned his wife and two small children. And on July 14, 1951, while performing at a dance hall in Austin, Texas, Choates was arrested by the local police for the desertion and nonsupport of his wife and children. He was thrown in jail without bail.

While imprisoned, Choates allegedly slipped into a coma. On July 17, he was pronounced dead. His family was given no account of the circumstances surrounding his death. The official cause of death was reported to be "Fatty metamorphosis of the Liver and Chronic Interstitial Nephritis"—both of which are generally associated with excessive intake of alcohol. Other reports contended that he had suffered an epileptic fit. The most popular theory, however, is that he had been beaten to death by unidentified sources. He was twenty-eight years old.

Mel Street was forty-five years old, and like the others included here, died without realizing the full extent of his great promise. Born King Malachi Street on October 21, 1933, in Grundy, West Virginia, he didn't score his first hit single until he was thirty-nine—"Borrowed Angel" in 1972. Over the next six years, he had twelve Top 20 hits. His final record entered the *Billboard* charts the week of his death. It was entitled, ironically, "Just Hangin' On" and chronicled the life of a man at the end of his rope.

On Saturday, October 21, 1978, Mel Street walked down the

In the 1970s, some thought that Mel Street had the best voice in country music next to his idol, George Jones. Jones later sang "Amazing Grace" at Street's funeral.

stairs of his Nashville home and sat down at the family breakfast table. It was his forty-fifth birthday. It was also an exciting time to be in Nashville. October was, as it always is, "Country Music Month," which is annually accompanied by a seemingly endless parade of parties, awards shows, and miscellaneous conviviality. And bemused gossip about Tammy Wynette and the mysterious masked gunman who choked her with a pair of pantyhose was rampant in the industry. Every day, it seemed, the newspapers were full of stories about additional threats made on the life of poor ole Tammy.

But, unlike many others, Mel Street was not laughing. He was lost in his own dark thoughts. Earlier that year, he had moved out of the family home, reportedly because of his excessive drinking. He returned home in March but by summer's end had resumed his addiction to the bottle. Said his wife, Betty, "The week before Mel's death—two weeks really—were a complete and total breakdown of his mind." On the eve of his birthday, Mel had been scheduled to perform at George Jones's Possum Holler nightclub in downtown Nashville. However, he telephoned his manager and friend Jim Prater and explained that he would not be able to make the performance. Prater responded, "Fine, I'll take care of it," to which Street replied, "I know you will. You've always done it, and I've always loved you for that." Prater later reflected, "That was the only time he ever used that word to me. Then he just hung up."

Street finished his conversation with Betty and his brother Cleve and excused himself from the breakfast table. He then walked up the stairs, put a .38 in his mouth, and blew his brains out, all over the façade of domestic perfection. He was pronounced dead at Nashville Memorial Hospital at 11:10 A.M.

He cried while listening to George Jones records. He was rich and talented and sad, a prince without a palace, and seemed, somehow, to embody the paradox of American youth in the late 1960s and early 1970s. He was a handsome stallion of spirit, speeding with poetic gait across a breezy, lush, country field in search of peace and purpose and resolve. Somewhere along the journey, however, he stumbled upon worldly temptations. And instead of freeing the world of its ugliness, he ingested its poisons and slowly but surely destroyed his mind and then his body.

Gram Parsons was a deeply sensitive, equally troubled young

Gram Parsons, with the youthful, unmistakable glint of promise shining in his eyes.

son of the South. His father, "Coon Dog" Connor, an amateur musician, committed suicide on Christmas Day when Gram was thirteen. His mother, more a proponent of southern money than southern soul, married millionaire Robert Parsons and died of malnutrition associated with alcoholism on the day before Gram graduated from high school.

Upon acceptance to Harvard University, Gram decided to major in theology. As he later commented, "I was into God then." However, within a few weeks, he grew disillusioned by the heavy chains of age-old books and nonsensical regulations and dropped out of school.

He wanted to soar. One way was with acid, the drug of a generation. Another way was with music. *His* music. He wanted to sit on the stars and conduct the orchestra. He wanted to fuse the whites with the blacks and the rednecks. He wanted to fuse the rockers with the shitkickers and the hillbillies. He wanted to fuse rock and roll with country. And he did. Only almost no one recognized it at the time.

After his country group, the International Submarine Band, disbanded in 1967 with an unsuccessful album (*Safe at Home*) to its credit, Gram joined the celebrity rock/folk group the Byrds. He almost immediately swayed the creative direction of the group with his decidedly country leanings. An album, *Sweethearts of the Rodeo* (1968), resulted. It was the first country/rock album in recorded history.

Still, almost no one listened. In July 1968, as the other Byrds flew off to South Africa, Gram boycotted the trip and flew the proverbial coop in protest of apartheid (unheard-of in 1968). He quit the band and roamed the streets of London, a boy and his guitar, and was befriended by Keith Richards and other rolling stones of all musical persuasion.

Following his trip to Europe and beyond, Gram returned to Los Angeles and formed another extension of his musical soul, the Flying Burrito Brothers. A critically well-received album, *The Gilded Palace of Sin*, resulted. Still, almost no one listened. Shortly following the album's release, Gram fell off his motorcycle and tumbled onto a California highway. With his beauty bruised and his determination dulled, he hobbled back to Europe, where he slipped and slid between purity and debauchery on the playground of youth. He was twenty-three years old.

Upon his return to southern California, which kept pulling him back by parting its legs with the promise of stardom, Gram recorded a solo album, *GP.* During the sessions, he reportedly fell to the floor more than once, drunk with the best tequila and

Gram Parsons

Grievous Angel

Before there were Willie, Waylon, the Eagles, Linda Ronstadt, and Emmylou Harris, there was Gram Parsons, the troubled pioneer who invented country/rock. Virtually ignored during his lifetime, it wasn't until several years after his death that his voice would really begin to be heard.

chemicals that money could buy. For, although his musical career floundered between critical acclaim and public obscurity, Gram was able to summon wealth from the generous trust fund that had been allocated to him by his stepfather. With *GP*, which received critical, if not commercial, success (again), Gram introduced to the world a new singer with the voice of a fallen angel. Her name was Emmylou Harris.

It was Gram's increasingly close relationship with Emmylou that reportedly signaled the end of his marriage, which had already been teetering on the cold and jagged rocks. Reportedly, during one of their fights over Emmylou, Gram's wife, Gretchen, slashed his face with a coat hanger and chipped away a piece of his ear, leaving him partially deaf. Following the completion of *Grievous Angel*, another album that featured Emmylou, Gram fled the ties that bound him to Los Angeles and checked into a small desert retreat at Joshua Tree, California. He was accompanied by a friend, Michael Martin, and two women, Margaret Fisher and Dale McElroy.

He spent the afternoon of September 19, 1973, at various Joshua Tree taverns drinking tumblers of tequila and shooting pool. That night, while the others went out for pizza, or some other delectable atrocity, Gram sat in a chair in Room 10 of the Joshua Tree Inn and ingested morphine and cocaine and amphetamines and more tequila. He stared at the desert through his motel room window and swallowed his delusions and bedraggled idealism as a killer swizzle stick swilled around the dulled cells of his brain. When his friends returned, bellies full, Gram Parsons, the Prince of Promise, was dead. He was twenty-six years old.

Two days later, at Los Angeles International Airport, Gram's corpse was stolen and stashed into a hearse. His stepfather, Robert Parsons, had summoned the body back to New Orleans, but Gram's friends plotted otherwise. Phil Kaufman, his manager, and Michael Martin, still belching pizza, intercepted the corpse and carted it back to Joshua Tree—reportedly fulfilling a pact that Kaufman had made with Gram a short time before. There, under the burning desert sun, Gram Parsons bowed to his public and ascended in a burst of hot, brilliant passion and flames.

It wasn't exactly tantamount to a cowboy's last ride into a Technicolor horizon, but it was, even by country music's grandiose, rhinestone standards, pretty damn spectacular.

> In my hour of darkness,
> In my time of need
> Oh Lord, grant me vision,
> Oh, Lord, grant me speed
> —Gram Parsons and Emmylou Harris
>   "In My Hour of Darkness"

ENCORE . . .

You got to have smelt a lot of mule manure, before you can sing like a hillbilly.
  —Hank Williams

BIBLIOGRAPHY

BOOKS

Allen, Bob. *George Jones: The Saga of an American Singer* (New York: Dolphin, 1984).

Bart, Teddy. *Inside Music City USA* (New York: Aurora Publishers, Inc., 1970).

Byworth, Tony. *The History of Country & Western Music* (Los Angeles: Exeter, 1984).

Caress, Jay. *Hank Williams: Country Music's Tragic King* (Briarcliff Manor, NY: Stein and Day, 1979).

Causey, Warren B. *The Stringbean Murders* (Salt Lake City: Quest Publishing Inc., 1975).

Cornfield, Robert, with Marshall Fallwell Jr. *Just Country* (New York: McGraw-Hill, 1976).

Country Music Who's Who (Record World, 1972).

Current Biography (New York: H. W. Wilson, 1969).

Gentry, Linnell. *A History and Encyclopedia of Country, Western and Gospel Music* (St. Clair Shores, MI: Scholarly, 1972).

Howard, Jan. *Sunshine and Shadow* (New York: Richardson & Steirman, 1987).

Hume, Martha. *You're So Cold I'm Turnin' Blue* (New York: Viking, 1982).

Hurst, Jack. *Nashville's Grand Ole Opry* (New York: Harry N. Abrams, Inc., 1975).

Lewis, Myra, with Murray Silver. *Great Balls of Fire* (New York: Quill, 1982).

Morris, Edward. *The Journal of Country Music* (1986).

Nash, Alanna. *Dolly* (Newton, MA: Reed Books, 1978).

Nashville Men (YMCA, 1902).

Nassour, Ellis. Patsy Cline (New York: Leisure Books, 1985).

Nelson, Susie. *Heart Worn Memories* (Austin, TX: Eakin Press, 1987).

Number One Country Songs of the 70's & 80's (Wauwatosa, WI: Hal Leonard Publishing Corporation, 1984).

Rollie, George, and Ralph Jerry Christian. *Nashville: A Pictorial History* (Norfolk, VA: Donning Company, 1981).

Tosches, Nick. *Hellfire: The Jerry Lee Lewis Story* (New York: Delacorte Press, 1982).

Williams, Hank, Jr., with Michael Bane. *Living Proof* (New York: Putnam, 1979).

Wren, Christopher S. *Winners Got Scars Too* (New York: Dial Press, 1971).

Wynette, Tammy, and Joan Dew. *Stand By Your Man* (New York: Simon & Schuster, 1979).

ARTICLES

Allen, Bob. "George Jones, Country Music's Tragic Hero," *Hustler*, May 1980.

Allen, Bob. "Freddy Fender, Bright Lights and Lonely Nights." *Hustler*, June 1981.

Anders, John. "Who Was That Masked Man?," *Dallas Morning News*, Dec. 13, 1975.

Anderson, Patrick. "The Real Nashville," *New York Times Magazine*, Aug. 31, 1975.

Andrews, Stephen. "Makin' Nashville Country Again," *Hustler*, Nov. 1987.

Axthelm, Pete. "Sharing Something American," *Newsweek*, June 20, 1983.

Bane, Michael. "David Allan Coe's Long Hard Ride," *Country Music*, January/February 1985.

"Barbara Mandrell Has Surgery on Leg After Head-on Crash," *Nashville Banner*, Sept. 12, 1984.

Blanche, Ed. "Kris Not Cured But In Control," *The Tennessean*, May 2, 1978.

Braudy, Susan. "The Queen of Country Music: 'Stand by Your Man,'" *Ms*, March 1973.

Braun, Saul. "Good Ole Boy," *Playboy*, Nov. 1970.

Brown, M. Eileen. "Campbell Speaks His Mind—But Not So Gently," *Arlington Heights Herald*, Jan. 7, 1983.

Burger, Frederick. "Country's 'Outlaw' Hustler Settles in on Big Pine Key," *Miami Herald*, Aug. 19, 1979.

Burke, Tom. "Kris Kristofferson's Talking Blues," *Rolling Stone*, Apr. 25, 1974.

Burke, Tom. "Kris Kristofferson Sings the Good-Life Blues," *Esquire*, Dec. 1976.

Burton, Charlie. "We Don't Smoke Marijuana in Muskogee. We Steal.," *Rolling Stone*, March 18, 1971.

Campbell, Glen. "My Good Times and Bad," *Ladies Home Journal*, Feb. 1970.

Canfield, Clarke. "Singer Paycheck Arrested in Ohio Tavern Shooting," *Nashville Banner*, Dec. 19, 1985.

Carlisle, Dolly, "Barely Afloat in a Sea of Troubles, C and W Star George Jones Plots His Own Rescue," *People*, Jan. 15, 1979.

Carlisle, Dolly. "The Fall and Rise of George Jones," *Penthouse*, Nov. 1980.

Carrigan, Shaun. "Cash Holdup Suspects Arrested," *Nashville Banner*, Jan. 4, 1982.

Cash, Johnny. "Singer Johnny Cash: Why Country Music Has Swept U.S.," *U.S. News & World Report*, Feb. 27, 1978.

Caulfield, Deborah. "Marie Osmond—The Mormon Madonna?," *Los Angeles Times*, Oct. 27, 1985.

Cramer, Richard Ben. "The Strange and Mysterious Death of Mrs. Jerry Lee Lewis," *Rolling Stone*, March 1, 1984.

"Crossover Artist, Glen Campbell, Comes to Town," *The* (Plant City, Florida) *Courier*, Feb. 27, 1986.

Crowe, Cameron. "The Kristoffersons Make It," *Rolling Stone*, Feb. 23, 1978.

Cunningham, Laura. "The Very Long Nights of Kris Kristofferson," *Esquire*, Nov. 1981.

Demaret, Kent. "Buck Owens Roamed While His Fiddler Burned, But Now He's Back on Bended Knee," *People*, July 18, 1977.

Demaret, Kent. "Rick Nelson 1940–1985," *People*, Jan. 20, 1986.

Edwards, Joe. "Barbara Mandrell Is Just Waiting," *The Nashville Banner*, Nov. 15, 1985.

Eipper, Laura. "A 'Bad Guy' Image in a Sensitive Man," *The Tennessean*, May 26, 1978.

Eipper, Laura. "Loretta Lynn Tells of Drug Addiction, Cure," *The Tennessean*, March 8, 1978.

Eipper, Laura. "Porter's Bitter Remarks Turn Dolly's Happiest Hour Sour," *The Tennessean*, Oct. 12, 1978.

Erickson, Michael. "Jones Wants Fans to Know 'I'm Tryin,'" *Nashville Banner*, July 19, 1982.

Flippo, Chet. "Waylon Jennings Gets off the Grind 'Em Out Circuit," *Rolling Stone*, Dec. 6, 1973.

Flippo, Chet. "David Allan Coe: Don't Fence Him In," *Rolling Stone*, July 18, 1974.

Flippo, Chet. "Tanya the Teenage Teaser," *Rolling Stone*, Sept. 26, 1974.

Flippo, Chet. "The Mysterious Rhinestone Cowboy," *Gallery*, Dec. 1974.

Flippo, Chet. "Waylon Jennings," *Penthouse*, Sept. 1981.

Gallagher, Kathleen. "Waylon Back on Stage After Drug Arrest Charge," *The Tennessean*, Aug. 25, 1977.

"Gatlin Illness Cancels White House Concert," *The Tennessean*, June 22, 1984.

"George Jones," *Country Music*, January/February 1984.

Goldman, Stuart. "Asleep at the Wheel, America's Hottest Country Band," *Hustler*, Oct. 1980.

Goldman, Stuart, (with profile by Mark Humphreys). "Jerry Lee Lewis, White Wild Man of Rock," *Oui*, May 1981.

"Grand Opry," *Newsweek*, Oct. 18, 1943.

Greenblatt, Mike. "Jerry Lee Lewis, Killer on the Loose," *Gallery*, July 1987.

Grissim, John, Jr. "California White Man's Shit Kickin' Blues," *Rolling Stone*, June 28, 1969.

Grissim, John, Jr. "Jerry Lee Busted and on and off Wagon," *Rolling Stone*, March 18, 1971.

Grobel, Lawrence. "Dolly Parton Interview," *Playboy*, Oct. 1978.

Hance, Bill. "Music Row Sees 'End' of Coe," *Nashville Banner*, Apr. 8, 1977.

Hance, Bill. "Gatlin Responds to Criticism in 'No Autographs' Fuss," *Nashville Banner*, July 14, 1978.

Hance, Bill. "Loretta Tells of Her 'Other Lives,' " *Nashville Banner*, Jan. 19, 1980.

Harvey, Lynn. "Never Said I Killed, Irate Rhinestone Cowboy Says," *The Tennessean*, Dec. 16, 1975.

Henry, David. "West, Metcalf Reach Divorce Settlement," *Nashville Banner*, Apr. 2, 1981.

Henstell, Bruce. "How the King of Western Swing Reached the End of His Rope," *Los Angeles Magazine*, June 1979.

Hickey, Neil. " 'If There Is a Hatchet, Let's Bury It,' " *TV Guide*, Oct. 8, 1983.

Hilburn, Robert. "Nothing Can Take the Place of the Human Heart: A Conversation with Johnny Cash," *Rolling Stone*, March 1, 1973.

Hilburn, Robert. "Kristofferson's Latest Obsession: Politics," *Los Angeles Times*, Apr. 26, 1987.

Hughes, Betty. "Nashville," *Los Angeles Times*, Sept. 28, 1986.

Hume, Martha. "The Highway of Life," *Rolling Stone.* May 5, 1977.

Hurst, Jack. "Whole Lot of Changin' Going On," *The Tennessean*, Dec. 12, 1970.

Jahr, Cliff. "Marie Osmond: On Her Own at Last," *Ladies Home Journal*, Nov. 1985.

Kay, Elizabeth. "The Memphis Blues Again," *Rolling Stone*, Nov. 21, 1985.

King, Larry. "David Allan Coe's Greatest Hits," *Esquire*, July 1976.

Logan, Joe. "Kristofferson Has a New Act and a Rosy Outlook," *Denver Post*, Aug. 18, 1985.

Loggins, Kirk. "New Arrest Seen in Jennings Case," *The Tennessean*, Aug. 26, 1977.

Lomax III, John, and Robert K. Oermann. "The Heavy 100 of Country Music," *Esquire*, Apr. 1982.

"Loretta Lynn," *Penthouse*, March 1980.

Malone, Pat. "Happy Glen and Tanya Confess They Fight Like Beasts," *San Antonio Express*, Dec. 21, 1980.

"Mandrell Files Suit over Crash," *The Tennessean*, Sept. 12, 1985.

"Mandrell Is Injured in Collision," *The Tennessean* Sept. 5, 1984.

"Marie Osmond's Husband Is Censured by the Mormons as the Singer Heads Back to Mom," *People*, Dec. 10, 1984.

McCall, Michael. "Larry Gatlin Admits Drug Problem Almost Month After Seeking Help," *Nashville Banner*, Jan. 1, 1985.

McGee, Mike. "Gatlin Minus the Cocaine, a Refreshing Change," *The Southern Standard*, Feb. 7, 1987.

McMurran, Kristin, and Dolly Carlisle. "A Battered Tammy Wynette Relives the Macabre Abduction That Nearly Killed Her," *People*, Oct. 23, 1978.

Means, Andrew. "Glen Campbell," *The Arizona Republic*, Dec. 25, 1983.

Moynihan, Maura, and Andy Warhol. "Dolly Parton Interview," *Interview*, July 1984.

Neese, Sandy. "An Outspoken 'Outlaw,' " *The Tennessean*, July 9, 1983.

Neese, Sandy. "Larry Gatlin in Drug Abuse Rehabilitation," *The Tennessean*, Jan. 4, 1985.

O'Donnell, Red. "Cash Denies Drug, Marital Rumors," *Nashville Banner*, Sept. 4, 1979.

Oermann, Robert K. "Old Report Tells of Hank Williams' Last Hours," *The Tennessean*, Dec. 16, 1982.

Oermann, Robert K. "Waylon: The Outlaw Who Went for Broke," *The Tennessean*, Nov. 5, 1983.

Oermann, Robert K. "After 21 Years, Waylon Says He's Drug-Free," *The Tennessean*, June 16, 1984.

Oermann, Robert K. "Choked-Up Barbara Back: 'I Thank God I'm Alive,' " *The Tennessean*, Jan. 4, 1985.

Oermann, Robert K. "For Marie Osmond, A Busy 3 Years," *The Tennessean*, Feb. 23, 1985.

Oermann, Robert K. "Alternative Music in Nashville: Past, Present, and Future," *Music Row*, May 1986.

Oermann, Robert K. "Battle-Scarred Paycheck Returns to the Ring," *The Tennessean*, May 31, 1986.

Oermann, Robert K. "Man in Black Without a Label," *The Tennessean*, July 16, 1986.

Oermann, Robert K. "Superstar Cash Still Speaks for the Hearts of Americans," *The Tennessean*, April 26, 1987.

Osborne, Robert. "The ABC's of Glen Campbell," *Sky*, Dec. 1972.

Palmer, Robert. "The Devil and Jerry Lee Lewis," *Rolling Stone*, Dec. 13, 1979.

"Paycheck Labeled Heavy Coke User," *The Tennessean*, June 21, 1980.

"Pentecostals in Heat," *Village Voice*, May 12, 1987.

Plummer, William, (reported by Louis Armstrong). "Cathy Stone's Life Has Gone from Jumble to Jambalaya Since She Learned Her Dad Was Hank Williams," *People*, Sept. 2, 1985.

Pond, Neil. "David Allan Coe Hits the Mainstream," *Music City News*, Apr. 1985.

Pond, Neil. "Go Johnny Go!," *Music City News*, May 1987.

Pond, Steve. "Elvis Remembered: His Final Days," *US*, Aug. 24, 1977.

Prime, John. "Merry Widow of Country Legends," *Los Angeles Times*, Sept. 20, 1987.

"Sadly the Troubadour," *Newsweek*, Jan. 19, 1953.

Sanderson, Jane. "In the Wake of His Fifth Wife's Death, Jerry Lee Lewis Takes Bride Number Six, Kerrie McCarver," *People*, May 18, 1984.

Schulze, Cathy. " '85 Big Money Year for Some Country Musicians," *Nashville Banner*, Jan. 1, 1986.

Schwed, Mark. "The 'Possum' Lying Low After Squabble," *Nashville Banner*, July 22, 1981.

Scott, Vernon. "How My Husband and I Saved Our Marriage," *Good Housekeeping*, May 1985.

Sharp, Amanda. "Lewis Acquitted; IRS to Press for Back Taxes," *The Tennessean*, Oct. 19, 1984.

Sheff, David. "Glen Campbell's Third Marriage Is on the Rocks, but Young Tanya Tucker Cushions the Fall," *People*, June 30, 1980.

Sheff, David. "Even Rhinestone Cowgirls Get the Blues," *People*, May 4, 1981.

Shoulders, Carolyn, and Sandy Neese. "Cause of Mandrell Wreck Puzzles Police," *The Tennessean*, Sept. 12, 1984.

Smith, Mark. "During Robbery, Cash Plotted Escape Try," *The Tennessean*, Jan. 4, 1982.

Smith, Timothy K. "Nashville Is Booming, and a Little Worried How It Will Turn Out," *Wall Street Journal*, Jan. 7, 1987.

Snyder, Bill. "Doctor Tells Nichopoulos Jurors Lewis Hospitalized For Drugs," *Nashville Banner*, Oct. 20, 1981.

"Special Report: Country Music," *Hollywood Reporter*, Apr. 6, 1987.

"Tammy Wynette," *Penthouse*, Sept. 1980.

Thomas, Susan, "Music City's 'High' Life," *The Tennessean*, Sept. 2, 1984.

Thomas, Susan. "From Country Boy to Cocaine Crazy," *The Tennessean*, Sept. 3, 1984.

Thomas, Susan. "Blackouts Drugs' Price, Cash Says," *The Tennessean*, Sept. 6, 1984.

Thomas, Susan. "Waylon's New High: Family, Not Drugs," *The Tennessean*, Sept. 7, 1984.

Thomas, Susan. "They Carried Him Away," *The Tennessean*, Sept. 9, 1984.

Thomas, Susan. "He Blames Music Industry," *The Tennessean*, Sept. 10, 1984.

Thomas, Susan. "His 'Family Tradition' Almost Killed Hank Jr.," *The Tennessean*, Sept. 13, 1984.

"Where Art Is an Imitation of Life," *The* (Enterprise, Alabama) *Ledger*, Feb. 12, 1986.

Wilson, Susan. "Loretta Lynn," *Boston Globe*, July 27, 1984.

Windeler, Robert. "Glen Campbell, Riding High Again, Shops for a Diamond, Not a Rhinestone," *People*, March 29, 1976.

Winston, Catherine. "Musically Inclined Spade Cooley Family Enjoys Valley Life," *Antelope Valley Press*, Nov. 6, 1960.

Wiseman, Rich. "David Allan Coe's Death Row Blues: Rhinestone Ripoff?" *Rolling Stone*, Jan. 1, 1976.

Zibart, Eve. "Plagued by Troubles, Audrey Williams Dies," *The Tennessean*, Nov. 5, 1975.

Zibart, Eve. "Tammy on a Tightrope," *Washington Post*, Oct. 26, 1978.

PHOTO CREDITS

Billboard
Pages: 32, 168
Personal Collection of Billie Jean Williams Horton
Pages: 34, 37
NBC-TV
Pages: 43, 85, 112, 176
CBS-TV
Pages: 51, 61, 66, 83, 152, 176, 181, 202
RCA Records
Pages: 60, 100, 111
Warner Brothers
Pages: 63, 73, 225
United Artists
Page: 65
MCA Records
Pages: 76, 81, 138, 203, 222, 253
UPI/Bettmann Newsphotos
Pages: 93, 240
Kathy Gangwisch & Associates
Page: 96
20th Century–Fox
Page: 107
Columbia Records
Pages: 110, 137, 160, 162, 164, 170
Sire Records
Page: 110
The Academy of Motion Picture Arts and Sciences
Pages: 114, 115
Bill Spencer Collection
Pages: 118, 131, 258
University of California at Los Angeles/Dept. of Special Collections, Los Angeles Times *Photograph Collection*
Page: 122
Regional History Collection/Dept.of Special Collections, University of Southern California
Pages: 122, 123, 124
The Jim Halsey Co., Inc.
Page: 128
Capitol Records
Page: 130, 197
Home Box-Office
Page: 140
Aristo Music Associates
Page: 143
Lee S. Mimms & Associates
Page: 144
ICM/Kragen and Company
Page: 147
Hearst Newspaper Collection/Special Collections, University of Southern California Library
Pages: 166, 234, 256
Rhino Records

Page: 170
Nashville Metropolitan Police Dept.
Page: 174
Hendersonville Police Dept.
Pages: 177, 178
Paul Schrader Collection
Page: 194
Variety Artists
Page: 200
Mercury Records
Pages: 207, 211, 245
Plantation Records
Page: 213
Beech Tree Books/Morrow, Photo by Stefani Kong
Page: 218
Troy Hess Collection
Page: 219
Gilley's
Page: 220
Tri-Star Pictures
Page: 235
Gerald Holly
Page: 237
Texarkana Gazette
Page: 243
Las Vegas News Bureau
Page: 251
Thomas Jacobs/From the book The Stringbean Murders *by Warren B. Causey*
Pages: 262, 263
Jerry Strobel/The Grand Ole Opry
Pages: 264, 265
Arhoolie Records
Page: 268
Mickey Welsh
Page: 275

INDEX